$12.50
NSF

Mari and Karana

MARI AND KARANA
Two Old Babylonian Cities

Stephanie Dalley

Longman

London and New York

Longman Group Limited,
Longman House, Burnt Mill, Harlow,
Essex CM20 2JE, England
and Associated Companies throughout the world.

© Longman Group Limited, 1984

First published 1984

ISBN 0 582 78363 1

British Library Cataloguing in Publication Data

Dalley, Stephanie
  Mari and Karana.
  1. Mari (Ancient city)   2. Karana (Ancient
  city)
  I. Title
  935   DS99.M3

  ISBN 0–582–78363–1

Set in 10/12 pt Linotron 202 Palatino
Printed in Great Britain
by Butler and Tanner, Frome & London

To the late André Parrot and to David Oates,
who uncovered Mari and Karana

"Who shall tell what may be the effect of writing? If it happens to have
been cut in stone, though it lie face downmost for ages on a forsaken
beach, or 'rest quietly under the drums and tramplings of many
conquests,' it may end by letting us into the secret of usurpations and
other scandals gossiped about long empires ago:– this world being
apparently a huge whispering-gallery."

George Eliot, Middlemarch

Acknowledgements

I am grateful to all those who have helped me in so many ways, especially with encouragement and discussion; in particular to Professor Jean Bottéro who suggested that I write a general book; to Professor David Oates who showed great faith in entrusting his tablets to a very inexperienced epigraphist in 1967; to Dr Joan Weir of Edinburgh who read various drafts with great patience, kindness and intelligence, and helped me to improve the text enormously; to Dr Roger Moorey of the Ashmolean Museum, Oxford, who read an early draft and gave precious time for many stimulating discussions; to Rob Pring of Instron Ltd and to Rosalind Howell-Caldicott for three splendid drawings; to all those who have so generously provided photographs, and finally to the publishers for their enthusiasm and productive work.

This book is based almost entirely on the results of laborious researches undertaken by numerous scholars of various nationalities over nearly half a century. It is impossible to acknowledge adequately the meticulous patience and aggressive perseverance with which cuneiformists have tackled the clay tablets, but their labours form the basis for this synthesis. Future work will certainly modify the present account, for thousands of tablets are still waiting to be edited and interpreted, and they will add new material and insights beyond our present scope. The author takes full responsibility, however, for errors and omissions in the awareness that a complete and accurate book on this subject can never be written.

Contents

List of figures

Note to Readers

Throughout the text, abbreviated marginal references are employed to refer to texts which will be of interest to specialists in the field. These references are listed against the key to editions of texts on pages 208 and 209.

Prologue

Nebuchadnezzar II, King of Babylon, was confronted by Daniel in the early sixth century BC, and Belshazzar saw the writing on the wall in 539 BC. Sennacherib and the Assyrians came down like a wolf on the fold a mere century and a half earlier. These are the episodes which our knowledge of the Old Testament usually brings to the fore when Babylon and Assyria are mentioned. If we have heard the name of Hammurabi, King of Babylon, who wrote a code of laws, we tend to associate it with those other familiar names, and we may be surprised that the span of time between Nebuchadnezzar and Hammurabi is as great as that which divides us from Alfred the Great. Nor did the great lawgiver live at the dawn of Mesopotamian civilisation, but roughly halfway through it. To Hammurabi, the heroic tales of Gilgamesh were already of great antiquity. The enormous time span of Mesopotamian civilisation, some 3,000 years, is approximately equal to that covered by the rule of the Pharaohs in Egypt.

Mesopotamia, with its kingdoms of Sumer, Babylon and Assyria, is scarcely connected with Egypt in the minds of most people until late in their histories. Until quite recently the evidence of archaeology seemed to show that these two centres of early civilisation were isolated, islands in a sea of barbarism. No longer can such a view be upheld. The Minoan palace at Knossos was uncovered in Crete in 1900, the great palace at Mari on the Middle Euphrates in 1934, and the riches of Ebla near Aleppo in Syria in 1974. A variety of new evidence now links those spectacular discoveries in space and time and shows that the whole of the Ancient Near East, together with Egypt and Anatolia, was urban, highly civilised and often literate from at least 2300 BC.

The overall picture is thrilling, yet too often the inquiring reader is discouraged from finding out more because the time-scale is dizzying and the bare names of innumerable kings are unfamiliar and daunting. It is rare indeed to be able to make the acquaintance at first hand of any of the prominent men and women of the time; too often a dry collection of names, deeds and objects confronts the persevering reader, a lifeless history. But by an enormous piece of good fortune there were discovered in the excavations at Mari and Karana, two small kingdoms in north-west Mesopotamia, large archives of clay tablets containing not only day-to-day palace records but also letters written by the royal families and their adherents in the years shortly before the growing power of Hammurabi dispossessed them around 1815 BC.[1] The period is the 19th century BC, at a time when the Wessex culture flourished in Britain and when the Minoan palace at Knossos in Crete was first laid out in monumental grandeur. Nowhere among the world's early civilisations has such extensive written information emerged at so early a period.

The palace correspondence seems fluent and often easy to understand today. There are several reasons for this. The translator has put the words into a modern idiom as far as possible, and naturally enough has not selected for this book passages of text which cannot yet be understood. Another factor is that this is one of the very rare periods when cuneiform writing recorded the living, spoken language. But perhaps most important of all, the culture revealed in the texts is in the mainstream of the tradition which we have inherited both through the Bible and through Classical civilisation.

Yet apparent familiarity should not mislead the reader about the extent of our present ignorance. There are still many words, phrases and customs that remain enigmatic. Some important questions are not raised in this book because neither archaeology nor the tablets give the evidence to answer them. The texts are bound to give a patchy, biased picture, for they were never intended to give us an objective view of their milieu. Many big cities are named in the following chapters, but you will not find some of them on the map at all because they have not yet been located with any accuracy, even though we may possess letters written by their king and know quite a lot about this period of their history. Even the date given for Hammurabi is approximate, and may be wrong by as much as a century.

Our period falls within the Middle Bronze Age, when most tools and weapons were made out of a copper alloy, and the working of iron had not yet developed. The whole of the Bronze Age in this area lasts from about 3200 to 1200 BC during most of which time Mari and Karana flourished. They are Bronze Age cities which were both abandoned in the Iron Age. In Classical times Dura Europos took the place of Mari.

Mari and Karana are not backwaters in the history of mankind. They mark the exchange of ideas between eastern and western culture within the Near East, between Mesopotamia and the Old Testament, Babylon and Jerusalem. They also link Sumer and Babylonia with the Hittites and Phoenicians, to whom Greek culture owed a considerable debt. The customs of Zimri-Lim, King of Mari, and Aqba-hammu, King of Karana, have affected the ways in which we think and behave in western Europe even in the 20th century. The palace records are fascinating to read because they are in tune with European culture in so many ways, despite the passage of almost 4,000 years between them and us. The selective processes of evolution had already fashioned a product in which we recognise ourselves.

Note

1. In this book the "long" chronology is used, following the study of P.J. Huber et al., "Astronomical dating of Babylon I and Ur III", in *Occasional Papers on the Near East, 1/4* Malibu, June 1982.

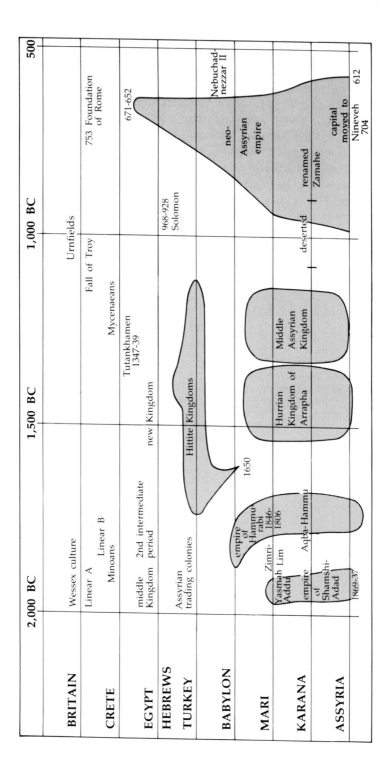

	2,000 BC	1,500 BC	1,000 BC	500
BRITAIN	Wessex culture			
CRETE	Linear A Linear B Minoans		753 Foundation of Rome	
EGYPT	middle 2nd intermediate Kingdom period new Kingdom	Mycenaeans Tutankhamen 1347-39	Fall of Troy Urnfields	671-652
HEBREWS			968-928 Solomon	
TURKEY	Assyrian trading colonies	Hittite Kingdoms		Nebuchad-nezzar II
BABYLON	empire of Hammu-rabi 1846-1806	1650		neo-Assyrian empire
MARI	Zimri-Lim Aqba-Hammu Yasmah Addu			
KARANA	empire of Shamshi-Adad	Hurrian Kingdom of Arrapha Middle Assyrian Kingdom	deserted renamed Zamahe	capital moved to Nineveh 704
ASSYRIA	1869-37			612

Guide to Kingdoms and royal families around 1850–1800 BC

ASSYRIA, capital city, Ashur.

Shamshi-Adad I (1869–1837 BC) His elder son, Ishme-Dagan, the crown prince was viceroy in S. and E. Assyria. His younger son, Yasmah-Addu, was viceroy at Mari and northwards.

Ishme-Dagan I succeeded to the throne of his father, but lost much of his empire.

MARI

Yahdun-Lim, son of Yaggid-Lim.

Sumu-yamam, driven out after a brief reign, perhaps by the Assyrians.

Yasmah-Addu, son of Shamshi-Adad I, ruled as viceroy.

Ishar-Lim, governed the Upper Habur for Yasmah-Addu and then usurped his throne.

Zimri-Lim, drove out the Assyrians, regained the throne of his father, Yahdun-Lim. Defeated by Hammurabi of Babylon.
> *Shibtu* his wife, mother of twins and many daughters.

KARANA (Tell al Rimah) *

Samu-Addu, probably a vassal of Shamshi-Adad.
> *Ashkur-Addu* his son
> *Iltani* his daughter

Hatnu-rapi, usurped the throne when Zimri-Lim drove the Assyrians from Mari.

Ashkur-Addu, son of Samu-Addu, regained the throne of his father from the usurper; was ousted by his brother-in-law and took refuge in Mari.
> *Bini-shakim* his son

Aqba-hammu, a professional diviner, drove out Ashkur-Addu, became a vassal of Hammurabi of Babylon.
> *Iltani* his wife, daughter of Samu-Addu.

BABYLON

Hammurabi (1848–1806 BC), at first a vassal of Rim-Sin of Larsa, late in life established an empire that included Mari and Karana.

RAZAMA a small city state somewhere near Karana

Sharrum-kima-kalima, familiarly known as Sharriya, ally of Hatnu-rapi. He may have been defeated by Aqba-hammu after a siege.

*The identification of this site is still not quite conclusive, but is assumed throughout this book.

Figure 1 (left) Diagram of chronology and geographical spread of cultures

ESHNUNNA (Tell Asmar) east of the Tigris.

Ibal-pi-el II during Zimri-Lim's reign tried to win back the empire of his father, Dadusha. Twice invaded towards Mari and Karana, but was repulsed.

Dannum-tahaz enjoyed a short reign.

Şilli-Sin invaded upper Mesopotamia, was involved in the siege of Razama. Was eclipsed by the rising power of Babylon.

YAMHAD the most powerful kingdom in Syria centred on the city Halab (Aleppo)

Yarim-Lim father-in-law of Zimri-Lim, gave refuge to the exiled Zimri-Lim during the reign of Shamshi-Adad.

Gashera his wife

Hammu-rabi his son, who coincidentally bears the same name as the king of Babylon.

CARCHEMISH (Karkamish)

Aplahanda, encouraged Yasmah-Addu's taste for wine.

Chief Officials at Mari

Bahdi-Lim in charge of the palace when Zimri-Lim was absent
Kibri-Dagan governor of Terqa
Yaqqim-Addu governor of Saggaratum
Mukannishum in charge of palace workshops
Yasim-Sumu in charge of personnel and records
Ama-dugga lady in charge of kitchens and foodstuffs

Figure 2 (right) Dynastic chronology

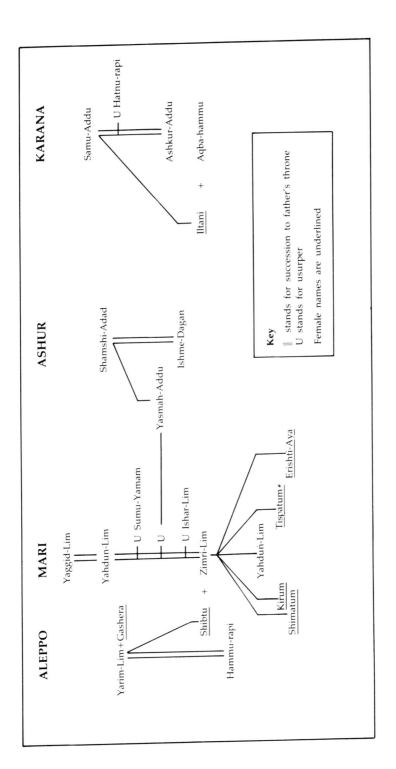

Chapter One
Discovering Mari and Karana

Historical Background

The land called Mesopotamia, which lies between the two great rivers Tigris and Euphrates, grows an abundance of food when it is irrigated. Early in the history of mankind the people who inhabited Mesopotamia learned how to produce plenty to eat and how to build cities with mud brick and baked brick. Having ensured their basic material needs from the resources which abounded in their homeland, they found time to spare, and they longed for wealth and ornament, diversions and comforts. But their land was devoid of all metals, all good building and furniture timbers and all coloured gemstones. Those coveted materials had to be imported from foreign lands. For this reason commerce and the trading caravan have always been the most honourable means of livelihood throughout Mesopotamian history up to modern times.

Many fine cities grew up, each with a central temple devoted to its patron deity. The god from his temple and the ruler from his palace provided the capital for traders who brought back foreign luxuries to embellish the palace and temples of their city. The merchant, his bankers and his agents became pillars of society, and were welcomed by royalty in palaces.

Because the rivers Tigris and Euphrates cover so many hundreds of miles, joining north to south, making contact possible from the Arabian Gulf almost to the Mediterranean Sea, they were two vital arteries along which trade flowed. So most of the great cities grew up on a river bank: Babylon, Ur, Ashur, Nineveh, Mari and Carchemish. Where land routes prevailed, caravans of donkeys, mules and (later on) camels plied regularly through mountain passes, along foothills, or across the deserted wastes of semi-desert. Smaller towns mark these land routes, for they are the country stations on the lines between the main cities. Such towns are Erbil, Karana and Harran.

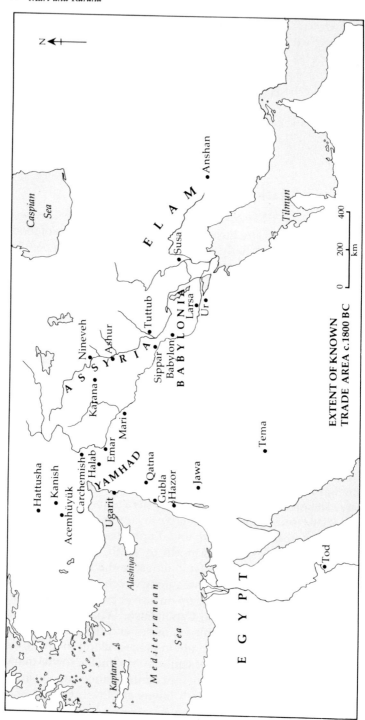

EXTENT OF KNOWN
TRADE AREA c.1800 BC

Urban civilisation began around 3500 BC in Mesopotamia. Recent discoveries have shown that this city culture was not restricted to Lower Mesopotamia, but that it flourished also on the upper reaches of the Euphrates. By the Early Dynastic period (c.2600 BC onwards) kings were busy acquiring foreign goods for their delight. The royal tombs at Ur are full of imported metals, semi-precious stones, and exotic furniture, although the foreign timbers from which they were made have perished completely[1]. They represent an astonishing standard of living that was not exceptional or narrowly restricted in geographical extent. Many travellers' tales circulated widely, recounting the adventurous expeditions which were sponsored by Gilgamesh and Enmerkar, kings of Uruk, to far-off lands whose kings would exchange materials and craftsmanship for cereals. At that time several large cities boasted a strong ruler and the land was not yet united. Then came unity under Sargon of Agade and his dynasty (2380–2167), but still the royally-sponsored trading ventures continued, and new stories of daring enterprises in strange countries took their place in the repertoire of entertainers.

Disruption brought to an end that long period of prosperity. Mountain people called Gutians invaded Lower Mesopotamia and they sacked or raided many of the wealthy cities. To what extent this broke up the pattern of trade outside Lower Mesopotamia we cannot yet tell, but a century later, when the kings of the third dynasty of Ur arose and established another widespread empire, trade with foreign countries flourished with renewed vigour. When that empire too disintegrated after a century of cohesion, Mesopotamia returned to its old tradition of many cities with many kings, and foreign trade continued unabated in the period known as Old Babylonian (c.2081–1576).

Patterns of Trade

Patterns of trade were set long before the Old Babylonian period by particular sources of supply and by the nature of the terrain. Outstanding among the needs of the Bronze Age was tin, that relatively rare metal which makes the best bronze when it is alloyed with copper. During the third and second millennia, when the cities of Karana and Mari were at their

Figure 3 (left) Map showing known trade area, c. 1800 BC

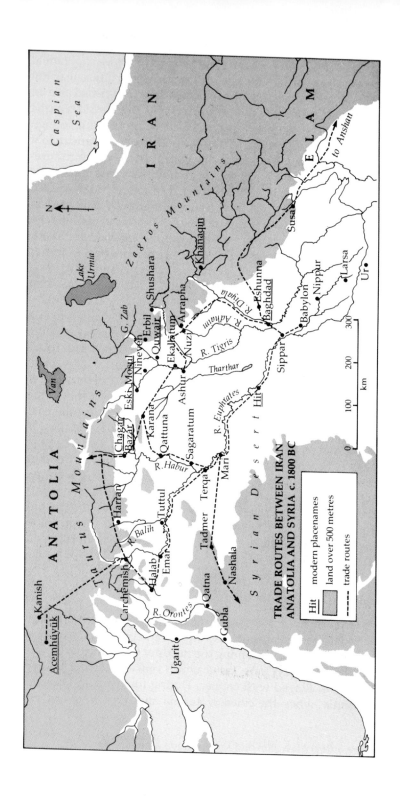

TRADE ROUTES BETWEEN IRAN
ANATOLIA AND SYRIA c. 1800 BC

Hit — modern placenames

land over 500 metres

--- trade routes

height, supplies of the metal *annakum* "tin"[2] entered
Mesopotamia from still unknown sources in the East. The tin
came through the land of Elam, whose king in the time of
Hammurabi of Babylon was called Siwe-palar-huhpak (in
Mari they had trouble with this foreign name, and called him
Sheplarpak). Siwe-palar-huhpak ruled both Susa, the
traditional capital of Elam, and Anshan, the ancient city which
lies near Persepolis, some 2,000 km from Mari by land. The tin
caravans journeyed through Anshan and Susa and entered
Mesopotamia through the Khanaqin pass into Eshnunna, up
to Arrapha, then across to the Tigris and over the river at or
near Ashur. The city of Ashur, traditional capital of Assyria,
owed its original wealth and position to this land route as
much as to the passage of goods up and down the Tigris. It was
a middle-man merchant city that sent its own traders far
abroad.

The merchandise which travelled on from Ashur went up
the Tigris to the Wadi el-Qasab, avoiding stretches of the
Upper Tigris including Nineveh which were sometimes
disrupted or controlled by the fierce tribe of Turukku; and then
along the road that connected all the towns such as Karana
which lie south of the dominating Sinjar mountain. From there
it continued on its way either over the mountain pass towards

Figure 5 The Upper Tigris at Eski-Mosul, viewed towards the
north-east. Its crossing was probably controlled by the fierce Turukku

Figure 4 (left) Map showing trade routes between Iran and Anatolia
and Syria, c. 1800 BC

Figure 6 Sinjar mountain range viewed from the south

Chagar Bazar, or else, keeping south of the mountain, westwards towards the Habur river, where the river port that served Karana and its neighbouring towns seems to have been Qattuna. Then it took the road up into central Anatolia to Kanish where, until the expansion of the Hittites in the 18th century BC forced Assyrian traders to abandon their colonies abroad, Assyrian families, natives of Ashur, inhabited their own, segregated quarter of the town.[3] They made a living by receiving and redistributing the goods, especially tin, and by sending back on the return journey locally produced merchandise, in particular textiles.[4] Our knowledge of them comes from a rather restricted group of private business records found on Turkish excavations at Kanish, and their connections with caravans of kings and of semi-nomads is not yet clear.

The Lebanon was a rich source of many timbers, not least the famous cedars. Ever bigger public buildings throughout Mesopotamia created a demand for larger, stronger beams than could be found locally; skilled craftsmanship in furniture demanded a variety of timbers, and aromatic resins became popular as perfumes. Many kings from Mesopotamia, Egypt and northern Syria sent expeditions to fetch timber from the Lebanon and from the Amanus mountains. To make the journey to Mesopotamia the timber usually joined the Euphrates at Carchemish or Emar and then travelled downstream in company with wines and millstones from northern Syria. Copper mined in Cyprus probably took the same route.

Other metals, timbers and stones came from the East, joining the two great rivers at the head of the Arabian Gulf and then travelling upstream along them. Carnelian, lapis lazuli and sissoo-wood[5] were among many commodities which probably entered Mesopotamia by this route.

Although the river valleys were the chief and obvious routes for trade, an alternative route had already developed from the Middle Euphrates to southern Syria and to Palestine. The desert road which later ran from Dura Europos through Palmyra to Damascus, or through Palmyra and Qariyatein to v 23 Homs was already in use in 1850 BC.[6] Mari occupied the position that later gave Dura Europos its importance; Palmyra was called Tadmer and Qariyatein was Nashala.[7] The ancient name of Damascus at this period has still not been identified, but Homs was called Qatna. Mari and Qatna shared a common frontier which ran across this desert route, so that they had to v 15 negotiate pasturing rights across a border which was not marked by any natural feature. Semi-nomads roamed the area, and may have played a part in organising the trade. Possibly the area was then less desiccated than it is now. Certainly in recent times the desert journey is very difficult without the use of camels, and there is no good evidence of their having been domesticated pack animals in this area at this period. Caravans travelling from Mari through Tadmer to Qatna therefore probably managed the journey with donkeys and mules.[8]

Population

During the Old Babylonian period Upper Mesopotamia, including the kingdoms of Mari and Karana, was mainly occupied by three groups of people: Akkadians, Amorites and Hurrians. Akkadian is the east Semitic language of the Babylonians and Assyrians; Amorite is a precursor of Biblical Hebrew (a west Semitic tongue), and Hurrian is a language that is neither Semitic nor Indo-European (which is the group of languages to which English, Greek and Hittite belong).

The way in which different elements in the population may be analysed is this. A list is drawn up of all the personal names from a group of texts. Many of the names are in the form of a phrase which is composed of two or more elements, and these are usually easier to analyse than the single element names.

Whether they are Akkadian, Amorite or Hurrian, compound names will have a meaning such as "The storm god Adad is my lord", "The sun god Shamash protects", "Servant of the goddess Ishtar". A deity almost always forms a part of such names, and the nationality of the deity is usually known; that is the first indicator. The other element in the name can be analysed linguistically, both for grammatical elements and for vocabulary.[9] Finally, the general assumption is made that the language of the name is the mother tongue of the person named.

The overall result from the analysis of personal names is that Amorites are found to be more common than Akkadians at Mari on the Middle Euphrates, and that Hurrians there are often working as prisoners of war in palace workshops, and are seldom found in positions of responsibility. At Karana, on the other hand, Hurrians were a part of the indigenous population, found in various social strata, and Akkadians outnumbered Amorites. If we take similar information from tablets found on excavations at other sites, we can draw a map to show an approximate distribution of linguistic groups.[10]

The population of Upper Mesopotamia was not all sedentary and urbanised at this time. There was a very considerable semi-nomadic element consisting largely of sheep-breeding pastoralists who lived sometimes in tents, sometimes on the outskirts of towns, finding employment as mercenaries in royal armies or as casual labour, or living by banditry. Some of them were subjected to the census and worked for the crown on palace land in the kingdom of Mari; RA 60 others are found in charge of huge caravans of donkeys in Upper Mesopotamia.[11] For the most part these semi-nomadic tribes use Amorite personal names. Several terms are found which describe different groups of them, and the distinctions are not always clear-cut; but in general it is true to say that the Sutu are found south of the Middle Euphrates between Mari and Qatna, whereas the Haneans and Yaminites (who used to be translated into English as Benjaminites[12]) are found within the homeland of Mari, along the Lower Habur, around Harran and in the kingdom of Yamhad. Within these groups there were smaller groups; in terms of their social structure they cannot always be distinguished clearly from the rest of the population.

Figure 7 (right) Map showing areas of major language groups, c. 1800 BC

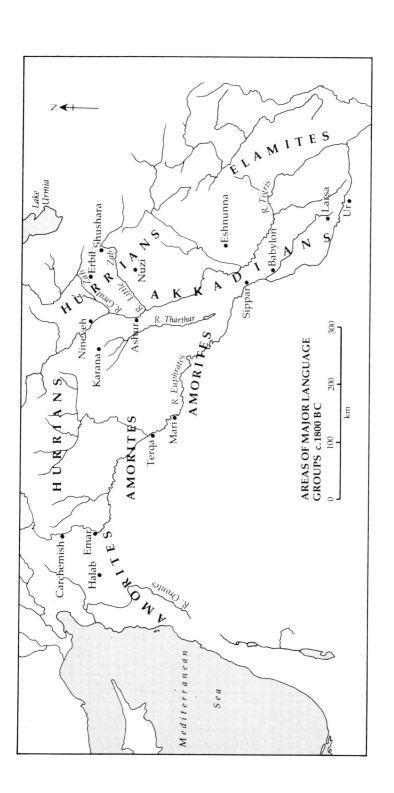

AREAS OF MAJOR LANGUAGE
GROUPS c.1800 BC

The excavations at Mari

Central to our interest is the city of Mari itself. In August 1933 a French lieutenant on a tour of inspection in the region of Abu Kemal came upon a group of Bedouin digging stone out of a mound of ancient ruins called Tell Hariri. A few days later a local man came to the lieutenant's office in Abu Kemal to report the discovery of a statue at Tell Hariri. The lieutenant went back to the site to investigate, and examined a headless statue which bore an inscription in cuneiform. Realising the importance of the discovery, he transported the statue to Abu Kemal, and informed the higher authorities.

Less than a month later word had reached specialists in Assyriology at the Louvre in Paris, who understood the potential wealth of the site from a single find, and acted swiftly. Some three months later a team arrived from France in Syria with a permit to excavate and the necessary finance, and before Christmas in the same year the first spadeful of earth was turned. During the second season's excavations the director André Parrot and his team began to uncover the great palace of Zimri-Lim. He directed more than twenty seasons of work, achieving some of the most sensational discoveries in Mesopotamian archaeology.[13] He recovered the entire plan of the huge Old Babylonian palace, and unearthed thousands of cuneiform records which document the life within it in great detail.

Mari was a large city of great antiquity. It lies close to the south bank of the Middle Euphrates near modern Abu Kemal, not far from Dura Europos, where the river meanders through a wide valley. The city stands at the lower end of this valley; both upstream and downstream of the valley the river has cut down through steep banks, and is flanked by stony soil. The land around the city was fertile enough to grow food for a flourishing population, and canals which collected water from both the Euphrates and the Habur greatly extended the acreage which could be irrigated.

Its first dynasty of kings featured in the Sumerian king list, very roughly 2500 BC[14]. It was a key point in the campaigns and strategies of the great kings of Akkad, Sargon I (2380–2335) and Naram-Sin (2310–2274). The astounding new discoveries of tablets at Ebla near Aleppo, which date to that time, show that Mari was also of exceptional importance to the new-found kings of Ebla, their contemporaries.[15]

The reasons for its importance are not hard to find. First, it

Figure 8 An aerial view of the palace

was a river port which took a tax from all the goods which passed along the Euphrates between Lower Mesopotamia and Syria with its Mediterranean and Anatolian contacts. Secondly there is now no doubt that it was at the head of the trans-desert route that connected Upper Mesopotamia to southern Syria and Palestine, so that the kings of Mari had close ties with the rulers of Qatna[16] and Hazor.[17]

The modern visitor to Mari sees a very extensive mound of decayed mud brick, pitted with the excavations of half a century, and dominated by a reddish protuberance of mud brick known as *le massif rouge*. One kilometre long, the whole mound rises more than 15 metres from the level of the surrounding land; the broad, meandering Euphrates flows within easy sight of it. There is no range of hills to dominate the horizon, but a flat expanse of land on all sides with occasional mounds to mark ancient settlements. Relatively fertile close to the river where the soil is alluvial, the land merges into stony semi-desert in the distance. No trees alleviate the barren view. To picture the scene in Hammurabi's day one must conjure up a network of canals, a multitude of cultivated fields, orchards, ponds and pasture; quite different from the desolate, neglected appearance of today.

The Old Babylonian Palace

Almost the entire palace of the Old Babylonian period at Mari has been excavated, and from it we have a good idea of the surroundings in which a king of the early second millennium lived.[18] It was a huge building covering 2.5 hectares of land. Entirely surrounded by mud brick walls, it had an imposing entrance paved with baked brick, and protected by towers on each side. Internally the plan consisted of various different and sometimes identifiable units, each one being an open courtyard surrounded by rooms. All the reception rooms and grand throne-rooms or audience halls were on the ground floor, and it is doubtful whether there was an upper storey at all over many parts of the palace. The walls, both internal and external, still stood to a maximum height of 4 metres, with a width of up to 3 metres when they had been excavated. At least one of the courtyards was planted with palm trees, and very probably each one had some kind of plant growing in it; the internal garden as the central feature of a house has

Figure 9 (right) Map showing position of Mari

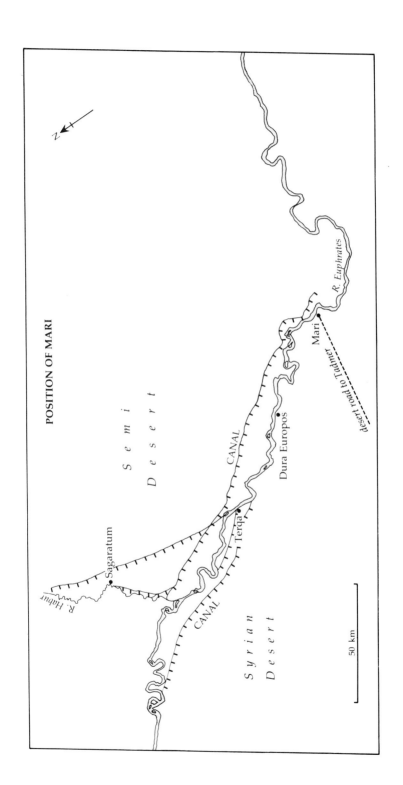

POSITION OF MARI

N

R. Euphrates

Mari

desert road to Tadmer

S e m i
D e s e r t

CANAL

Dura Europos

Terqa

CANAL

Sagaratum

R. Habur

S y r i a n
D e s e r t

50 km

remained traditional in the Near East ever since. The internal walls and door-frames within the palace were plastered and painted; sometimes they had plain red dadoes with black bitumen for the skirting area, and white for higher areas of wall; in other rooms scenes of ceremonial and mythological action were painted on the wall-plaster, each little scene framed with a decorative border.

The palace was first of all the residence of the royal family. Therefore it contained their private apartments as well as public rooms for audience and for entertainment. But it also served as the centre of local government, and this is the reason why so many records and letters have been found there. To the palace came the regular reports of officials who worked in other parts of the city of Mari, or who were stationed in VII 277 provincial towns. Each regional centre had a governor who lived in a "palace", for the word palace implies a Government House, not an exclusively royal residence.

Another function of the palace, scarcely less important, was as a caravanserai, to which foreign and local merchants brought their goods. The vast internal courtyards of the palace at Mari were obviously well suited to receive large numbers of VII 86 men and perhaps also their animals, and there is good textual evidence for this. The secluded nature of these courtyards

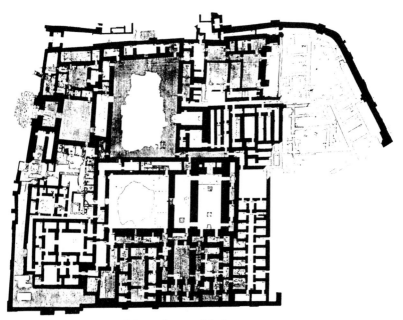

Figure 10 Plan of the palace at Mari

protected the luxury wares from casual pilfering or from raiding; and the whole palace was locked at night, so that even xiii 9 the highest officials could not gain access. Such security was also necessary because the palace served as a repository for taxes: one text tells us that taxes were collected together in a vii 217 bedroom in the presence of the king. Some goods such as wine and dried vegetables were kept sealed in rooms within the palace.

Because the palace contained much foreign merchandise and local produce, it is scarcely surprising to find that it contained a retail unit, a suq or bazaar, where goods were redistributed. This part of the palace plan closely resembles the plan of a modern bazaar in the Near East, and it was called *kār ekallim*, "palace market".[19] But we do not know to what extent, if at all, the general public had access to it.

To a lesser extent the palace served as a centre of production in the manufacture of goods when the processes involved were not noisy, smelly or dangerous. Most textile work was done inside the palace: spinning, weaving and stitching certainly were, although fulling and dyeing are more likely to have happened outside the palace walls. Much preparation of foodstuffs and cooking were done inside the palace, as many culinary ovens, found in various rooms, bear witness. Other kinds of production, such as metal working, were probably practised outside the palace walls; no furnaces were excavated, and a text speaks of bringing metalwork into the xiii 9 palace from outside. However, we know quite a lot about those skills, because all the records of work carried out on behalf of the palace were stored there, whether or not the work was actually done inside the palace walls. All this we know from the archives of cuneiform tablets.

The clay tablets

The French archaeologists who excavated at Mari uncovered more than 20,000 clay tablets in the Old Babylonian palace, for the palace contained all the offices of administrators who worked for the king. Letters of all kinds, ration lists, personnel lists, records of legal decisions, of tax collection, of groceries for the kitchens – all these and many more were found.[20]

Cuneiform tablets are usually cushion-shaped pieces of clay, of various sizes. When they are discovered, they are entirely unprepossessing, for they resemble the rubble of mud brick in which they are found. Yet they reveal the ancient

civilisation in a fuller sense than the purely archaeological record can ever hope to do. They are written in the Akkadian language, mainly using a syllabic script in which one
cuneiform sign represents one syllable. A few words, mostly
common nouns, were normally written logographically: that
is to say that one sign or group of signs represents a whole
word without any syllabic function. Some two hundred signs
were used, for the alphabet, so much more economical in its
use of signs, had not yet been invented. The script reads from
left to right (like English) and is the only Semitic language to do
so.

Sometimes letters and business documents were sealed
with an envelope of clay to keep the contents private and to
prevent fraudulent alterations. Such envelopes were normally
broken open as soon as they arrived at their destination; the
shattered fragments would have been swept up, and perhaps
even recycled. Very few have been found. But a letter was
found at Karana still sealed in its envelope, unopened. It was
addressed "To Dadu-rapi", and was written by Aqba-hammu,
whose seal was impressed upon the envelope. The first
sentence of the letter reads: "I have written to you five times
like the first time". Perhaps Dadu-rapi, knowing all too well
what the letter would say, had not even bothered to open it.

The skills of the scribe were specialised, and the palace may
have contained a school in which apprentice scribes were
trained.[21] Since most officials who had to record their business
and compose letters were not trained as scribes, the palace
employed a number of scribes who worked with administrators. Letters, therefore, had to be dictated and, when they
reached their destination, the recipient's scribe would read
them out aloud. So each letter begins with instructions to the
scribes such as: "Speak to the king; thus says the governor",
which corresponds to our more direct mode of address "Dear
So-and-so; Yours sincerely, So-and-so."

Many different kinds of tablets were kept in the palace. First
of all, huge registers were kept of all the people in a district
who were registered in the census. From that list groups of
names were abstracted for use in more specialised lists, for
instance ration lists for kitchen staff. Then, every delivery to
the palace and every outgoing from its stores had to be
recorded on a tablet, whether it was of gold or garlic. When a
caravan arrived at the palace, the names of all the men
accompanying it were noted down on clay. Records of legal
disputes concerning any of the palace's large staff were kept
on the premises. The king's administrators, whether they

Figure 11 Some tablets: (a) *in situ;* (b) close-up view

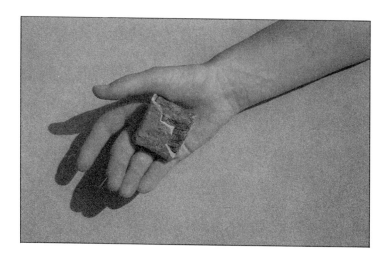

Some tablets (c) as a group

worked in a palace office or helped to govern in the provinces, sent daily reports to the king in the form of personal letters. To cope with this huge volume of correspondence, the king had a deputy who represented him and received letters for him in his absence.[22] He also had a personal secretary to help him.[23]

Perhaps because writing was used to convey daily trivia the written language at this period seems to have reflected spoken language quite closely, even to the point of indicating small differences of dialect and pronunciation. It was relatively free of conservative formality, so we can discern the moods and worries, the furies and irritations that beset kings and courtiers while they were dictating to their secretary-scribes. At most other periods of ancient Mesopotamian history this was not the case; formality or a deliberately archaic, even cryptographic, system of writing obscures the flow of language.

We know from the texts themselves that tablets were stored x 12 in baskets or boxes along with other objects in sealed rooms, and that they could be retrieved for reference.[24] Therefore there must have been a systematic method of storage. Although the Mari tablets were found in many distinct groups in separate rooms, those groups did not prove to have much significance when they were examined more closely. Tablets from different reigns were jumbled together; the letters of a legitimate king along with those of his usurper. Food lists lay cheek-by-jowl with letters from foreign rulers. Almost identical menus for the king's meals came from quite separate places. No attempt had been made to destroy the records of an illegitimate or unpopular régime, as if changes in political power scarcely interrupted the flow of internal bureaucracy. But probably some of the tablets had been scattered and jumbled when the palace was ransacked by the victorious Babylonians who brought the power of Mari to an end.

Careful reconstruction of many types of dated record is still continuing, and soon the orders of month names and year names will be established completely so that we shall find out more about methods and timing of record-keeping, and the chronology of officials; we should gradually be able to establish who succeeded whom in important posts, and to distinguish the work of a man in an earlier job from his work in a later job after a promotion. At present there is still much difficulty in separating the functions of different bureaucrats in the palace, and already it seems clear that they were not as specialised as one might have expected. To add to our difficulties, the dating of all the letters and the events which they describe remains problematic, because they are never dated with the day, month and year as administrative records always are. Since years were named after an important event, and were not given a numerical order, it is a long task indeed, and one that is still incomplete, to work out their order for each king and for each city. Only gradually is it proving possible to apply to the letters the hard-won chronology of the records, and many episodes described in the letters may never be put into their proper place. Largely for such reasons of internal chronology it is not yet possible to describe the hierarchy of officialdom, or how the organisation worked.

When the palace of the Old Babylonian period had been excavated in its entirety, the French expedition began to dig to find out what lay beneath. To their astonishment they found an earlier palace, no less magnificent than its successor, and a very few records from its daily administration. This showed that the later palace continued a lifestyle which was much older: the kings of the Old Babylonian period were following a tradition of palace life which was already at least six hundred years old. What is new and exciting is the range, diversity and detail of the Mari archive, the unparalleled opportunity which it has given us to explore the past.

The excavations at Tell al Rimah/Karana

Tell al Rimah, "mound of spears", is a hill of ruined mud-brick in northern Iraq. It contains the weathered and eroded remains of a small trading city named Karana which flourished in the late third millennium and during all of the second millennium BC. Today its position, 17 km south of the modern town of Telafar, is mystifying: like several other mounds of similar size and position in that area it lies too far south of the mountains to benefit from a regular water supply draining off them, nor is it situated anywhere near a permanent river. Therefore irrigation played little part in its ancient economy. In summer it is dependent on wells and a stable water table. Modern farming and grazing there are unreliable, since rainfall is not adequate or predictable each year and there is no evidence that the climate has changed in the last 4,000 years. The short springtime in March is luxuriant and beautiful, with

Figure 12 (right) Map showing position of Karana

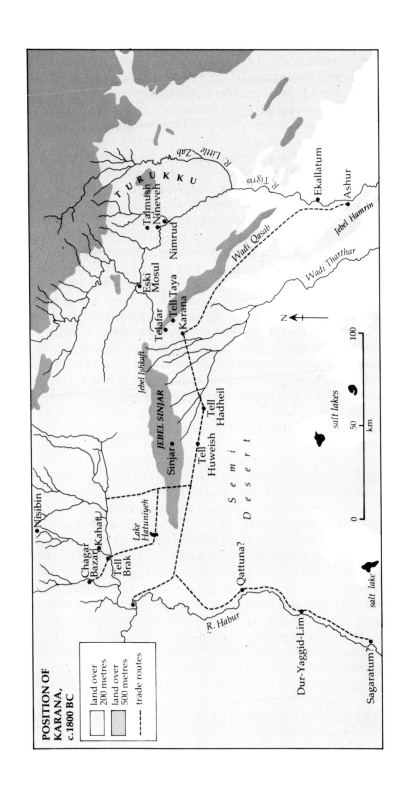

POSITION OF
KARANA,
c. 1800 BC

land over
200 metres
land over
500 metres
trade routes

T U R U K K U

Talmush
Nineveh
Nimrud

Eski
Mosul
Tell Taya
Telafar
Nimrud
Karana

R. Little Zab

R. Tigris

Wadi Qasab

Jebel Hamrin

Wadi Tharthar

Ekallatum
Ashur

Jebel Ishkaft

JEBEL SINJAR

Sinjar

Tell
Hadheil

Tell
Huweish

S e m i
D e s e r t

N

100

50
km

0

salt lakes

Nisibin

Chagar
Bazar
Kahatu
Tell
Brak

Lake
Hatuniyeh

Qattuna?

R. Habur

Dur-Yaggid-Lim

Sagaratum?

salt lake

rich grass and bright wild flowers, but within six weeks the earth turns to dust that lifts and shifts with every wind, and is reduced to a gigantic mud-bath whenever there is a rainstorm. In autumn and winter the thick mud can render the tracks almost impassable, and the patient foot has an advantage over the power-driven tyre.

Such conditions as these were surely not found there during the third and second millennia BC. In this marginal zone the precarious ecology has been changed by the intrusion of man and his domesticated animals, and perhaps too by a slight change in the vital rainfall, or in the level of the water table;[25] modern population is very sparse and poor compared with the people who live in the foothills, in Telafar and Beled Sinjar.

Surface survey and excavation have combined to show that this area was populated in prehistoric times, which means in Mesopotamian terms before about 3000 BC. But it was with the building of a line of trading cities south of the hills, probably in the early third millennium, that the region began to enjoy its greatest prosperity. Those cities attracted the attention of Seton Lloyd, who made a thorough survey of them in 1938, on behalf of the British School of Archaeology in Iraq.[26] Then in 1964 David Oates chose Tell al Rimah from among several similar sites with a view to increasing our very scanty knowledge of that area at that period. He conducted excavations for six seasons between 1964 and 1971, the first three seasons in co-operation with a team from Pennsylvania.[27] In 1967 his team began to uncover a palace which was contemporary with the palace at Mari, and discovered cuneiform tablets too. Great was the joy when the name of the well-known king of Mari, Zimri-Lim, was first read on a letter from Tell al Rimah; gradually evidence from the texts accumulated to show that Tell al Rimah was probably ancient Karana, a city which is often mentioned in the Mari texts.[28] Indeed, letters from the kings of Karana had already been found at Mari and had been published by the Franco-Belgian team. Mari no longer stood in isolation; the ancient kings were in communication.

The modern visitor to Karana, approaching the site from Telafar, sees a mound on which the central ziggurat and temple ruins stand out clearly, as does the nearly circular wall that surrounded the town. It is a mound of weathered mud-brick, devoid of stone, with a ditch encircling it to carry off the devastating floodwaters which cause damage to mud-brick so much faster than to stone. On a clear day one can

Figure 13 The ruins of Karana. In the foreground stands a small kiln. The contour of the temple mound is clearly defined, with excavations in progress

see across the flat plain to the similar, circular-walled mounds of Tell Hadheil and Tell Huweish, and to the gaunt ridge of the Jebel Sinjar. Here stand the mounds representing other merchant towns of the Old Babylonian period; although they have not yet been identified, we can be sure that their ancient names are all familiar to us from tablets found at Mari and Karana.

We know that the area was only sparsely settled in the first millennium BC. The neo-Assyrian kings tried to rejuvenate it by building new towns which they populated with deported people from various parts of their huge empire. But these new towns were short-lived, and the reason for their failure can be seen not only in the inadequacy of a neglected land surface, but also in a major change in trade routes between the second and first millennia which went hand-in-hand with the change from the Bronze Age to the Iron Age. There have been no towns of notable size in the area ever since.

It is quite clear that the wealth of Karana was dependent on goods, especially tin, travelling from east to west and crossing the Tigris near Ashur. The major change which took place some time at the end of the second millennium was that the main track of east-west trading caravans no longer continued to come westwards from Arrapha to use that river crossing.

Instead they more often continued northwards along the foothills of the Zagros mountains through Erbil, an area which had become much more stable and controlled, crossed the Upper Zab at Quwair or near Kalak, and went westwards to cross the Tigris at Nineveh. Also, with almost total state control of trade during the long period of the Assyrian empire, all goods tended to converge on Nineveh and Ashur, and there was much less transit trade than formerly.

As a result, Ashur declined as a trading city, although it continued as a river port for traffic up and down the Tigris; and it rested on its laurels as the traditional seat of Assyrian religion and kingship. The neo-Assyrian kings of the early first millennium themselves moved northwards with the main trade route, and founded new capitals where they could take direct advantage of that trade and its roads, in Nineveh, Nimrud and Khorsabad. No doubt there were other reasons for these new capitals: a better, cleaner water supply; a better marshalling point for the untiring campaigns north, east and west; fine spacious positions for new palaces, away from the over-crowded citadel at Ashur; but the change in the trade route was important too.

Although the tin route was vital to Karana, there were probably other lines of communication about which we are less well informed by the texts. On the Tigris at its closest to Karana the two ancient mounds of Eski Mosul (about 30 km from Karana) and Nineveh (40 km away) have occupation levels which are continuous throughout the third and second millennia. The Tigris is not safely navigable upstream from Eski-Mosul, but the two river ports must have acted both as crossing points for traffic needing to go from one bank to the other, and as starting points for river journeys down to Babylonia. Karana must have benefited from her proximity to Nineveh and Eski Mosul whenever local conditions were peaceful.

Another feature of Karana's position which calls for attention is her placing at the head waters of the Tharthar, the "third river" of Mesopotamia. During wet weather the water which runs off south of the mountains is very considerable, and it drains down into the Tharthar. It is an inland river, sometimes brackish, with only very small seasonal tributaries, and it runs parallel to the Tigris on its western side, draining into a marshy inland depression. It was bordered by a strip of vegetation which was permanent, not seasonal, and which supported a varied fauna including wild cattle and ostriches.

Wells were very frequent. Those wells must certainly have served semi-nomadic travellers with their merchandise who preferred to avoid the transit taxes levied by Ashur on the professional, river-based traders.

The Assyrian king Tukulti-Ninurta II (890–884 BC) made a journey westwards from Ashur to the Tharthar, then southwards down it, and he gives us our only description of this area from ancient records, albeit nearly a thousand years later than the Old Babylonian period.

"I crossed the Wadi Tharthar, pitched camp and spent the night... I exhausted(?) 470 wells in the vicinity... On my expedition along the banks of the Wadi Tharthar I killed eight wild bulls."

Only a small part of the Old Babylonian palace at Karana was excavated, for it lay many metres below the ground level,

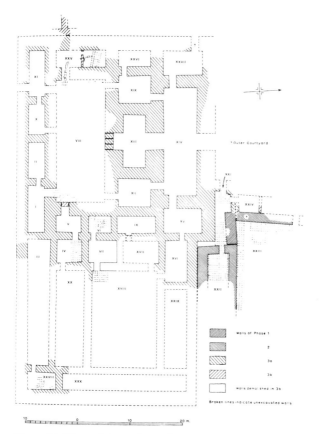

Figure 14 Plan of the palace of Karana

EXCE and was far less accessible than the palace at Mari.[29] But from a Mari letter we know that the palace at Karana was particularly fine; a Mari official wrote to his king to report that he visited the king of Karana, saying: "We went into a really splendid palace."

The main group of tablets which was found inside its walls consisted of about 200 letters and administrative records which directly concerned the queen Iltani, wife of the ruler Aqba-hammu, spanning perhaps four years. As at Mari, there was no obvious meaning to the tumble of tablets. Iltani's records and letters lay in confusion in the bathroom. Tablets of the usurper Hatnu-rapi were left over from several years previously, and had not been cleared away when his reign terminated abruptly; they were lying casually in another room of the palace. Within the debris that covered two other rooms were found the remains of a royal wine archive, mixed in with a letter fragment. So two particular aspects of life which added to the picture given in the Mari tablets were the role of the queen, and the allocation of wine. Most of the tablets were in very good condition, and they have all been published by a British team of scholars.[30]

The excavations at Chagar Bazar and Shemshara

A site called Chagar Bazar lies in marvellously fertile country in the eastern part of the triangle made by the branches of the Upper Habur river. Its ancient name remains uncertain. It was excavated between 1932 and 1937 by a British expedition led by Mallowan with his wife, Agatha Christie.[31] They found some rooms which were almost certainly part of a palace similar to the palaces at Mari and Karana. In those rooms they discovered about a hundred tablets which were administrative records from the department of the palace which dealt with barley: barley for bread, beer, fodder for all kinds of animals and birds, rations for all types of palace personnel, issued during the reign of Shamshi-Adad I, King of Assyria. Mari and Chagar Bazar probably both belonged to a single province that was governed by the younger son of that king. The records span just a few years, but they have supplied some very valuable information, particularly about livestock, which complements the more cosmopolitan tablets from Mari and Karana, and they are exactly contemporary with one of the groups of Mari tablets.[32]

There is a fourth site called Shemshara, ancient Shusharra, which has produced tablets that add to our knowledge of this period. In 1957 a Danish expedition excavated an ancient mound which was to be flooded by a new dam in the mountains near Ranya, east of the Tigris. They found 146 letters and records, but since few of them have been published, only a small amount of information is available for inclusion here. They are exactly contemporary with the tablets from Mari and Chagar Bazar, and will eventually provide us with much additional detail from a very different part of the Old Assyrian kingdom.[33]

It was an age of small states and ambitious minor kings, an age of beautiful palaces, close communications, queens who played a distinct role in palace life. Above all it was an age when people wrote frequent letters both personal and official and kept records of all transactions. If one combines the evidence from all these excavations and their many groups of tablets, a remarkably balanced and lively picture emerges of palace life in the early second millennium.

Notes to Chapter One

1. Woolley, "The Royal Cemetery", *Ur excavations Vol II 1934.* For an updated account, see Woolley and Moorey, *Ur of the Chaldees,* London, 1982.

2. In some contexts and at some periods there is a possibility that *annakum* may mean lead as well as tin. The later, Persian, word *anuk* may mean both tin and lead; see J. W. Allan, *Persian Metal Technology 700–1300 AD,* (London 1979), p. 25.

3. Kanish is no longer unparalleled as the only excavated city with a colony of foreign traders. Excavations at Acemhüyük to the west of Kanish have revealed a similar city. Among the most remarkable finds are clay sealings from consignments sealed by dignitaries who are already known from Mari: Shamshi-Adad, King of Assyria; Aplahanda, King of Carchemish, and a daughter of Zimri-Lim, King of Mari. See also note 24 to Chapter 2.

4. There are three good studies of this colony: P. Garelli, *Les Assyriens en Cappadoce,* Paris 1963; K. R. Veenhof, *Aspects of Old Assyrian Trade,* Leiden 1972; M. T. Larsen, *Old Assyrian Caravan Procedures,* Istanbul 1967.

5. This is timber from the large tree *Dalbergia sissoo,* which is still commonly used for furniture in Afghanistan and Pakistan. It

resembles ebony in colour, and it is often carved with intricate patterns.

6. For an Old Babylonian tablet discovered at Dura Europos and sealed with the seal of a king of Hana, see F. J. Stephens, "A cuneiform tablet from Dura Europos", *Revue d'Assyriologie* 34, 1937, p. 183ff.

7. See B. Groneberg, *Répertoire Géographique des Textes Cunéiformes Band 3*, Wiesbaden, 1980.

8. Mari records speak of copper from Tema (*Revue d'Assyriologie* 64 p. 25). If this is correctly identified as Tayma in Arabia (which is still disputed), the copper deposits of the Wadi Arabah area were finding a first market in Arabia, and the desert route Tayma – Petra – Qatna may also have existed at this time. Petra (Semitic name Raqmu) has not yet been found in these cuneiform records.

9. The best overall analysis of Akkadian names is still by J. J. Stamm, *Die akkadische Namengebung*, Leipzig 1939. (Mitteilungen der vorderasiatisch – aegyptischen Gesellschaft no. 44.) For Amorite names from Mari see H. B. Huffmon, *Amorite Personal Names in the Mari Texts*, Johns Hopkins Press 1965.

10. Elamite, the language of south-west Iran, is not represented in the indigenous personal names of Mari and Karana.

11. J. R. Kupper, *Les nomades en Mesopotamie au temps des rois de Mari*.

12. This is an example of early attempts to connect Biblical names and events too closely to the Mari letters.

13. Preliminary reports of the excavations have been published in the journal *Syria*, from no. 16, 1935 onwards.

14. See Pritchard, ANET third edition, p. 265ff.

15. P. Matthiae, *Ebla, an empire rediscovered*, London 1980.

16. For excavations at Qatna, see Le Comte du Mesnil du Buisson, "Les Ruines d'el Mishrifé", *Syria* 7 1926 p. 289ff., and "L'ancienne Qatna", *Syria* 9 1928, p. 66ff and p. 81ff.

17. Y. Yadin, "Hazor", Schweich Lectures, 1970, published London 1972.

18. A. Parrot, *Mission de Mari II* Le palais 1. Architecture (1958) 2. Peintures murals (1958). 3. Documents et monuments (1959).

19. See S. I. Feigin, *Legal and administrative texts of the reign of Samsuiluna*, Yale Oriental Series, Babylonian Texts vol XII no. 70.

20. So far 16 volumes of these texts have been published in the series Archives Royales de Mari (ARM) Paris 1950 onwards, by G. Dossin, C-F. Jean, J- R. Kupper, J. Bottero, G. Boyer, M. Birot, A. Finet, O. Rouault and H. Limet. Indexes to all those volumes and to texts published separately in journals can be found in Birot, Kupper and Rouault, ARM XVI/1, *Répertoire Analytique*, Paris 1979; and J. G. Heintz, ARM XVII *Index documentaire des textes de Mari*, Paris 1975. See specialised bibliography, "Editions of the texts" page 208.

21. The excavator identified room 24 with its little mud-brick stool-like benches as the scribal school. This has since been questioned, for school exercise texts have not been found; the benches would be equally suitable for tailors.

22. See J-R. Kupper, "Bahdi-Lim, préfet du palais me Mari", *Académie royale de Belgique, Bulletin de la classe des lettres*, 5° série, tome XL, Brussels 1954.

23. See Birot, ARM XIII, p. 47.

24. In particular see F. Thureau-Dangin, *Sur les etiquettes de paniers à tablettes provenant de Mari*, Symbolae P. Koschaker, Leiden 1939, pp. 119–120.

25. Short-term, marginal climatic changes at such a geologically recent period cannot yet be traced independently of archaeological evidence. The problem is well summarised by M. Rowton, "The Physical Environment and the problem of the Nomads", in *Compte rendue de la XVe Recontre Assyriologique Internationale*, Liege 1967.

26. S. Lloyd, "Some Ancient Sites in the Sinjar district", *Iraq* 5 1938, p. 123ff.

27. Preliminary reports of the excavations were published in the journal *Iraq* from No. 27 1965 to No. 34 for 1972. For further bibliography see Meissner etc., *Reallexikon der Assyriologie s. v. Karana*.

28. A problem is raised by the name Karana, which resembles the Akkadian word *karanum* "grapevine, wine". Indirect evidence suggests that the deity to whom the temple was dedicated was Geshtin-anna, originally a Sumerian goddess whose name can be translated "grapevine of heaven". *Karanum* is an Akkadian translation of the Sumerian word *geshtin*. The vicinity of Karana, however, is not a wine-growing district in modern times and the ancient texts do not attest viticulture there; so it is possible that the connection is coincidental.

29. It is still too early to try and estimate the extent of the kingdoms or the size of the two cities' populations.

30. S. Dalley, J. Hawkins and C. Walker, *The Old Babylonian Tablets from Tell Rimah*, London 1976.

31. M. E. L. Mallowan, "The excavations at Tell Chagar Bazar", *Iraq* 3 1936, p. 1ff, No. 4 1937, p. 91ff.

32. C. J. Gadd, Tablets from Chagar Bazar *Iraq*, 4 1937, p. 178ff and *Iraq* 7 1940, p. 22ff; O. Loretz, "Texte ans Chagar Bazar" in *Lišan Mithurti, Festschrift for W. von Soden*, 1969.

33. J. Laessøe, *The Shamshara tablets, a preliminary report*, Copenhagen, 1959.

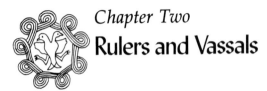

Chapter Two
Rulers and Vassals

The whole of Mesopotamia from the north to the south contained many fine cities of great antiquity, each with its own ruler and his palace, and each with a prominent temple which housed its patron deity. The history of those cities throughout the Bronze Age from the earliest historic times is one of friction, encroachment and ambition which led to shortlived empires and shifting centres of power. The archives from Mari and Karana cover a relatively brief period, perhaps less than fifty years in total; yet during that time we can trace many political and military changes which must have seemed overwhelming to the people who lived through them. At the time when we begin our story, the two cities that happened to be dominant were Eshnunna and Larsa.

Eshnunna and Larsa

Shamshi-Adad I (1869–1837 BC) lived in exile in Babylonia before he came to the throne of Assyria. At that time his ancestral homeland was largely occupied by the power of Eshnunna, an ambitious kingdom lying to the east of modern Baghdad, whose kings had expanded northwards along the east bank of the Tigris, seizing Assyrian towns and taking control of the trade routes.[1] Meanwhile to the south in Babylonia the great power of the moment was the kingdom of Larsa, ruled by its long-lived king, Rim-Sin I (1878–1819 BC), whose empire included most of the great cities of Babylonia. Among his vassals he counted the grandfather and father of Hammurabi of Babylon, and subsequently Hammurabi himself, a minor monarch in a second-rate city with a nonentity of a god called Marduk.

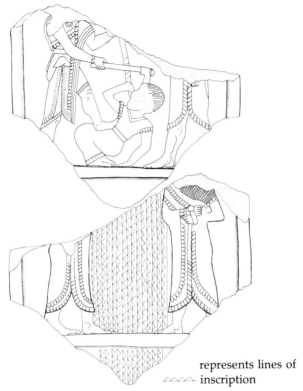

represents lines of
inscription

Figure 15 The victory stela of Dadusha (?), King of Eshnunna. The face of the defeated enemy was probably damaged deliberately. The inscription is written along lines which are turned through 90°, as is usual on stone monuments of this period. Height 0.45 m

Assyria and Larsa

Success did not come swiftly for Shamshi-Adad when he decided that the time was ripe to re-enter his native land, to drive out the invaders from Eshnunna and to usurp the throne of Ashur.[2] He captured the town Ekallatum[3] "Palaces", which lies a mere 18 km from Ashur on the other bank of the Tigris; but it was three years before he managed to take control of Ashur itself, whereupon he was crowned king and initiated an extensive building programme on its dilapidated temples. During his thirty-three-year reign he acquired an empire and displaced Eshnunna as the leading power of the Upper Tigris. He expanded so far westwards that he was able to erect his

Figure 16 Ashur, capital city of Shamshi-Adad I, on the Middle Tigris

victory stelae on the shores of the Mediterranean Sea; northwards too his influence was felt upon the kings of Tukrish, a mountain land north of Elam, who sent tribute to him.

Rather than appoint governors from among his commanders and officials, he divided his empire into three parts, took charge of one part himself, and set his sons Ishme-Dagan and Yasmah-Addu over the other two. Ishme-Dagan was responsible for the land that lay east of the Tigris and so his capital was Ekallatum, a city well placed for the task. His name, Ishme-Dagan, was expressed in its Akkadian form, for Akkadians outnumbered Amorites in that part of the kingdom. The younger brother, Yasmah-Addu, controlled the western empire from the city of Mari, whence the local dynastic family had been driven by Shamshi-Adad. Because Yasmah-Addu's territory was populated largely by Amorites, his name took an Amorite form. Shamshi-Adad himself ruled from an unlocated capital city called Shubat-Enlil somewhere 17 in the north of his kingdom; Nineveh was already an important city under his control.[4] Since he ruled both Akkadians and Amorites, his name is expressed in two ways: in its Akkadian form, Shamshi-Adad, and in its Amorite form Samsi-Addu.

While the tripartite kingdom of Assyria continued to flourish under Shamshi-Adad and his two sons, Larsa retained its hold south of Mesopotamia, and Eshnunna remained dormant, although it would soon make two attempts to regain its ancient glory. Babylon still played only a minor role upon the world stage. From that historical background comes the early group of letters from Mari, the records of the Assyrian interregnum.

The two princes, Ishme-Dagan and Yasmah-Addu, who helped their father to administrate the Assyrian empire were very different in character, as we know from the letters found at Mari that Shamshi-Adad and Ishme-Dagan wrote to Yasmah-Addu. Yasmah-Addu was a dilatory administrator, fond of good wine, and his brother was a paragon, an energetic leader who dealt promptly with both military and domestic problems. Shamshi-Adad expressed in no uncertain terms his irritation with his younger son:

I 61 "Speak to Yasmah-Addu, thus says your father Shamshi-Adad. I have read your letter that you sent me. People have been gossiping about Mubal-shaga for the last three years, but you have taken no action either to defend or to condemn him; you have shown complete indifference towards him. Are you still a child? Have you no beard on your chin? Even in the prime of life you haven't organised a proper household. Ever since Uşur-awassu died, who has been running your household? Promise that you will appoint an official within two or three days, so that the post will not just vanish. I can't understand why you didn't appoint a man to that post on the very day that it fell vacant. And you wrote to me about Sin-iluni saying: 'Sin-iluni is too young.' I suppose you didn't realise that he was too young for his previous post! But why do you listen to Sin-iluni's gossip and take no action about Mubal-shaga? Who is there here that I can appoint to your post? You should know your own subordinates: appoint one man who pleases you."

Yasmah-Addu found a kindred spirit in the king of Carchemish named Aplahanda. Carchemish was in a main
v 6 wine-producing district, and Aplahanda, knowing Yasmah-Addu's partiality for wine, wrote to him: "If you have no good wine to drink, write to me, that I may send you some good drink. Even though your city is so far away, keep writing to me whenever you want anything at all, that I may give you what you want." It seems that Yasmah-Addu did indeed make requests, for another letter from Aplahanda says: "Now, I

have sent you by the hand of Abi-Addu and Yawi-ila fifty jars
v 13 of wine, of the sort that I drink; fifty jars of honey (or syrup),
one linen tunic and five talents of assorted stones."

Ishme-Dagan, the virtuous elder brother, often wrote to
i 131 Yasmah-Addu to report on his military achievements in some
detail. "Speak to Yasmah-Addu, thus says your brother
Ishme-Dagan. When I had captured the towns of Tarram,
Hatka, and Shunham I approached Hurara, and I surrounded
that town; I brought a siege tower and a battering ram up
against it, and I captured that town within a week. Good
news!" Yasmah-Addu resented his brother's prowess and his
father's relentless criticisms. In his letters to Shamshi-Adad,
whom he addresses as Addaya, "daddy", he tries to exculpate
himself, or tries to anticipate his father's next strictures.
i 108 "Speak to Daddy; thus says your son Yasmah-Addu. I read
the letter that Daddy sent me, in which you said: 'How much
longer must we keep you on a leading rein? You are a child,
you are not a grown man, you have no hair on your cheek.
How much longer will you fail to direct your own household
properly? Don't you see that your own brother is directing vast
armies? You just direct your own palace and household
properly!' That is what Daddy wrote to me. Now, how can I be
like a child and incapable of directing affairs when Daddy
promoted me? How can it be, that although I have grown up
with Daddy ever since I was little, now some servant or other
has succeeded in ousting me from Daddy's affections? So I am
coming to Daddy right now, to have it out with Daddy about
my unhappiness."

Yasmah-Addu was so lacking in confidence that he had to
iv 59 be reminded by his brother to carry out sacrifices at festivals,
and once, when he was worried about the result of taking a
liver omen (from which the outcome of a particular future
action could be predicted) he sent the liver, or a model of it, to
iv 54 Ishme-Dagan, who wrote back to tell Yasmah-Addu that his
interpretation was wrong, and that there was no cause for
alarm.

Shamshi-Adad realised that the immaturity of his younger
son might cause him to direct his army rashly, and so he wrote
to warn him to control his impetuosity, quoting a proverb
which is known in ancient Greek,[5] and which later became
widespread in Europe:
i 5   "You keep looking for a chance to kill the enemy and you
prowl around him, and the enemy does the same to you, he
keeps looking for a chance and prowls around you – like

wrestlers each one keeps looking for a chance against the other. But take heed of the old proverb which says: 'The bitch is in such a hurry that she bears blind puppies', and don't you act in the same way!"

Mari

Before Shamshi-Adad rose to power in Assyria, Mari had been an independent kingdom ruled by a strong king named Yahdun-Lim. Yahdun-Lim had controlled both banks of the Euphrates including Terqa and Tuttul, the two great cult centres of the god Dagan, and he increased the productivity of his land by building a new canal which connected the Habur river with the Euphrates, naming it after himself.

"I opened up canals, and made those who draw water from wells unnecessary", he claimed in a royal inscription.[6] To protect his people he built new forts and defensive walls for his cities, and he led an expedition to the cedars of Lebanon to obtain valuable timbers, stopping at the shore of the Mediterranean Sea to offer a sacrifice to the Ocean and to give his soldiers the opportunity for a swim in the sea. Many neighbouring kings fell before his aggression, and he availed himself both of their labour as prisoners, and of their wealth as booty.

Yahdun-Lim had a son named Zimri-Lim, who was destined to succeed his father only after long troubles and many years spent in exile. For Yahdun-Lim was succeeded for a brief time by a man named Sumu-yamam, who may have been a usurper; his ancestry is uncertain.[7] He soon made way for the conquering Assyrian, and his throne was seized and occupied by Yasmah-Addu.

While the Assyrians ruled as conquerors at Mari, the royal family of Mari, descendants of Yahdun-Lim, took refuge probably in Halab, capital of the great kingdom of Yamhad, and Zimri-Lim married a daughter of the king of Yamhad. He remained in exile there for many years. Even when Shamshi-Adad died and his empire began to crumble, Zimri-Lim did not depose Yasmah-Addu directly,[8] for a man named Ishar-Lim[9] took advantage of the unrest to seize the throne for a very brief period.

Eshnunna: attempted revival

The time of Shamshi-Adad's death was one of great upheaval and unrest in northern Mesopotamia. The ruler of Eshnunna, Ibal-pi-el II, invaded northern Mesopotamia with a large army, no doubt hoping to fill a power vacuum, and hoping also to augment his army by means of an alliance with Hammurabi of Babylon. This hope did not materialise. Ibal-pi-el invaded at least twice after the death of Shamshi-Adad; on the first occasion Yasmah-Addu and the Assyrians were still clinging to power in Mari and Samu-Addu was enjoying his last days as ruler of Karana. [10]

IV 26   "Speak to Yasmah-Addu, thus says Ishme-Dagan your brother. I wrote to you before to say that I had gone to Karana to help Samu-Addu. The ruler of Eshnunna, together with all his troops, his courtiers and his friends, has assembled and is staying in Upe; [11] and he kept writing to the ruler of Babylon (Hammurabi) to meet him in Mankisum, but the ruler of Babylon did not agree."

The appearance of an army from Eshnunna so soon after the death of Shamshi-Adad must have triggered off numerous changes in alliances and regrouping of loyalties.

Perhaps this event was the coup-de-grace for Assyrian power at Mari, for now Zimri-Lim of the old ruling family at Mari finally made a successful come-back to his ancestral throne, perhaps with help from his powerful father-in-law, and drove the Assyrians out of Mari. [12] Zimri-Lim was the last independent king of Mari, and he is the best known because most of the tablets from the palace at Mari belong to his reign.

Karana

At about the time when the correspondence between Shamshi-Adad and Yasmah-Addu was written and deposited in the palace at Mari, Karana was ruled by a man named Samu-Addu. He had a son, Ashkur-Addu, and a daughter named Iltani (of whom we shall hear much more) among several other children, and he was a vassal of Shamshi-Adad, King of Assyria. [13]

Samu-Addu of Karana was so closely allied with the Assyrians that when their power diminished his days as king were numbered, and his throne was seized by a usurper named Hatnu-rapi. While these two new rulers, Zimri-Lim and Hatnu-rapi, were finding their feet at Mari and Karana, Ibal-pi-el of Eshnunna invaded again, only a year after his previous invasion.[14]

Assyria was no longer a force to be reckoned with. Ishme-Dagan succeeded his father Shamshi-Adad as king, and thought that his alliances were powerful enough to enable him to fend off rivals who would try to encroach upon his father's territory. So confident was he that he had boasted to his brother Yasmah-Addu soon after his coronation saying:

IV 20 "When I sat upon the throne of my father's house at first, I was in a turmoil, and so I did not write to you to say how I was. But now, you are my brother and I have no brother apart from you. Do not worry at all; my throne is your throne, and I hold Adad and Shamash in my hand. I hold the halter of the king of Elam and the king of Eshnunna. Do not worry at all, as long as you and I are alive, you will always sit on your throne."

Events were to prove him wrong, to show that his assurance was over-confident: he lost his father's empire and became a petty ruler of little account. He is scarcely mentioned in the letters of Zimri-Lim at Mari, and never finds his way into the correspondence from Karana. Much of his eastern and northern empire was taken over by the Turukku, fierce Hurrians of the foothills.[15]

Samu-Addu was driven from power by an upstart named Hatnu-rapi at Karana, and it is probably at this point that the whole royal family, including the daughter Iltani, went into

K 119 exile to Eshnunna, east of the Tigris, driven to seek shelter with the ally who had failed them. Hatnu-rapi, being an enemy of Assyria and Eshnunna, joined a coalition that included Zimri-Lim of Mari, and he was present at the sack of Shubat-Enlil, once the royal residence of Shamshi-Adad, an event which marks the final blow to early Assyrian power in northern Mesopotamia. During the looting he took some of

K 5 the booty that was due to his ally Zimri-Lim, and was reprimanded for his lack of fair play by the king of a neighbouring state. Hatnu-rapi was a tricky character, not to be trusted, and his loyalty to Zimri-Lim, in the face of the second threat from Eshnunna, was suspect, according to a letter sent from Yaqqim-Addu, governor of the river port of Saggaratum on the Habur, to his lord and master Zimri-Lim at Mari. It tells how Hatnu-rapi opened negotiations with Ibal-pi-el after that ruler had killed some men in Razama. The

XIV 106 king of Razama was frightened into joining forces with Ibal-pi-el, and his near neighbour Hatnu-rapi was tempted to do likewise. But the aspirations of Eshnunna were doomed to disappointment, and its army withdrew without territorial gains.

Several letters received from neighbouring rulers by Hatnu-rapi at Karana were uncovered in the palace at Karana. From them we receive corroborating evidence that Hatnu-rapi's particular friends among adjacent city-states were Sharriya of Razama and Bunu-Ishtar (also known as Bina-Ishtar), whose exact territory is still unknown.[16] These three kings Hatnu-rapi, Sharriya and Bunu-Ishtar organised a coalition to help Zimri-Lim:

K 4 "Speak to Hatnu-rapi, thus says Bunu-Ishtar your brother. When you have read this letter, you, Sharriya and the other kings who are on your side get together and muster 4,000 men between you. And I from here shall muster 2,000 men. The former plus the latter, 6,000 good men, let us muster between us, and let us send them quickly to the help of Zimri-Lim; indeed, let us act to save Zimri-Lim. This is not a matter for neglect; let us apply ourselves to this, that we may the sooner send these troops to Zimri-Lim. May my brother not neglect this message of mine!"

Hatnu-rapi may not have ruled for long on the throne of Karana; perhaps his vacillating nature caused the overlord at Mari to engineer his downfall. Probably then a firmly pro-Zimri-Lim man was put on the throne, none other than Ashkur-Addu, son of the old king Samu-Addu, perhaps newly returned from exile in Eshnunna. Ashkur-Addu ruled Karana during much of Zimri-Lim's reign at Mari. He was the king who embellished the palace at Karana, which became a royal residence worthy of comment abroad.[17]

Ashkur-Addu remained in power at Karana for most of the rest of Zimri-Lim's reign. His sister Iltani presumably lived there too, married to a *bārûm*-priest, a man who divined the future from entrails.[18] The allegiance of Ashkur-Addu to Zimri-Lim was rewarded with protection; on one occasion his
II 63 territory was raided by a ruler who was a vassal of Zimri-Lim, but Zimri-Lim ordered him to give back the property stolen in the raid. For about twenty years Zimri-Lim's domination ensured the peace of Upper Mesopotamia, and trade flourished.

The rise of Babylon

Hammurabi of Babylon (1848–1806 BC) remained in the shadows between Rim-Sin of Larsa and Shamshi-Adad of Assyria for the first decade of his reign. Nor did he exploit the death of Shamshi-Adad, which occurred during his tenth year of rule, to his own advantage, although he was soon corresponding with Zimri-Lim. It was another twenty years before he overthrew the king of Larsa and began to build an empire of his own; then for a brief span Mari and Babylon were the two super-powers of Mesopotamia, led by Zimri-Lim and Hammurabi.

Figure 17 The ruins of Babylon with a view towards the Euphrates flood plain

    A new ruler came to the throne of Eshnunna, Şilli-Sin (his
II 43 name means "the moon-god is my protection"), who revived old ambitions to win power in northern Mesopotamia; he invaded the area of Karana, and laid siege to Razama, whose king, Sharriya, had been a good friend of the Karana kings. [19] These events provoked a crisis of leadership in Karana;
II 39 Ashkur-Addu tried to remain faithful to Zimri-Lim, who sent a detachment of soldiers to help him; but his brother-in-law, Aqba-hammu, believed that the balance of power was shifting
VI 62 away from Zimri-Lim. He drove out Ashkur-Addu, who went to Mari, and became king in his stead, a usurper. He was soon

paying a heavy tribute to Hammurabi of Babylon. This is the period to which the main group of tablets from Karana belongs. He wrote to his wife:

K 70   "I shall take many garments with my tribute to Babylon; I have collected together all the garments that are available here, but they are not sufficient."

For Hammurabi had marched up to Mari and tried to impose vassaldom on Zimri-Lim; when this attempt failed he sacked Mari, burnt the great palace, and became the unrivalled ruler of much of northern Mesopotamia.

Figure 18 Hammurabi, King of Babylon, before the sun-god Shamash, Lord of Justice. Hammurabi's famous law code is inscribed below

The archive of Iltani at Karana

To mark his servitude, Aqba-hammu of Karana had a new cylinder seal cut; whereas his old seal had proclaimed him as "Aqba-hammu the diviner, the son of Himdi-Samas", the new seal added to this, "the servant of Hammurabi".[20] His wife Iltani continued to give him support in the very palace in which he had usurped her brother.

Figure 19 Impression from a cylinder seal found at Alalakh in northern Syria. The inscription shows that it belonged to a subject of Aqba-hammu, King of Karana; the head of Humbaba links it directly with the excavated temple; the arrow-shaped spade, symbol of Marduk of Babylon, suggests that Aqba-hammu was already a vassal of Hammurabi

The Karana tablets tell chiefly of the lives of the royal couple Aqba-hammu and Iltani. Aqba-hammu spent much of his time travelling, both within his kingdom and outside it. The area of his dominion may have been wider than that of his predecessors; it is likely that Qatara, Razama and perhaps Andarik[21] were under his rule, even though the latter two at least had been independent city-states ruled by Sharriya and Qarni-Lim respectively in the time of Ashkur-Addu and Zimri-Lim. Hammurabi of Babylon apparently ruled Mari – what was left of it after he had sacked it – directly, and its importance was drastically diminished. Never again did it become a city of any great importance. Mari is hardly mentioned in the archive of Iltani, Zimri-Lim never. The focus of Aqba-hammu's attention is southwards, to Ashur, Babylon and Sippar. This is the end of a long period of trade between Ashur and Kanish in Anatolia that passed through Karana.

One of Iltani's most regular correspondents was a man named Napsuna-Addu. He may have been her brother, put in charge of one of the towns near to Karana within the kingdom. "Speak to Iltani, thus Napsuna-Addu. May Shamash and Marduk grant you long life. You wrote to ask how I am: I am well. News of the ruler has arrived from Babylon. All is well. May news from you be regular." Another letter that connects Karana with Babylon says: "Speak to Iltani, thus Re'um-El your son. I am well, I reached Babylon safely and have seen the king Hammurabi in a good mood. Following this letter I shall return to Karana. Rejoice!"

K 135

We hear of Aqba-hammu's military exploits mainly indirectly, and one success was against the kingdom of Shirwun, probably just a small local principality.

K 72

"Speak to Iltani; thus Aqba-hammu. I have brought to my side all the land of Shirwun. All the troops have been enjoying

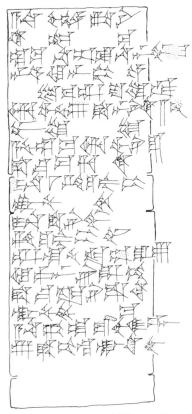

Figure 20 Copy of a letter to Iltani which mentions Mari and Kanish

the booty, and I am about to return to the homeland full of
presents. Rejoice!''

The king of Shirwun, now a vassal king with his coffers
sadly depleted by the looting, had to visit Karana as a subject
bearing a tribute.

K 82   "Speak to Iltani; thus Aqba-hammu. The king of Shirwun
has arrived; he asked the caravan that was going out of
Karana, but it had no garments fit for presents available. Now
send me quickly any garments that you have available,
whether of first-rate or second-rate quality, for presents.'' So
Aqba-hammu had to provide his own vassal with the first
instalment of tribute or presents for himself, just to keep up
appearances!

The tablets do not tell what caused Aqba-hammu's reign to
end, and what brought about the destruction of his palace at
Karana. It would be simple to suppose that the Iltani archive
marks the last years before the catastrophe. But both at Mari
and at Karana groups of tablets have been found within the
palaces that are definitely much earlier than the date of
destruction. The letters of Iltani show that Hammurabi of
Babylon came up into northern Mesopotamia, and so did a
Babylonian army, and that this caused anxieties:

K 68   "Speak to Iltani: thus Aqba-hammu. You wrote to me about
the thousand troops that came up from Babylon and have
entered Andarik. Why did you not ask your servant, who
brought that news, for a fuller account?''

Another correspondent writes to her:

K 147   "You wrote me a letter about your anxiety. Previously when
I passed by, I was in a hurry and so could not come to you.
Now the army's approach towards us draws near; I shall
indeed come and take counsel with you. But if not, if I cannot
meet you, do not worry; as long as I have not taken counsel
with you, I shall not go elsewhere. Until the day when I reach
you, do not open your mouth to anyone; be ready, and do not
keep fretting.''

Perhaps connected with the troop movements that caused
Iltani such anxiety was the plundering of the neighbouring
town of Andarik. Whether it was still an independent
city-state by now, or whether it was incorporated into the
kingdom of Karana is not clear, nor do we know who
plundered Andarik.[22] There is only a letter from one of Iltani's
K 153 female correspondents saying: "It was indeed a good sign
when a servant woman came into Andarik, and you had sent
Azzu-ena's wool! Surely you know that we have been

plundered and defeated? If you really love me, do organise some provisions for me." On the other hand, the letter of Re'um-El shows that his visit to Hammurabi in Babylon was once favourably received; and that Aqba-hammu was conscientious in collecting his tribute of textiles, at least for one year.

To his subjects in northern Mesopotamia, Hammurabi of Babylon was a distant overlord. From our own standpoint we know that he became an exceptionally powerful man, rather late in life, in an age of small city-states, that he promulgated a Code of Laws quite late in his reign, and above all that Babylon became then, for the first time, the most important city in southern Mesopotamia, and remained so for 1,500 years. Hammurabi promoted the city god, Marduk, to become a major deity in the Mesopotamian pantheon, and an echo of this promotion is to be found in the letters from Karana, written by Napsuna-Addu to Iltani. "May Shamash and Marduk grant you long life," is a greeting that recurs even in local letters, by which the supremacy of Babylon and the new prominence of its god are acknowledged in far-flung vassal kingdoms.

Yamhad and the west

Hammurabi's prominence has drawn our attention to Babylonia at the expense of the west, partly because no big western sites of that period have been excavated, no fine buildings uncovered, no archives deciphered. The Mari archive alone has redressed the balance: we now know that Syria had cities and monarchs equal in power and civilisation to Larsa and Babylon. Its mightiest kingdom was centred on Aleppo, ancient Halab in the state of Yamhad, ruled by Yarim-Lim and then his son, another Hammurabi. The great god Adad – or perhaps he was known by his Amorite name Addu or Adda – was supreme there; but temples and palaces probably lie far beneath the modern and mediaeval city, and cannot be excavated. We know that Halab was the mightiest of many kingdoms in Zimri-Lim's day from a Mari letter which states:

AREP 117 "There is no king who is mighty by himself. Ten or fifteen kings follow Hammurabi the ruler of Babylon, a like number Rim-Sin of Larsa, a like number Ibal-pi-el of Eshnunna, a like number Amud-pi-el of Qatanum, but twenty follow Yarim-Lim of Yamhad."

Figure 21 Aleppo, ancient Halab, capital of the most powerful kingdom in Syria in the 18th century BC. The castle was probably built over the ruins of the great palace of Yarim-Lim

Qatna

Scarcely less important was the kingdom of Qatanum, later known as Qatna. Ruled by Ishi-Addu, who bred horses, it was the home of the goddess Belet-ekallim, and was directly connected with Mari by the desert road which ran through Tadmer. Both these cities, Halab and Qatna, enjoyed close ties with Mari: regular exchange of envoys, marriage alliances arranged between members of the ruling families, and flourishing trade.

Carchemish

Carchemish (kar-Kamish) "Quay of the god Chemosh", situated on a vital crossing of the Euphrates, was ruled by the bibulous Aplahanda, who grew rich on the trade between Syria, Mesopotamia and Anatolia. The site was excavated by Sir Leonard Woolley just before the beginning of the First World War, but he did not dig deep enough to reach this early period of occupation. However, several of Aplahanda's letters were discovered at Mari, and the seal of his daughter Matrunna is in

Figure 22 The ruins of Carchemish on the Upper Euphrates, where the bibulous Aplahanda once ruled

a private collection. Although the native tongue of Aplahanda would probably have been some form of Amorite, he followed the convention of the time by writing in Akkadian, the language of international correspondence; and his letters show a definite "foreign accent", noticeable to modern scholars who read his letters. The seal of Matrunna is dedicated to the goddess Kubaba, who was known much later in Classical times as Cybele, a mother goddess who was often depicted holding a mirror.[23] So we know from this seal inscription that Kubaba was already the patron deity of Carchemish, despite the name "Quay of Chemosh" which implies that Chemosh was a leading god when the city was first established and given its name.

Figure 23 Design on the cylinder seal of Princess Matrunna, daughter of Aplahanda

Aplahanda's commercial interests were certainly not restricted to Mari. His seal impression has been uncovered by excavation at the great trading centre Acemhüyük in Anatolia, some 300 km away.[24] Carchemish was only one of several independent Syrian kingdoms that prospered in trade with it, and the presence of the king's own seal there shows that he himself was involved with the transactions. Perhaps indeed he personally sealed and exported wine, for some of the best vines in the world of that time were cultivated in his kingdom, and we know from his correspondence with Yasmah-Addu that he had good wine to spare.

These were the great western cities in the days of Hammurabi. If Babylon stands out as the greatest among them, that is due largely to its eminence and Biblical connections many centuries later. Mari, Carchemish and Yamhad were no less prosperous and cosmopolitan than Babylon. If Karana presents a sharper profile than Acemhüyük and Andarik, that may be due to our luck in excavation and identification. The value of the tablets from Mari and Karana is to show that an enormous expanse of western Asia was a network of well-established, prosperous kingdoms, each busily trading and often fighting each other for brief periods of ascendancy.

Notes to Chapter Two

1. The king of Eshnunna named Dadusha may be the author of a fragmentary stela with an inscription recording conquests, which was probably found in the vicinity of Karana, although some scholars think that Dadusha's predecessor Naram-Sin (also King of Eshnunna) or Shamshi-Adad (King of Assyria) was the author. See A. K. Grayson, *Assyrian Royal Inscriptions* Vol. I, Weisbaden, 1972, pp. 25–6.

2. Shamshi-Adad's father was named Ila-kabkabu. He was a king, but not king of Assyria; possibly he ruled to the West of Assyria. He negotiated a treaty of alliance with Yaggid-Lim (grandfather of Zimri-Lim), but broke the agreement when Yahdun-Lim his son succeeded to the throne of Mari (I 3). See Grayson, op. cit., p. 18ff, and *CAH* (second edition) vol II/1, p. 1ff.

3. Ekallatum has been identified with Tell Heikal, chiefly on the similarity of the names. There is not conclusive evidence. See Groneberg, *Répertoire Géographique*, p. 68; and D. Oates, *Studies in the ancient history of N. Iraq*, p. 38 n. 5.

4. The site of Chagar Bazar has been suggested as Shubat-Enlil because palace records were found there. But we now know that every small, provincial town of this period had its palace with written records, so that argument alone is no longer valid.

5. It occurs in a fragment attributed to Archilochos. W. Moran, "Note brève sur ARM 15: 11–13", in *Revue d'Assyriologie* 71, 1977, p. 191.

6. F. Thureau-Dangin, "Iahdun-Lim, roi de Hana", in *Revue d'Assyriologie* 33 1936, p. 49ff.

7. G. Dossin, "Archives de Sumu-Yamam", in *Revue d'Assyriologie* 68 1974, p. 91.

8. A new analysis to be published by M. Anbar in *Israel Oriental Studies* 9 will suggest that Yasmah-Addu may have retained the throne at Mari for several years after the death of Shamshi-Adad.

9. Our knowledge of this comes from a single year name: "Year when Ishar-Lim entered into kingship." He was a military general who served under Shamshi-Adad, and may have been responsible for the census in the districts around Chagar Bazar (A 950, A 929, V 51). G. Dossin in A. Parrot, *Studia Mariana*, Leiden, 1950, p. 53.

10. For a close analysis of these events see Dalley, *OBTR* pp. 1–11, and the remarks of Anbar in *Bibliotheca Orientalis* 35, 1978, p. 209.

11. Upe is Opis on the Tigris, at its nearest point to Sippar.

12. See note 9. The new analysis would alter this possible synchronism.

13. At some time during this period Karana was probably supervised by a provincial official named Hasidanum, who kept watch over vassal kings and reported directly to Yasmah-Addu at Mari (V 35–45). Dalley, *OBTR*, pp. 32–33.

14. A different reconstruction puts this invasion of Eshnunna some four years or more after the first.

15. We will learn more about this when the Shemshara tablets have been published fully.

16. Sharriya is a nickname for Sharrum-kima-kalima, which means "The king is equal to anything". His inscribed foundation disk was discovered during the excavations at Karana. C. Walker, *OBTR*, p. 193.

17. See Chapter 1 p. 26.

18. See Hawkins, *OBTR*, p. 253.

19. There may have been two different sieges of Razama, both quite close together in time. Dalley, *OBTR*, p. 7ff.

20. Hawkins, *OBTR*, p. 253.

21. All three towns remain unidentified, but lie in the vicinity of Karana.

22. Iltani's sisters lived there (K 100) and several of her personnel problems show that there was much coming and going between Andarik and Karana.

23. The seal is mentioned by G. Dossin, "Aplahanda roi de Carchemish", in *Revue d'Assyriologie*, 35 1938, p. 115, and C. Virolleaud, *Syria* 19, 1928, p. 94. It is now in the collection of Mrs W. H. Moore, and has been republished by G. A. Eisen, Oriental Institute Publications 47, Chicago 1940, as no. 103.

24. N. Özgüç in E. Porada, *Ancient Art in Seals*, Princeton 1980, especially pp. 62–67.

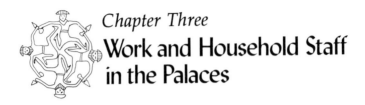

Chapter Three
Work and Household Staff in the Palaces

The Old Babylonian palace was a centre for organising production of articles made from metals, wool, stone, timber and leather. Nowhere is this better shown than in the lists of goods, in the records with the names of professional craftsmen and their rations and in the letters which give orders, accept deliveries and record complaints. The palace at Mari was ransacked thoroughly by Hammurabi when he brought Zimri-Lim's reign to an end, so the fine ornaments of precious stones and metals are gone; time and decay have taken their wholesale toll of textiles, leather and wood. The texts alone can bring the ancient craftsmanship back to life. At Karana too the palace apartments had been stripped of their riches, and only the clay tablets were left, because they had no intrinsic value to the looters.

It is a remarkable feature of the Mesopotamian Bronze Age that even in the wealthiest palaces and temples virtually no metalwork has been recovered by excavation. Copper, tin, silver and gold were all imported at great expense, and they were recycled again and again. All the more vital, therefore, are the tablets with their detailed information, for the material remains give a deceptively poor picture.

Raw materials and industry

Two men emerge from the records as workshop directors at Mari: Mukannishum, whose connections with textiles and metalwork are particularly fully documented; and Yasim-Sumu, whose department is called *bīt Yasim-Sumu*, literally "the house of Yasim-Sumu", and may be a room or group of rooms in the palace, or a workshop outside the palace walls with a separate "office" inside the palace. Other men too had their departments: Qishti-Mama the smith, for example, and

XII 17, 263
XII 263

Zikratum the banker, and Bahdi-Lim who took charge of the whole palace whenever Zimri-Lim was away.

The goods and materials that entered the palace and its workshops came from far and wide. Caravans came from V 14 Tilmun (Bahrain) in the Arabian Gulf; a particular kind of copper came from Tema, perhaps modern Tayma in Y 641, 6 north-western Arabia.[1] The great caravanserai on the citadel at Jawa in the Jordanian desert dates from this period and implies that profitable trade across barren desert was flourishing in the hands of semi-nomads.[2] A characteristic drinking vessel, VII 239 perhaps a type of rhyton, came from Tukrish, which lies to the v 63 north of Elam. Tunip in northern Syria supplied a particular IX 20 kind of oil; Tuttub, (modern Khafaje in the Diyala region east XVIII 12 of Tigris which has been excavated) supplied a special textile or garment, and so did Yamhad, including a kind of carpet; "tin" ain 64 97 came to Mari via Anshan, which lies in Iran near Persepolis,[3] K 122 and through Eshnunna. Kanish in central Anatolia supplied K 33 special kinds of cloth or garments and perhaps some rare dyes. Copper came from Alashiya (Cyprus); and Kaptara (Crete) sent weapons, goblets and sandals.[4] There was apparently a style or pattern of trim that was made in the Yamhad style, perhaps favoured especially during Zimri-Lim's reign because Iraq 39 the queen came from Yamhad. Lapis lazuli came from mines in VII 265 north east Afghanistan;[5] carnelian from the Indian subcontinent. The Hittites were already established at their capital city RHA 35 Hattusha, and were trading in various unspecified luxury goods, *ašlalû*, with the Mari palace.

Textiles

Textiles – fabric, clothes, trim for clothes such as fringes, tassels and ornamental border strips, coverings and hangings, blankets and rugs – are among the commonest items manufactured and traded even in modern times. They are relatively light, they do not perish easily, and with their enormous range of local variation, life can be made more colourful and interesting; prestige as well as profit can be gained by trading in them.

There are many different terms for the textiles which were made in the workshops of Mari and Karana. Often it is impossible to discover from the word that is written exactly what type of garment or cloth or textile was meant, but wool was the main material, linen being used very rarely, and cotton still unknown. Usually they were graded as two

qualities: first rate and second rate. Particular kinds were
Iraq 39 imported; one text tells how wool sent from Babylon was used
XIII 10 for making some curtains. The word for carpet has been
identified as *mardatum*, although we do not know whether it
was a woven or embroidered rug, or a patterned pile carpet. In
a letter from Zimri-Lim to Mukannishum, the king announces
that he intends to take the Yamhad-style carpet that is being
made at Mari to Babylon, a good instance of royal presents as
XVIII 12 the outlet for luxury goods.[6] Another text, an administrative
list, mentions a textile of a particular type for a bed, "with two
faces", presumably meaning a reversible bedspread or
something similar; next to it are listed four first-rate blankets
and a particular type of hanging also "with two faces".

Some garments were adorned with beads or sequins made

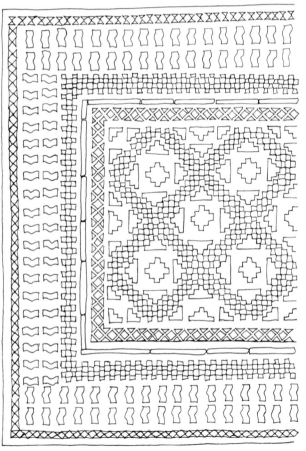

Figure 24 A frit inlay with a carpet-type pattern

of coloured stones or perhaps metals, and an example of cloth with tiny beads sewn on it has been excavated at Acemhüyük in Anatolia. We can connect this archaeological find with a letter from Iltani to Aqba-hammu containing a technical term that has been clarified only recently:

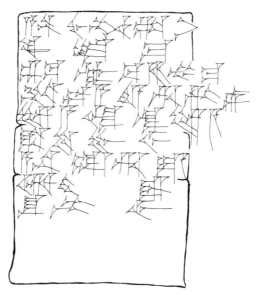

Figure 25 Copy of a tablet of Aqba-hammu, ordering Iltani to send decorated garments

K 80   "Send me quickly the garments, both with appliqué and without appliqué, which you have made."

There is some precise information about the size of stock at a given moment. From Mari comes a letter to Mukannishum XVIII 11 from Zimri-Lim requesting 200 purple garments, 100 blue, 100 white, 100 black and 100 green. At Karana Aqba-hammu writes to Iltani (perhaps her establishment was not quite large enough to rate a workshop director) saying:

K 57   "Now, I have sent you 50 minas of wool for 50 garments." The relative sizes of the workshops at Mari and Karana can be estimated from the ration lists: Iltani had 15 women and 9 men who are specified as being textile workers, whereas a Mari list XIII 1 gives 58 men and 29 women in only one of five departments that used textile workers. These huge numbers almost certainly reflect the military success of Zimri-Lim, in particular his capture of the city Ashlakka, which took place not long before this list was compiled. Aqba-hammu, on the other hand, was a vassal of Hammurabi of Babylon, so that his scope for enlarging the labour force by conquest was very limited. But we cannot be entirely certain that these lists from Mari and Karana are strictly comparable; very few lists were found at Rimah, and they may well be extracts from larger lists.

Dyes

The textile workshops must have stocked dyes and mordants,[7] or the raw materials from which they were made, but there are difficulties about identifying the specific terms. It may be significant that Zimri-Lim writes to Mukannishum to say that he will get three kinds of alum or fullers clay from the rulers of Karana and neighbouring Razama, which shows that even such materials as these were the concern of rulers and exchanged at a royal level of trade. It also suggests that Karana specialised in acquiring and stocking such goods.

XVIII 15

"Tyrian purple", the crimson dye which is obtained from the murex sea snail off the coast of Syria, definitely formed the basis of a flourishing dyes and textiles industry at Ugarit some 250 years later, for excavations have found heaps of discarded shells as well as tablets which list red-purple dyed fabrics. Almost certainly that same murex-based industry prospered at this period too; the Kingdom of Ugarit was already well established, and is mentioned in the Mari texts. No doubt other coastal towns made use of this inexhaustible natural resource too. But present evidence does not allow us to isolate the term for murex-dyed fabric, and we can only infer the existence of it at Mari from the later, Ugaritic evidence.[8]

Semi-precious stones

Much less is known about working in semi-precious stones and in leather, perhaps because some groups of tablets from Mari are not yet published.

One record tells of lapis lazuli coming via Eshnunna on its long journey from the mountains of Afghanistan:

"$\frac{1}{3}$ mina 3 shekels of lapis lazuli worth $\frac{2}{3}$ mina 6 shekels of silver."[9]

IX 254

Iltani commissioned her sister to find and buy a necklace of lapis lazuli in Ashur, but her sister wrote back to say that she was still unable to find one. Alabaster and mother-of-pearl were used in Mukannishum's workshops; pieces of inlay have

XIII 12

been found in the palace by excavation; and Inib-shina (probably the wife of Zimri-Lim's second-in-command Bahdi-Lim) sent to Zimri-Lim a present consisting of a chair and footstool inlaid with alabaster. Carnelian was imported for VII 265 fine jewellery; very little survived the pillage and was found XVIII 8 in the palace at Mari. A yellow stone was used with gold to make a headdress. One word, *hašmānum*, which means both a stone and the green/blue colour associated with that stone, may possibly be turquoise. Turquoise is rarely identified on excavations in Mesopotamia, perhaps because sunlight and changes in humidity cause it to fade and turn crumbly.[10] The Egyptians used turquoise from mines in Sinai from a very early date; it was almost certainly exported from Sinai to Upper Mesopotamia too.

Leather

As for leather, the records describe the many mundane uses of I 17 this flexible material. Leather boots or sandals were issued, sometimes together with waterskins, to men who were going on a journey. Leather was used for the bags in which wool and K 195, 196 fabrics were stored. It is found in the form of drumskins, on VIII 86 drums which were played at a ceremony in the king's presence. It was probably used in armour too, although there VII 161 is still no definite evidence for this. Leather harnesses, reins and blinkers for horses, mules and donkeys were made; a golden yellow may have been the colour most favoured, for this is the only descriptive term used in the few records available.

Wood

Wood is essential for good furniture, for construction work – especially doors and roofing – for boats, carts and wagons, and for such special goods as lyres, bows and battering rams. Since the area around Mari was almost certainly not wooded four XVIII 17, 21 thousand years ago, timber was imported from far and wide into the workshops. Carpenters were employed in the palace, and in provincial towns. One letter from Mari, written by Yaqqim-Addu the governor of Saggaratum to Zimri-Lim, tells how the former has gathered a total of 13 carpenters from various towns and villages in his district to send to Zimri-Lim, XIV 47 presumably for a large project.

"I asked Bazilum," continued Yaqqim-Addu, "and he told

me that 200 planks of juniper wood, two (trunks?) of cedar wood 15 m long; and 8 juniper (trunks?) 12 m long are being detained in Carchemish.''

The king was concerned personally in the timber business at all stages; in this letter, Mukannishum wrote to him saying:

"My lord wrote to me about having the cedar door made opposite the door of the gate of Uṣur-pi-sharrim. The pivot for xiii 7 the door, which they brought from Carchemish – I will not touch that pivot until my lord has examined it. I have measured the total length of the door at the gate of Uṣur-pi-sharrim, with (?) the pivot, and it is 6 m by 3.25 m.''

xviii 44　A record from Mukannishum's administration tells of doors made from a valued timber called *elammakum*.[11] The doors were probably for the king's bedroom, and were to be decorated with silver stars, using about 43 g of silver.

One of the most highly prized timbers for use in furniture was *musukannum*, sissoo, the dense, dark wood that resembles ebony.[12] This sissoo wood was often imported to make chairs, ii 47 tables and beds; Bahdi-Lim wrote to Zimri-Lim saying that he had sent sissoo wood to a man named Nabu-malik, who was xviii 26 very pleased with the consignment. A letter to Mukannishum tells how the king ordered from Mukannishum's workshops a bed or couch with knobs on, together with a footstool of sissoo wood; the chief carpenter, Qishti-Nunu, was to make them for vii 181 the king's travels. There were possibly four carpenters in Mukannishum's department, of whom Qishti-Nunu and xiii 20 Habdu-Hanat worked together to make five lyres for the king. It is not easy, however, to discover how the different departments were organised; the same two carpenters feature in a letter of Yasim-Sumu to Zimri-Lim:

xiii 40　"I have not neglected to gather labour for the palace's harvest, as my lord wrote to me. And as for what my lord wrote to me concerning the carpenters who are working on the doors, saying: 'If you have taken the carpenters who are working on the doors for the harvest, release them and let them finish their doors' – the carpenters who were working on the doors had no work to do, but the carpenters working under Qishti-Nunu and Habdu-Hanat, together with the coppersmiths who are working under Yashub-Ashar are busy with the work on the wagon.''

These texts show that the departments of Mukannishum and Yasim-Sumu overlapped in the use of workmen and in the royal instructions sent to workshop managers.

XIII 11 Other woods were also imported: ebony *ušum* was used as a veneer on boxwood *taskarinnum*.[13]

XIII 12 Inlay was done in alabaster and mother-of-pearl, and the remains of an inlaid wooden chest were actually found during excavations in the palace at Mari, the geometric pattern still visible. A list of finished wooden objects from Mari says:

IX 20 "1 bed, 8 chairs, 1 *kaniškarakkum*-style tray, 1 tray of *elammakum*-wood, 1 tray of pistachio wood, 1 footstool and 1 chest."

There is direct evidence of wood being used in the army's
XVIII 17 equipment: for battering rams and for bows in Mukan-
XVIII 21 nishum's workshops. The palace used timber in several ways:
XIII 138 it was heated with log fires or braziers (or perhaps this "timber for burning" was for workshop furnaces and kitchen ovens), which again seems to have been the responsibility of Mukannishum; he acquired firewood from the governor of Terqa. Buildings or new wings of the palace had to be roofed with timber beams, and Kibri-Dagan again helped to supply the palace at Mari:

III 23 "My lord wrote sternly to me about beams for roofing the walls, but there really were no beams available. Now, by hunting right and left among the country folk I have obtained 50 beams that are 6 m long and 250 beams that are 5 m long, and I have despatched them straight away, downstream to my lord."

There is much less evidence from the Karana texts, possibly because Iltani was not concerned with carpentry or furniture-making; possibly because the extant records do not happen to cover that aspect of palace production; or perhaps because much more woodwork was done in the palace at Mari
K 170 than at Karana. However, one text mentions a footstool, which is known from many texts to have been an extremely common
K 204 item of furniture. Another text is a list that includes "5 wooden mixing-bowls of fruit", which shows that the solid wooden fruit bowl was in fashion; maybe fruit salad too.

Metalwork

There is much evidence about metalwork, mainly from the
XIII 6 records of Mukannishum. He wrote to Zimri-Lim to tell him that there was not enough red gold for the goldsmith's work. He kept the gold locked and sealed, and was responsible for inspecting it. It is difficult to estimate what amounts of gold

Figure 26 (a) Some popular decorative themes from objects found in Mari;

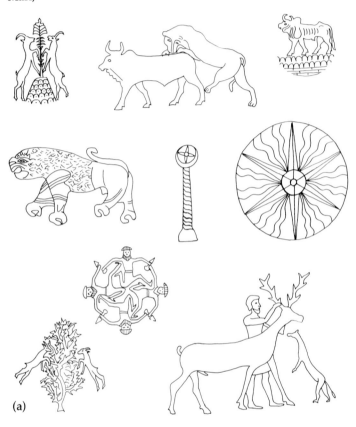

(a)

(b) decorative motifs from objects found at Kanish

(b)

and silver were at the disposal of the palace workshops. Perhaps the best indication of quantity comes from two Mari letters in which gifts are to be exchanged between the royal families of Assyria and of Qatna, on the arrangement of a dynastic marriage. Shamshi-Adad arranged to send a total of ten talents, some 300 kg of silver, and he certainly expected to receive presents of equivalent value.

The man who worked both gold and silver was the *kutimmum*, and he was entirely separate from the copper-smith, *qurqurrum*. There was a coppersmith called Ibbi-Adad, and, according to another letter of Mukannishum, he was making a surround of some kind for the "courtyard of palm trees", which is now identified with court 131 of the palace at Mari. Prancing *lamassum*-figures were to go with it, probably here winged bulls that served as protecting deities. Such figures are well known in gigantic stone form, dignified (never prancing), on guard over the gateways of late Assyrian citadels and palaces; here the material is not specified; perhaps they were painted on the walls, or perhaps they were copper ornaments, since there may be a connection with the coppersmith.

Gold and Silver

Statues were sometimes plated with gold; indeed, fragments of gold leaf were found in the throne room in which smashed statues were uncovered. Drinking vessels were made of gold and of silver, often with theriomorphic designs that make us think of much later Achaemenid work – this is simply because no examples of the Old Babylonian work survive, whereas some Achaemenid ones are extant. Mukannishum sent to Zimri-Lim from his workshops:

"2 drinking vessels of silver in the form of a bull's head, weighing 650 g; 8 drinking vessels in the form of an ibex head and 1 drinking vessel of red gold, weighing (nearly) 3 kg, 1 silver drinking vessel in the form of a gazelle's head weighing 200 g, weighed with the king's personal set of weights." Suddenly we are given a glimpse of the royal banqueting table, laid with precious drinking vessels in a variety of animal designs. The drinking vessels were probably not studded or inlaid with precious stones.

Drinking vessels and rhyta in the shape of animals' heads were commonly used by ordinary folk in Syria and Anatolia at this time, but they were usually made of terracotta. Many have been excavated at the Assyrian colony site of Kanish; the

Figure 27 Silver (?) drinking vessels from Anatolia, the closest parallels to those described in clay tablets from Mari. Height both 18 mm

Figure 28 Two Anatolian rhyta; terracotta vessel in the form of a bull's head, from Kanish; broken lion-head rhyton from Alishar, height about 70 mm

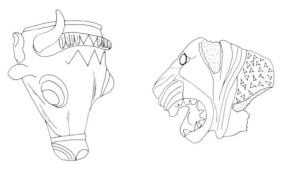

sturdy material and crude design show that they belonged outside the royal court; they may have imitated roughly in pottery what the palaces enjoyed in silver and gold. The vessels of precious metals were manufactured not only in Mari at this time, but also in Tukrish, an unknown country which lay north of Elam. The people of Tukrish were already famed for their craftsmanship in Zimri-Lim's time; perhaps their reputation spread after Shamshi-Adad, King of Assyria, received tribute from them. Certainly the style of Tukrish was

Figure 29 Pottery rhyton from Tell Kerab, near Carchemish, showing that luxury drinking vessels of precious metals were imitated in clay (Dimensions: height, 155mm; length, 225mm; width 166mm)

VII 239   notable enough for a silver bull's head cup from Mari to be described as "of Tukrish", and some 350 years later, when the Kassites ruled Babylon, their textile work was among the most coveted in ancient Mesopotamia.

A record from Karana shows that drinking vessels were put into a stand which in turn was kept in a royal box or coffer.

K 214   "2.5 kg is the weight of silver for making 7 drinking vessels of silver and 1 silver coffer for a drinking vessel stand, property of Burraganum. (Nearly) 2 kg of silver which are from the king's coffer. Total (about) 4.5 kg of silver for 32 drinking vessels each weighing 120 grams, which was given to Ibbi-Ilaba for manufacture."

In a letter Aqba-hammu wrote to Iltani:

"May the horses promptly deliver the case of silver drinking
K 85   vessels which are placed in the care of the cupbearers, to the bearer of this letter of mine", implying that Iltani, in addition to her work concerning food and textiles, authorised the removal of the vessels from the palace precinct.

The stand in which drinking vessels were placed was itself a work of art. A letter from Yasim-Sumu to Mukannishum suggests that the two workshop directors were co-operating.

XIII 55   "The king has instructed me about the ornaments for the drinking vessel stand; the heads of lions, the horns of roebuck and stags, saying: 'Put them on!' So I said: 'They are being put on.' Now, as soon as you have read this letter, have them put on immediately – the heads of lion, roebuck and stag."

Ivory was used occasionally; one text lists some stands for
VII 264   drinking vessels made of ivory, plated with gold and silver, in one case inlaid with two stars of lapis lazuli. There is not yet any evidence to show where the ivory came from; it is not often mentioned in the Mari texts, but the excavations at Acemhüyük in Anatolia have unearthed quite a lot.[14]

Bronze

There are only scattered allusions to bronze work, and to the manufacture of armour, which must have taken up much of the bronze-smith's time; but these are sufficient to show our dependence on which groups of records survived to be discovered, and which have been published.[15] When a list of textiles given to particular people also contains some kind of bow, we may deduce that some of the textiles at least were
XVIII 61, 63, 66   body armour. Hauberks are found, described as "Akkad-style" or "Aleppo-style", of first or second quality. However,

XVIII 28 either the military arsenal of Zimri-Lim was not within the palace walls at Mari, or the evidence is still lacking, for these references are few and tantalising. The bronze-smith, *nappāhum*, was probably a man of considerable standing in K 25 society. A Karana text shows that he owned a slave-girl, and in the Mari ration lists the only smith who is included, named Shamash-tukulti, received the larger standard of bread ration.

Yasim-Sumu sent bronze to Mukannishum in order to make XIII 54 tools at the urgent request of the king – axes, chisels and spades. It is likely that the work, although supervised by Mukannishum, was done outside the palace walls, for no bronze-smith's furnace or slag was found in the palace. Perhaps surprisingly, only a single bronze-smith is found in XVIII 5 the ration lists, yet a letter written by Zimri-Lim to Mukannishum suggests that the latter was indeed closely concerned with arms manufacture.

"Speak to Mukannishum; thus your lord. As soon as you have read this letter, have made 50 bronze arrow-(head)s of 40 g weight each, 50 arrow(head)s of 24 g weight each, 100 arrow(head)s of 16 g weight each, and 200 arrow(head)s of 8 g weight each. Make it a priority, so that it is finished quickly. It looks as if the siege of Andarik may be prolonged, and that is why I am writing to you for those arrows."

Tin

Tin, that rare metal, had to be supplied from far abroad, from a source still unidentified.[16] There are several unresolved problems connected with tin and the manufacture of bronze at this period. Although there is no doubt that, in some contexts, the word *annākum* does mean tin, in other contexts it may mean lead.[17] We certainly cannot assume that a single word in Akkadian has a single equivalent in English. Analysis of pieces of bronze from good strata on excavations seems to show that arsenic-bronze, not tin-bronze, was still much in use at this period,[18] which does not seem to tally with the interpretation of *annākum* as tin being imported in large amounts. To complicate the issue further, there is firm evidence that lead in the late Bronze Age was used as an alloy with copper in addition to tin.[19] Very little bronze from Mesopotamia in the time of Hammurabi has yet been analysed. Lead occurs naturally and plentifully in Anatolia, so that it would not have had to be imported into Anatolia by Assyrians; it makes nonsense to suppose that lead was the mainstay of the Old

Assyrian trading colony at Kanish – it was so common locally that very often figurines were made of solid lead, and they have been found in considerable numbers at Kültepe. Nor yet is it possible to reconcile archaeological finds and their analysis with the written records. As for its sources, although there are a few known in Iran, it is not certain whether they were being exploited at the time; the discovery of cloves from Indonesia in the excavations at Terqa[20] is bound to reopen the possibility that Thailand, not Iran, was the main supplier. Because it came from far away, and perhaps because the sources were few, the flow of material must have been intermittent, reflecting unrest or interference at any point on its long journey.

K 109   "There is no tin available", wrote Kiṣṣurum to Iltani at Karana; yet some years earlier, Mari under Zimri-Lim was receiving such a plentiful supply that tin was sent on from XIII 144 Mari to the city Talhayum, capital of the state Idamaraz which lay to the NNW of Mari, so that new tools could be made. This occurred probably just after Zimri-Lim had annexed its people to Mari.

There is an administrative record that shows the quantities in which tin was stocked at one particular time.

VII 86   "33 kg of tin, item one, is in the courtyard; 2.5 kg of tin, item two, is in the . . . storehouse; 30 kg of tin, item three, is in the . . . storehouse; 2.5 kg of tin, item four, total 76 kg of tin, which I, Ahushina, have received."

VII 218   In the text quoted below (p. 65), tin is found with drinking vessels and rings given to high officials who are known to have carried out duties abroad as ambassadors from Mari or to have deputised at Mari in the king's absence. In the later part of the second and in the first millennium tin is well known from texts as a currency metal alongside silver, and this usage can now be seen also in Old Babylonian Mari.[21] There is another text, concerned entirely with tin, although it does not indicate the function of the tin. Even though the end of it is broken away, the amount of tin in total is colossal, some 480 kg. Moreover, RA 64 the text describes not only whence the tin had arrived and where it was stocked, but also whither it was to be redistributed. Some, the largest amount, comes from Mari; some from Hammurabi of Babylon is to be found in Halab; some is a delivery from Sheplarpak, the king of Anshan with the impossible name; some is "a present from Ishi-Dagan and Yatar-Addu", to be found in Ugarit. Of this tin, the second distribution is as follows: some to Shamshi-Adad the king of Assyria, some to Yarim-Lim, King of Aleppo, a separate and smaller quantity to his wife Gashera (Zimri-Lim's mother-in-law), some to three other men in Aleppo, the rest to other western towns including Hazor, and some to "the Cretan". This text gives a little insight into the complex patterns of distribution and redistribution when the Assyrians controlled Mari, and confirms the view that much trade was done in the form of presents exchanged at a royal or ambassadorial level, in raw materials such as metals as well as finished goods such as textiles.

Iron

Iron was known, and was used for ornamental work: for
I 244, 247 buckles and beads. Of course, the working of it to produce tools and weapons that were as good as bronze ones was not yet developed; it was 800 years or more before iron-working reached maturity in this area;[22] meanwhile the metal was known and used without having any great significance for the economy. An ivory casket recently excavated at Acemhüyük is decorated with studs of bronze, iron and lapis lazuli.[23]

Currency and rates of exchange

It is clear from the texts that the manufacture of drinking vessels and their stands in quite considerable numbers was common. This brings us to the question of currency in an age when coinage had not yet been invented, for it is evident that merchant palaces must have owned currency objects, and probably manufactured them also. The records from Mari show quite clearly what forms currency took in Mesopotamia during the Middle Bronze Age.[24]

There is one text which lists drinking vessels side by side with ingots of tin and rings of silver for particular people.[25] Rings are already known as a form in which silver was used as pre-coin currency.[26]

VII 218 "1 ring, 73 drinking vessels, Hammu-shagish, 2 (of which are) bull's head (vessels). 6 drinking vessels, Asqudum. 10 drinking vessels, 2 (of which are) bull's head (vessels), Yasim-Sumu. 7 drinking vessels, Habdu-Malik, 24 ingots of tin, Idiniatum. 6 drinking vessels, Yasim-Dagan. 57 drinking vessels, 3 rings, Bahdi-Lim, bull's head (vessels). 3 drinking vessels, 4 rings, Yasim-El." All these men were very high-ranking palace officials, some of whom had married into

Zimri-Lim's family. The payments may have been for them personally, or for them to distribute abroad as ambassadors, and to give to visiting dignitaries at Mari. In any case, the drinking vessels are clearly a form of exchange or payment. Another text tells how 7 drinking vessels in the shape of end IX 46 sections of horns, weighing a total of 1.17 kg of silver, were given to the men of the Babylonian commander-in-chief.

Payment seems also to have taken the form of silver-and-gold axes or axe-heads.[27] One text allots a garment VII 249 and a *haṣṣinnum*-axe, which is made with a stated weight of silver and plated with gold, to each of six different, named officials. Such an axe could never have been used as a tool. The weight of each man's axe presumably reflects the payment which was due. Only a single tablet so far published attests this practice, but it is particularly enticing as a parallel for the currency- or ingot-axes of Armorica (Brittany in France) in the early first millennium.[28]

There is a list of silver which seems to show that official travellers did not keep the so-called gifts which they received abroad.

VII 117   "2 kg of silver, rings in a pouch, . . . Abdu-Malik.

1 kg of silver pieces. . . . .

540 g of silver for the messengers.

2.38 kg of silver in a pouch . . . Yasim-El.

372 kg of silver, for the ransom of 4 servants of Kabiya.

88 g of silver, presents for the messengers in Tabatum.

1 drinking vessel in the shape of an end section of a horn of silver, present of Habdu-Malik when he came back from Hali-sumu . . . .

2 silver rings (weighing) 147 g, of Aqba-ahum, when he came back from Qarni-Lim (King of Andarik), from two journeys . . . .

1 silver drinking vessel (weighing) 80 g, of Habdu-Malik, when he came back from Hammurabi."

The summary at the end of the text shows quite clearly that they surrendered the so-called presents to the king, for it says: "Additions to the king's coffer." The king's coffer, then, *pisan šarrim*, was the royal purse or palace treasury.

Silver was the basic medium of exchange, and it was often stored or carried in the form of a thin coil or ring of wire or ribbon, such as has been found on excavations near Karana, at Tell Taya.[29] When the *nadītum*-women of Sippar paid for their acquisitions, the records state that they gave "from their silver ring"; in other words they snipped off the appropriate weight of silver from a long coil. Much of it was imported from Anatolia, in particular from the abundant silver mines of Cilicia, and presumably it was common and regularly supplied, and therefore the most suitable metal for currency.

These forms of metal in which payments were made – ingots, rings and drinking vessels – and also the royal coffer in which the currency was stored, can be illustrated with an Egyptian discovery known as the Treasure of Tod. This treasure consisted entirely of imported items, and was stored in a fine coffer which bore the cartouche of Amenemhet II, and so was perhaps a century or so earlier than the Mari texts.[30] Among the items were oblong ingots of silver, rough rings of silver, lightweight cups with simple fluting, and other cups which had been flattened and folded up quite deliberately, to be stored as pieces of sheet metal in the king's coffer. Details of workmanship and of seal cutting showed that some of the work was Aegean, some Levantine and some Mesopotamian. The items were various forms of metal currency, produced abroad and given in exchange for Egyptian exports. The drinking vessels of the Mari texts were more elaborate and varied in design, but largely served the same purpose, some of them being quite tiny (200 g), others at 3 kg hard to lift and drink from. The treasure also contained fragments of lapis lazuli, which may likewise have been used as currency.

Figure 30 A selection from the treasure of Tod: (a) silver ingots weighing between 124 and 133 grams, (gold ones were also found); (b) linked silver rings, weight approximately 85 grams; (c) silver coil-ingot with schematic decoration:

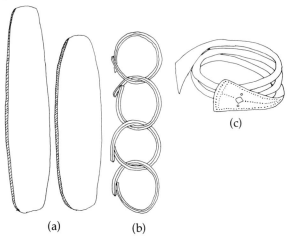

(a)   (b)

(d) silver cups and bowls, (one gold cup was found), weight varies between 17 and 111 grams. (e) deliberately flattened cups and bowls; (f) copper treasure box/coffer. Cartouche with the name of Amenemhet II on lid. (Now in Louvre)

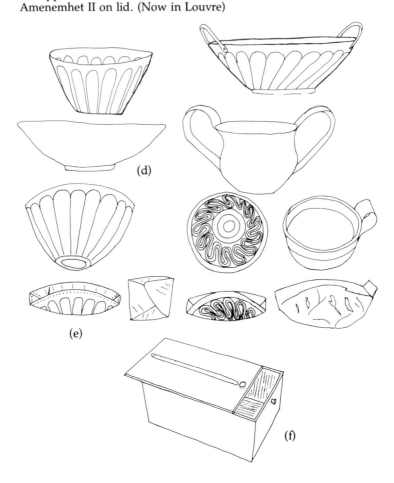

The post of chief cupbearer was important because he was in charge of the king's wine and perhaps tested it for poison. But if this information about the drinking vessels is interpreted correctly, he may have been responsible for a very large quantity of precious metals, virtually the palace treasury. In this capacity he would be in charge of drinking vessels as presents to guests who must be honoured (or insulted) by weight of metal and by craftsmanship according to their status, and who probably received the gifts during a royal banquet.

How was adequate exchange value arranged? There were certain theoretical rates of exchange for a few basic commodities, such as those proclaimed by Shamshi-Adad King of Assyria in a public inscription, and a different one, probably a few years earlier, by Dadusha, the king who compiled the lawcode of Eshnunna and included the list of exchange rates there.[31] These texts give the worth of such items as barley, oil and wool in terms of silver, and they were probably supposed to be applied throughout a kingdom or empire as a standard rate. Comparison with daily records seems to show that they were very optimistic rates, reflecting a propagandist's view of the world rather than fiscal reality.[32] How regional discrepancies in exchange rates were ironed out we have no evidence, but presumably bargaining and complaints were used to good effect.

The division of labour

The Karana texts have shown how the queen was closely concerned with palace textile workshops, and how it was only one of many duties for Iltani. The women's letters from Mari have shown that Queen Shibtu was, among many other functions, closely associated with food storage on a large scale. This lack of specialisation was not restricted to women. Yasim-Sumu, as well as using the two carpenters from Mukannishum's department and co-operating with him in producing metal objects, advised the king on how to choose a year formula.

At that time each year was named after an important event that had usually taken place the previous year; the events were usually cultic or military.[33] These appellations, in the absence of any formal historical writing, are an important source of information for the military and political history of the period. Perhaps Yasim-Sumu's involvement was a part of his stated profession of "archivist" ŠÀ.DUB.BA. He wrote to Zimri-Lim saying:

XIII 27 "The year that has just come in – let it be called 'Year when Zimri-Lim went to help Babylon, and went against the kingdom of Larsa for the second time.'" Before he wrote this suggestion to Zimri-Lim, he had discussed alternatives with a colleague named Shunuh-rahalu:

XIII 47 "About the name of the year, of which you wrote to me saying: '(As for the suggestion to call the year) "Year which

Zimri-Lim dedicated a large throne to the god Dagan" ' –
that throne still has not been dedicated. Now, I have sent a
letter to my lord, giving the name of the year as: 'Zimri-Lim
went to help Babylon and to Larsa for the second time.' Draw
the king's attention to that letter, and then write to me to say
whether or not he has accepted it."

XIII 40 Yasim-Sumu kept the king informed about men and
XIII 42 equipment for the harvest; dealt with a carpenter from Halab
who was to make a *lamassum*–statue of a protecting genius; sent
XIII 44 Zimri-Lim a leather-worker, and helped to arrange imports of
XIII 35 grain. So it is evident that the workshop managers did not
divide their work by craft, but that each was concerned with
many different trades. Mukannishum is found involved with
wool, finished garments, metalwork, oil, leather, meat, and
female prisoners. Just emerging is the possibility that work
was organised in sections that dealt with a particular area of
IX 127 trade, since there is evidence for "the office for Babylon" and
VII 283 "the office for Terqa".

Even with such a wealth of documents it is difficult for us to
tell how good the conditions of labour were for slaves. The
exact significance of the word *nepārum* is uncertain. Although
it is used in the sense of "prison" this may be a secondary
meaning. Usually it means a palace workshop in which both
prisoner-of-war slaves and free men worked. The origin and
etymology of the word are unknown. A different expression,
bīt ṣibittim, is used in one Mari letter for a prison in which
ORD criminal offenders were detained.

There is no definite evidence from Mari that free men could
be enslaved for debt, but we suspect that the texts would
seldom if ever mention such a thing. We may be misled by the
bias of the evidence into supposing that almost all slaves had
lost their freedom through capture in a war.

A slave could be given away as a present even after a lifetime
X 57 of service, but this was regarded as an insensitive thing to do.
The lady Adad-duri wrote:

"Dagan-ellassu grew up in this palace from a baby, and you
are going to give him away as a present to Sumu-hadim as he
reaches old age. The attendants his 'brothers' have gathered
together (to protest), and I cannot satisfy them".

Another letter from a woman to Zimri-Lim begs him not to
X 97 give away her ageing mother as a present. Presumably the
mother was a slave, but her daughter, whether also a slave or a
freed woman, could write to the king himself, to beg him to
change his mind.

K 133   There is no definite evidence that slaves were punished for
XIII 26 trying to escape: they were recaptured and brought back
again. Among so many detailed letters there is only one
incident in which some workmen tried to escape. It occurred in
the town of Șuprum within the kingdom of Mari. Zimri-Lim
wrote to Adad-duri saying:

"I have just read the letter that you sent me, in which you
wrote to say that some menials had tunnelled their way out of
X 150 the workshop of Suprum and escaped, but that they were
caught."

Zimri-Lim advised Adad-duri to act forcefully, so that
escapes should not become common; but we do not know
exactly what measures were taken. The reluctant worker who
made a habit of trying to escape might be guaranteed by his
fellow workers, who would have to pay jointly a large sum of
money to the palace if he escaped. It seems to have been a
VIII 63, 65 common habit to insure slaves in this way, and perhaps the
need for harsh punishment was obviated.

In Karana, where labour was particularly short, a worker
K 34, 76 could not be taken from one task for another without having a
K 101 replacement provided. There are only two records of slave
sales from Mari from this period,[34] and none from Karana.
Also, it is difficult to be sure exactly which workers were slaves
and which were free workmen, as slave names cannot yet be
distinguished from others at this period.[35] Nor is there usually
a distinction of word between "slave" and "servant, subject of
the king". We still do not know what proportion of the
population consisted of slaves, nor to what extent they were
treated differently from free people, although Hammurabi's
Code makes it clear that slaves sometimes paid the death
penalty whereas a free man paid for the same crime with a fine
of money.

The main source of labour in the palace was prisoners of
war. This means that production could quickly be increased by
enlarging the centralised labour force as the result of a military
victory. When a city or a palace was sacked, human labour was
as valuable a commodity as precious metals to the conquering
X 125 king, and it is clear from the Mari letters that a new influx of
prisoners was speedily absorbed into the palace workshops.
XIII 21 Other workmen, however, were skilled professionals of local
origin who had probably been trained by palace staff; though
unfortunately there is not any detailed evidence extant for
65 p. 54 apprenticeship, apart from one list which includes 11
talmēdu– apprentices with 19 builders.

Blind people, IGI.NU.GÁL, were employed in the palaces.
CB 42 At Chagar Bazar these blind men and women were listed on the palace ration lists and were allotted the standard ration. One of them was a reed worker, one a female miller, and two were gardeners. It is curious that their state is described in those laconic lists, since their name and profession suffices to distinguish them, and their ration is no different from that of workers who were not blind.

What the conditions of employment were in the service of the palace can be described only in part. If a ration list term
XVIII 55 ŠU.BAR.RA has been understood correctly, textile workers
V 71 were allowed time off, free days without work, although
IX 24, 25, 101 details are lacking. Wages were paid in clothes, in wool and cereal, and perhaps most commonly in cereal or bread, demarcation permitting!

"Speak to my lord, thus Bahdi-Lim your servant. The city
VI 39 Mari, the palace and the district are well. Now, I have been looking into the matter of the palace workers, and of the 400 palace workers, 100 have been given clothes and the other 300 have not been given clothes. So about the workers without clothes I asked Mukannishum and Bali-Erah, and Mukannishum replied saying: 'It is not my department; it is for Bali-Erah to give them clothes.' And Bali-Erah replied saying: 'I have given clothes to 100 of the workers. 100 is the total of my department, and Mukannishum should give clothes to the others'."

Every movement of goods, payment of workers and arrival from abroad was recorded in writing on a clay tablet. The tablets were stored in boxes, probably on shelves and the room was sealed by the king with his cylinder seal, the signature of his authority. Inibshina wrote to Zimri-Lim saying:
X 82 "In accordance with the message that you sent to me, I unsealed the tablet room, which had been sealed with your seal; Mukannishum and Tabat-sharrussu were present, and then Igmillum showed them the boxes for their information; I let them out with the boxes for all the census as their personal responsibility."

Seals were used also to seal food stores. The wine store at
X 133 Mari was locked with Zimri-Lim's own seal; he sent the seal to Shibtu his wife when he wanted her to take out some wine as a present for Hammurabi of Babylon. When she had resealed the room she was told to give the seal back to the king.

The mechanism by which rooms were sealed appears to

have been more symbolic than practical: a string or cord was stretched across the opening edge of the door, held in place at both ends by a blob of clay on which the relevant seal was imprinted. When the door was unsealed, the blobs of clay simply fell to the floor, where they sometimes accumulated in more or less stratified heaps, bearing witness to slovenly housekeeping – which is such a boon to the excavator, as long as his workmen recognise the importance of clay lumps with designs often impressed only faintly. No doubt this device for sealing doors was often supported by sturdy bolts.

Tablets keeping records of the workshops were carried not only from one part of the palace to another, but also from one town to another within a kingdom.

K 311 "Bring your tablets, make the journey and present the K 71 accounts of your barley," says a letter from Karana. Iltani took tablets with her on her travels, and perhaps then brought them back to her palace, together with letters that she had received while she was away.[36] Sometimes a letter would be sent only from one part of the palace to another. Either of these 16, 136 situations may result in the occasional discovery of two letters, XIII 10 one of which was written in answer to the other.

A1285 Several other professions are known from palace ration lists, apart from those already mentioned. At the humble end of the 26, 27 scale were the drawers of water, at Mari two girls called Behi and Abi-shamshi; and two men who "carried wood". There was a doorkeeper (women were doorkeepers at Chagar CB 44 Bazar), a barber, a throne-bearer and a reed worker who IX 25 would have made baskets, mats and fencing. There were XIII 16 gardeners who tended the palm trees in the great courtyard XII 267 and probably cultivated fragrant flowers in "the garden of the king", where *alappānum*-beer offerings were made to the goddess Ishtar. Curiously no potters are to be found in the I 740-6 Mari ration lists, although there are lists of different types of pots, their capacity or intended function stated. Two potters are found in the ration lists of Chagar Bazar.

12, 176 The official who was in charge of "the bitumen department" is not known, although this ubiquitous fixative and waterproofing agent had a whole room or department to itself at Mari. Perhaps the same man, or a man from the oil stores, was in charge of lighting the palace.

K 17 "1 litre of first-rate oil for the lamp that stands before the VIII 32 goddess," says an oil record from Karana; a Mari text contains X 86 the same word *šannūrum* for an oil lamp, and in a letter lamp wicks, *buṣinnum*, are sent with oil. A man (or women) whose

work included refining oil and making perfumes was the *raqqûm* or *luraqqum*, oil-presser or perfume-maker, and he was
VII 103 in charge of various aromatics: essences of cypress, storax, myrtle, cedar and juniper, with his own room or department. Probably these were used for anointing and cleaning both people and the statues of the gods.[37]

Although most of the written records concern work, there was also play in the palaces of Mari and Karana. We have already referred to the two lyres made under Mukannishum's direction, and to the drums made with palace leather. A little plaque of this period shows a lute player in action; musicians both male and female received rations of food and wine in the palace. A fragmentary letter from Mari shows that musicians
XIV40 K255 travelled with caravans, and a wine list from Karana reveals that female musicians were allowed wine. Jugglers and wrestlers are found in a ritual text,[38] displaying their skills to the goddess Ishtar in her temple, but they probably also
VII 161 performed in the palace. Mukannishum's section perhaps produced wrestlers' belts. A game perhaps akin to quoits was played in Court 31 at Mari, where the excavators found a square containing nine squares set into the floor. The edges were of plaster painted to look like marble. From other excavations in Mesopotamia we know that gaming boards and gaming pieces were popular, some of them being very beautifully made with intricate inlaid decoration; but the games which they played are not understood today. However, in general terms they were the forerunners of backgammon and chess.

Notes to Chapter Three

1. This identification has been disputed. J. Muhly, *Copper and Tin*, does not mention it at all (cf. p. 11 and note 390 to Chapter III), for he regards this Tayma as a different, unidentified place. The reference to Teima in the later versions of a text of Sargon (A. K. Grayson "The Empire of Sargon of Akkad", in *Archiv für Orientforschung* 25 1974–7, p. 60 line 48 and note on p. 64) is supposed to be an anachronism. But if the identification is correct, Tayma may have been the market or kingdom from which the mineral wealth of Sinai was distributed; evidence for copper mine working at this period has not yet been found in Sinai.

2. See S. W. Helms, *Jawa*, Methuen 1981, pp. 31–34.

3. For the identification of Anshan as Tel Malyan, see E. Reiner, *Revue d'Assyriologie* 67 1973, p. 57ff.

4. The various textual references to these items are listed in the Répertoire Analytique, *ARM* XVI/I under *noms géographiques*.

5. See Reallexikon, *lapis lazuli* entry.

6. Note that the Yamhad-style carpet was actually made at Mari; the name of a style does not, therefore, necessarily mean that the object was made in the place where the style originated.

7. Mordants are substances that "fix" dyes in fabric to stop them fading or washing out.

8. There is a curious term "sea locusts" or "shrimps" for something that was used in textile work. There is also a dye called *allānum* from central Anatolia, which may be the scarlet dye obtained from the Kermes oak tree that is native to Anatolia. According to K 122 it came from Kanish via Ashur to Karana.

9. The shekel of silver was roughly a manual worker's monthly wage at this period, and weighed about 8 grams. There were 60 shekels in a mina.

10. Conditions for its preservation are very much better in Egypt, where most material comes from well-built tombs. At Shahr-i-Sokhta in eastern Iran the excavator noticed that far more turquoise was recognised and found in tombs than in houses. See M. Tosi, "The problem of turquoise in protohistoric trade on the Iranian plateau", *Studi di Paletnologia, Paleoantropologia Paleontologia e Geologia del Quaternario* vol 2 (nuova serie) 1974.

11. The old identification of *elammakum* with sandalwood has been abandoned because it is now known that the timber was imported from the Lebanon, where sandalwood is not indigenous. See Dossin, "Inscription de Foundation de Yahdun-Lim", *Syria* 32 1955, p. 1ff, and A. Malamat, *Assyriological Studies* 16 1965, p. 368, "Campaigns to the Mediterranean by Lahdun-Lim and other early Mesopotamian rulers".

12. See note 4 on Chapter 1.

13. Walnut has also been suggested as the identification of *taskarinnum*; but the wood is so frequently found with ebony that boxwood may still be preferable, its white colour making a striking contrast with the blackness of ebony.

14. See e.g. N. Özgüç, "Belleten of the Türk Tarih Kurumu", *Contributions to early Anatolian Art from Acemhüyük* 43, 1979.

15. They are discussed in detail by J. Muhly, in Wertime and Muhly, *The Coming of the Age of Iron*, Yale UP, 1980.

16. For the difficulty that *annākum* may mean tin and lead, see note 2, Chapter 1.

17. *Annākum* is thought to mean only tin by J. Muhly, *Copper and Tin*, Archon 1973, and in Wertime and Muhly, *The Coming of the Age of Iron*, Yale UP, 1980. It is translated as "tin" here.

18. See P. R. S. Moorey in H. H. Coghlan, *Notes on the prehistoric metallurgy of copper and bronze in the Old World*, Oxford 2nd ed., 1975, esp. p. 41.

19. Coghlan, op. cit., p. 36.

20. See Chapter 4, p. 83.

21. In the trading colony of Kanish merchants used "hand tin", *annak qātim*, as currency for certain types of payment, e.g. for paying taxes and hiring lawyers.

22. For the slow introduction of iron-working into Assyria, see K. R. Maxwell-Hyslop, "Assyrian sources of iron", in *Iraq* 36 1974, especially p. 142.

23. M. Mellink reporting from N. Özgüç, *American Journal of Archaeology* 81 1977, p. 295b.

24. See J-R. Kupper, "L'usage de l'argent à Mari", in *Zikir šumim*, Assyriological studies presented to F. R. Kraus, Leiden, 1982, pp. 163ff.

25. For drinking vessels as currency in Old Assyrian, Cappadocian texts see *CAD* sub *kāsu*.

26. See J. Bottéro, *ARM* VII p. 332–3.

27. Currency axes are known from Nuzi a few centuries later; see *CAD* sub *haṣṣinnu*.

28. J. Briard, *The Bronze Age in Barbarian Europe*, translated M. Turton, 1979 pp. 206–7.

29. J. Reade, Tell Taya (1972–3): summary report, *Iraq* 35 1973, p. 165 and plate LXVIIa. For the possible connection of *kaspum* "silver" with the verb *kasāpum*, "to cut off", see W. Eilers, *Welt des Orients* 2 1957, pp. 322–337.

30. F. Chapoutier, *Le Trésor de Tod*, Cairo 1953. Its precise date is disputed.

31. The attribution of this lawcode to Dadusha was made by Landsberger in his article "Jungfräulichkeit", in *Symbolae iuridicae et historicae M. David dedicatae, Tomus alter iura orientis antiqui*, pp. 65–67.

32. See the remarks of A. K. Grayson, *Assyrian Royal Inscriptions* vol. I, Wiesbaden 1972, pp. 20–21, note 64.

33. According to M. Anbar's study (forthcoming) each year name had both a military and a cultic section, but frequently only one half of the name was used.

34. *ARM* VII 9 and 10.

35. Such a study has now been done on slave names of this period from Sippar: R. Harris, "Notes on slave names in Old Babylonian Sippar", *Journal of Cuneiform Studies* 29 1977.

36. A clay envelope was often used to safeguard a letter, which could easily be altered or damaged since it was of dried clay and was not usually impressed with a seal.

37. See Chapter 4, p. 86.

38. G. Dossin, "Un rituel du culte d'Ištar provenant de Mari", *Revue d'Assyriologie* 35 1938, p. 1ff.

Chapter Four
Food and Drink

The pleasures of the table

When Enkidu came out of the desert to be introduced to
Gilgamesh and city life, he lacked all the graces of a civilised
man. "When they placed food before him, he narrowed his
eyes and stared intently. Enkidu knew nothing of eating food,
he had no experience of drinking strong drink."[1] The ancient
Mesopotamians recognised that the pleasures of the table are a
sure indicator of sophistication. The Near East, whether in
recent times or in the mediaeval tales of the *Arabian Nights*, is
renowned for delicious dishes, spicy meats and aromatic
confections, with an emphasis on the variety of small,
tempting preparations and on pleasing the olfactory sense by
flavouring with clever combinations of herbs and spices. To
invite guests is to make an opportunity to display wealth and
good taste, and to give hospitality is the mark of duty,
generosity, pleasure and power. To what extent this tradition
has its origins in early antiquity can be discovered from the
remarkable cuneiform tablets of Mari and Karana.

The villagers who lived in the little kingdoms of Mari and
Karana produced most of the basic food that was eaten there
by their labour on the land. How much of that land was owned
by palace and temple we cannot yet say, although the texts tell
us that the palace owned and distributed some agricultural
equipment. Certainly plenty of food found its way to the
king's banqueting hall, and was recorded in writing on the
way.

With Yasmah-Addu's penchant for luxurious living already
established, it comes as no surprise to find that his dinner
menu is often much larger than that of his more austere
successor, Zimri-Lim.

XI 1   "900 litres of KUM-bread, 60 litres of bread made with
sammidatum-flour; 2,020 litres of 'sour' *emṣum*-bread made of

Figure 31 (a) Issue of best and second-best bread to Iltani when Lady Belaya came to stay; (b) issue of barley to Lady Azzu and to fisherman Zirashe, probably authorised by Iltani

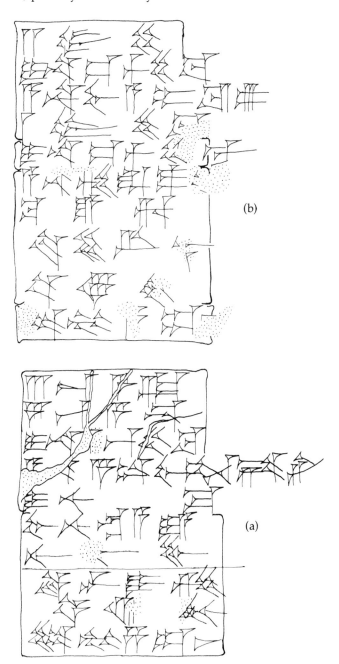

burrum-cereal, 950 litres of cake, 2,185 litres of 'sour' *emṣum*-bread made of barley, 940 litres of *alappānum*-mead, 100 litres of chick peas, 11 litres of *isququm*-flour, 6 litres of *sasqum*-semolina, 3 litres of *sammidatum*-flour, 70 litres of (linseed) oil, 3 litres of honey (or date syrup), 4 litres of linseed, [2] 5 litres of dates – meal of the king and his men in Mari on the fourth day of the month *kiskisum*."

Unfortunately we do not know how many men sat down to this feast; but compare the menu of Zimri-Lim, which is considerably less in quantity.

XI 70   "147 litres of KUM-bread, 102 litres of 'sour' *emṣum*-bread, 120 litres of cake, 10 litres of *alappānum*-mead, 24.5 litres of *šipkum*-cereal, 14 litres of (linseed) oil, 3 litres of honey/date syrup, 10 litres of linseed, 5 litres of dates, 2 litres of *buṭuṭṭum*-flour, 2 litres of *appānum*-pulses."

Of course, these menu lists do not give the whole story. They were the records from only one part of the palace kitchen supplies, and there are other texts which fill out the picture, so that the diet is shown to be less starchy.

Sources of protein

Meat was certainly eaten by people as well as being offered to the gods. There was a notable profession, that of animal-fattener, known from both palaces, a man who fed animals on barley. The Mari palace supported two, named
IX 27 CB 40   Shamash-tappe and Asirum. They fattened oxen, sheep, pigs,
V 46   deer and birds. One letter from Mari concerns a top quality,
IX 51   barley-fattened ox that would have to make a journey by boat for a religious offering; but in case the ox falls ill en route, a
XIV 6   member of the kitchen staff is to travel with it, so that he can butcher it and send the meat to the palace instead if necessary.

XII 747   A distribution list from Mari shows that cuts of mutton were given both to foreign envoys who were staying in the palace, and to musicians, workmen, a priest and a palace attendant. The palace at Chagar Bazar was a centre for the distribution of food, some of it meat from the department of the
A 994   animal-fattener. One text mentions a crate of meat which was taken from there to another town.

AREC   Hares were hunted for food, and on one occasion when the six men who had caught some brought them to the palace at Mari, they were rewarded with three shekels of silver for their
CB 15   pains. Gazelles too may have been eaten; or possibly they were caught for royal parks and fed in order to keep them alive

and well, not fattened for succulence. Certainly they were eaten at the court of King Solomon, according to the Old Testament.

Very little information is available for domesticated fowl at this period. The cockerel with his distinctive crest is known for certain in Assyria some four centuries later from a drawing on ivory; geese and ducks were certainly kept as domestic birds in the first millennium, and almost certainly very much earlier. But so far the Mari texts mention only professional bird-catchers, who capture fat TU.TUL-birds for the governor of Saggaratum, and he sends them on to Mari for Zimri-Lim. When ostrich eggs were discovered at some distance from Saggaratum by policemen who were tracking down miscreants, the eggs were collected and taken to the governor who sent them to Zimri-Lim; but perhaps so that the splendid shells could be used as vessels, rather than for the contents as food.

Then, as now, a plague of locusts was a chance source of protein. Kibri-Dagan the governor of Terqa under Zimri-Lim wrote to his king:

"Just as I was about to write to my lord, locusts descended on Terqa. Because the weather was too hot, they did not settle. But now I am sending to my lord as many locusts as were caught."

Fish was another source of protein. The nineteenth-century explorer and excavator Sir Henry Layard describes Lake Hatuniyeh, a fresh water lake that lies 120 km from Karana as the crow flies, just north-west of the Jebel Sinjar. "We traced the remains of cultivation, and the dry watercourses, which once irrigated plots of rice and melon beds. The lake may be about six miles in circumference. From its abundant supply of water, and its central position between the Sinjar and the Khabour, Khatouniyah must at one time have been a place of some importance. . . . It abounds in fish, some of which are said to be of very considerable size. As we approached, the Bairakdar, seeing something struggling in a shallow rode to it, and captured a kind of barbel, weighing above twenty pounds. Waterfowl and waders, of various kinds, congregate on its shores. The stately crane and the graceful egret, with its snow-white plumage and feathery crest, stand lazily on its margin; and thousands of ducks and teal eddy on its surface round the unwieldy pelican."³

In addition to natural sources of fresh fish such as this lake, artificial ponds and ditches were stocked with fish. The town

of Kahat in the Upper Habur had a ditch stocked with
girītu–fish. When Mari was under Assyrian occupation, Kahat
fell under the control of Yasmah-Addu, whose brother
Ishme-Dagan wrote to him to request some of those fish.

I 139   "There are some *girītum*–fish in the ditch of Kahat.
Have some caught and sent to me." A kitchen supply list from
IX 250 Mari states briefly: "15 *arzuppum*–fish, 80 *abatum*–fish, 30 *purādum*–
carp, 9 *kuppum*–eels." A fragmentary list of supplies for an
IX 251 evening meal mentions 60 fish and 23 birds from one man; 33
fish and x birds from another.

Some tablets from Karana show that both dried and potted
fish were known.

"Speak to Iltani; thus says Amur-sha-Shamash. May Adad
K 130 and Geshtin-anna grant you long life! Your fish roes in salt
water in Qaṭara have been turning yellow for a long time.
Now, why don't you dry the fish roes?"

Queen Iltani was sent a special container of shrimps by her
sister Amat-Shamash, who was a priestess down in Sippar.
Amat-Shamash wanted to be sent some slaves, and offered
presents as an inducement:

"The slaves whom my father gave me have grown old; now,
I have sent half a mina of silver to the king; allow me my claim
and get him to send me slaves who have been captured
recently, and who are trustworthy. In recollection of you, I
have sent to you five minas of first-rate wool and one container
of shrimps."

Sippar is far from the sea, so the shrimps must have been
preserved in some way to make the double journey: some
300 km from the sea to Sippar, then another 300 km to
Karana. A list of foodstuffs from Karana also includes a box of
shrimps.[4] But no doubt most fish were caught locally; Iltani's
K 204 palace kept a fisherman named Zirashe on the pay-roll, and he
K 188 probably maintained various natural and artificial ponds
stocked with fish within the kingdom. Little fish-hooks made
of bronze, looking just like modern fish-hooks, were found in
the excavation of the Mari palace.

Spices

Spices are a traditional way of preserving meat and fish as well
as flavouring them in the modern Near East. Some of them
have been introduced from Africa, America and the Far East in
relatively recent times, but many were known and used in the
XII 241 days of Hammurabi. Cumin and coriander often occur

together; both black and white cumin were used. Fenugreek
K 38 seeds were well-known. When quantities are stated in the
457, 577 Mari records they are very large: 240 litres of coriander, 20
litres of cumin, 20 litres of saffron from the yellow autumn
crocus, and 5 litres of ammi, which is similar to mint. A
common flavouring was provided by *samīdum*, which is still
unidentified. Cloves were discovered dating to this period in
recent excavations at Terqa; they must have come all the way
from Indonesia, a very remarkable journey. Their Akkadian
name is not known.

Various types of onion and garlic were used plentifully in
the food: the onion came in lots of 70 litres or even 120 litres;
733, 734 the garlic-like *hazannum* arrived in batches of up to 40 litres in
the kitchen, but when it had just been harvested it was taken
16, 136 up on the palace roof to dry in the sun in a batch of 1,200 litres.
Once it was dry, it was stored in *šuhurrum*-jars of 30 litres'
capacity. In charge of this operation was Queen Shibtu,
responsible to her husband Zimri-Lim, who ordered her to
seal the roof chamber with her own seal, no doubt to prevent
pilfering by the palace servants. *Šuhatinnum* was yet another
XII 734 kind of onion; *kasûm*, probably mustard, was very popular,
and arrived in the kitchen in a delivery of 120 litres.

Cereals and pulses

Peas, chick peas *appānum*-pulses are frequent in kitchen
records, usually in small amounts: 4 or 5 litres of chick peas is
common; peas usually come in two-litre consignments.
Perhaps they were already dried and stored in larger amounts,
and so not comparable with the herbs and spices which may be
represented only in the quantities of a harvest yield. There
were various preparations made out of pulses as well as
cereals: chick peas were crushed and made into a kind of bread
K 191 called *nagappum*. Probably these foods formed the basic diet of
poorer people; a tablet from Karana records the issue from the
palace of 10 litres of chick peas for serving-women. Payment
by the palace to its workers took the form of barley rations;
gayātum was a preparation made from roasted barley, and was
eaten at Karana; *mundum*-groats and *arsānum*-groats too were
perhaps eaten outside more often than inside the palace.

The chief cereals at that time were barley and emmer wheat.
Of the two, barley is by far the most frequent in the texts, and
the usual word for emmer wheat does not occur in the Karana
tablets at all. An unidentified cereal known as *burrum* was

common also; it is thought to be a kind of wheat. It sometimes occurs with another unidentified cereal called *zīzum kinītum*. A great variety of grades of flour was milled, but usually the exact meaning of the different Akkadian words eludes us.

The letters show that supply and distribution did not always go smoothly, and the edges of the kingdom suffered. xiv 33 Yasim-Sumu wrote to Zimri-Lim to inform him about a xiii 35 massive shipment of barley from Emar to Mari, no less than 360,000 litres. Ten boats and sixty men were required to xiv 74 transport this quantity. Another letter tells how some flour, ready milled for feeding some auxiliary troops at Saggaratum, had been ruined by ants; so Yaqqim-Addu the governor of Saggaratum wrote to Zimri-Lim to ask whether Yasim-Sumu could spare some to replace it. On a different occasion the xiv 43 tables were turned, and Yaqqim-Addu sent flour from Saggaratum to Zimri-Lim at Mari.

At least four kinds of bread are found in the texts. The loaves probably came in various shapes; one word *kakkarum* is known ix 115, 277 to denote a round loaf; another, *mersum* is a kind of cake that contained fat, dates and spices. Various kinds of porridge, gruel and semolina were eaten regularly at the royal table, not spurned as fare too lowly for the king.

Food preparation

There is less information about how foods were prepared, xi 13 mixed and cooked. One Mari text gives 120 litres of dates and 10 litres of pistachios for making *mersum*-cake. Fresh fruits k 204 were evidently made into confections: Iltani's palace took delivery of 5 mixing-bowls of fruit; at Mari the kitchen received xii 440 100 litres of apples and 10 litres of medlars "for the work of the kitchen staff"; another text records a consignment of 220 litres xii 573 of figs; probably such a large quantity was dried and stored. xii 738 The same may be true of 220 litres of pears which arrived "for the work of the kitchen staff".

Winter would have been a time of reduced variety in diet, particularly at a time when bottling, canning and probably also pickling were unknown, and so drying or salting were the only long-term methods of preserving food. Therefore the earliest fruits gave occasion for particular joy and the exchange of presents:

"I am sending you pistachio-nuts as the first fruits of the year", wrote Yataraya to Iltani. Ishme-Dagan sent to his brother Yasmah-Addu pears and pistachios as first fruits, *nissan šattim*.

An occasional delicacy was truffles. Yaqqim-Addu sent to Zimri-Lim a basket of truffles that had been brought in by a workman from a neighbouring locality; on another occasion he reported that his men had filled six baskets with specially good truffles. Perhaps Zimri-Lim was very fond of them; he III 28 received them also from Kibri-Dagan in Terqa.

Dates were common fare, although they were probably always imported from further south, since the date palm produces no good fruit in the latitudes of Karana and Mari. They were the basic material from which syrup was made; but here we have a problem, for the word *dišpum* in Akkadian means both date syrup and honey from bees. If we are to believe the inscription of a first-millennium governor in this area (see p. 203 below), systematic, advanced bee-keeping may not yet have been introduced into Mesopotamia. This does not exclude the collection of wild honey, or the use of "wild" beeswax for *cire perdue*, casting of metals, nor the encouraging of wild bees to build hives in strategically placed pieces of pipe. But probably date syrup was the main sweetening agent in cookery, with wild honey a rare treat. It does seem that cultivated honey was imported as a luxury into Mesopotamia, for Aplahanda, the king of Carchemish (a region where date-palms do not produce good fruit), sent to Mari 50 jars of wine together with 50 jars of *dišpum*; Yarim-Lim of Aleppo sent *dišpum* to Mari together with wine and olive oil, and Iltani received in Karana *dišpum* together with imported western goods, namely resinous extracts from pine and juniper. Presumably the wine was produced by local vines in the kingdoms of Carchemish and Aleppo; possibly the honey came from further west, for again, the bee is not found in Mesopotamian or north Syrian iconography of this period, the space-filling motifs of seals that include grasshoppers, water birds, hares, snakes and scorpions; nor do beads or other jewellery use the bee, although it is often hard to tell an old, colourless fly from a bee![5] This argument is not unassailable; but there appears to be no word in Akkadian for bee-keeper, nor do gardeners bring *dišpum* from the palace orchards in the many texts that have now been published.

Various oils and animal fats found their way into an important department of the Mari palace. Two men, Balumenuhhe and Ili-ashraya, were chiefly responsible for receiving, storing and distributing the vast supplies. At Karana, Iltani herself was apparently in charge of oil supplies. The most basic oil was *šamaššammūm*, literally "oil of plants", for which there are problems of identification. The word reminds one of sesame, and it was accepted without hesitation as sesame until modern archaeological seed analysis failed to produce a single sample or impression of sesame seed on any of several major sites of various periods in Mesopotamia. Linseed remains, however, proved abundant, and no common word for linseed was known in Akkadian. So many scholars now consider that *šamaššammūm* was linseed, until sesame was introduced at a much later date, and the new oil plant took over the old name.[6] Linseed to us has strong associations with paint and cricket bats, but of course it is perfectly edible.[7] Different processes in ancient Mesopotamia gave rise to special varieties produced in particular localities: oil of Mari, oil of Agade, oil of Tunip, sweetened oil and scented oil, no doubt all improvements on a plain commodity. In addition to linseed oil there were juniper and cedar oils, using an unknown base, but perhaps also perfumed linseed oil. Oil was used not only in the kitchen, but also for bandages, for lamps, for cleaning statues, for mechanical lubrication, for funerary rites, and for anointing people. Here are some extracts from tablets that illustrate these functions.

"One litre of first-rate oil for the lamp that stands in front of the goddess."

"11 litres and 40 g of first-rate oil for anointing the heralds who have come from Ishme-Dagan (to Yasmah-Addu)."

"10 litres of oil for anointing the female textile workers who are sick."

"One litre 120 g of first-rate Mari oil for the bandages of Anaku-ilumma."

"One litre of first-rate oil for Iddin-ili the doctor."

"40 g of cedar oil, 40 g of first-rate oil for the battering-ram."

"$\frac{1}{2}$ litre of juniper oil for anointing the king."

"One litre of pot oil, one litre of cedar oil for the grave of the lady Ahatani."

"80 g of first-rate oil to anoint the fugitive who has come from Tirzah."

"One litre of cypress oil, one litre of pot oil, one litre of cedar oil for the god Nergal, on the occasion of the Chariot of Nergal (festival)."

RA 69   "$\frac{1}{2}$ litre of linseed oil for washing (the statue of the goddess) Ninhursag. $\frac{1}{2}$ litre of linseed oil for washing (the statue of the goddess) Deritum."

VII 238   Olive oil was imported from northern Syria, ready-made in jars from Yarim-Lim the king of Aleppo, along with jars of wine and honey. It was definitely used for anointing the king and for anointing female textile workers. However, there is not yet direct evidence from the tablets that the olive as a fruit was imported for eating, or even that the oil was used in the kitchen.[8] As to quantity, a record states that 120 litres of olive oil were stored in the magazines of Mari.

Animal fats were used, although we have less information about the uses to which they were put. Butter or ghee, *himētum*, is only occasionally found on the menu. Cheeses have not been identified yet. Milk is never on the kitchen lists, but we know that it was used, for a single letter speaks of sending milk to the king. This serves to caution us against supposing that the lists contain every single foodstuff.

Mutton fat is found in smallish quantities, but lard or pig fat occurs in very large quantities in a list of groceries from Karana, a total of very roughly 1,000 litres. There is room for error in comparing quantities from Mari and Karana texts, however, because different systems of measurement were used in the two cities. Mari relied largely upon the Babylonian system of capacity measures, which are quite well known at this period, based on baskets and beakers, whereas the Assyrian system was in use at Karana, based on the homer or donkey-load, subdivided by jars of uncertain size.[9] Not only was there variety between different towns and different periods, even the sets of measures for weights could vary within one city, so that weights are often given with the location specified.

"6²/₃ litres of best beer according to the 10-litre measure of the household servants" is a record from the same findspot as another tablet that says:

"One litre of best oil according to the one-litre measure of Shamash."

So the modern equivalents used for translating in this book are not precise; they are useful only as guidelines.

Some dowry texts of this period that come from Babylonia proper have details to offer about how food was served and eaten in the houses of moderately wealthy people.[10] The wooden tray was used to carry food from the kitchen, and small bowls that served as spoons were given for individuals to eat from. A rich man probably had a tray inlaid with shell and stone patterns, a king presumably might have the same item made of a precious metal. The best quality eating bowls were made from the dark, lustrous sissoo wood, native to Afghanistan and Pakistan; and spoons were made of wood

XI 4, 11
II 140
K 204
K 205
K 18

Figure 32 Some culinary moulds of terracotta, found in Zimri-Lim's palace of Mari

too, although a king might possess ivory ones.

In Mari palace itself was found an astonishing variety of terracotta moulds. They have decorative patterns in high relief, and it is generally reckoned that they must have been culinary moulds, either for cooking shaped dishes, or for impressing a decoration on to a soft food. The latter is a tradition in modern Iraqi cookery, often using wooden pattern blocks. More than any other discovery in the palace, these kitchen moulds display a taste for refinement and luxury that lifts Mesopotamian life high above simple material sufficiency.

The housekeeper who was in charge of all the food stuffs in the palace was a redoubtable lady named Ama-dugga. She had made herself so indispensable to the orderly running of the kitchens under Yasmah-Addu that when he and his Assyrian followers were driven out, Ama-dugga was allowed to remain at her post under Zimri-Lim. Her seal is found authorising the incomings and outgoings of oil, in which the transactions were made by her subordinates Balumenuhhe and Ili-ashraya. Her seal too authorises the dealings in cereals of one Ilu-kanum.[11]

There is no doubt from these records that she was a female of high rank, in charge of male officials. Although she continued her career under Zimri-Lim, her early allegiance to Shamshi-Adad, the Assyrian king, was not forgotten, for she continued to use the cylinder seal on which the inscription proclaims her as: "Servant of Shamshi-Adad", and signally failed to have a new seal made that would have acknowledged her new master Zimri-Lim.

Drinking habits

Beer

Both at Mari and at Karana there is much good evidence about drinking habits. Beer was the chief drink, since it could be produced locally from cereals. At Mari a sweet, beer-based drink called *alappānum* was made from barley and was probably flavoured with pomegranates; it was on the menu for royal meals in enormous quantities, on one occasion more

II p. 13–14 than 1,000 litres. Another drink was *himrum*, made from fermented barley and perhaps flavoured with aniseed, or a similarly flavoured plant. Nowadays the aniseed that flavours the locally-produced spirit called arrak is grown in large quantities on the Middle Euphrates and is exported to make liquorice-like sweets and medicines. Whereas *alappānum*-mead and *himrum*-arrak were perhaps distributed only in the

VI 36 palace, a letter indicates that beer was distributed to troops, perhaps after a successful campaign. At Karana beer was made from barley in large quantities in the palace. Several receipts of grain by Samkanum, the palace brewer, were found. He

K 176-8 produced on a grand scale: 3,020 litres of barley (more than thirty homers or donkey-loads) was not an unusual amount in

K 176 his records. He seems to have worked directly under Iltani the

K 18 queen. At Karana beer was supplied for a courier who arrived from abroad, perhaps with an escort, since he received $6^2/_3$ litres of ordinary beer and $6^2/_3$ litres of best beer. A plaque of terracotta found at Mari suggests that, at least on a particular occasion and with one drink, people drank with long straws from a communal container that was placed upon the ground. Anyone who has tried to drink soup or beverages on an evening when the air (and soup and beverages) is alive with big bulbous bugs will understand this habit.

Wine

v 13 We have already seen how Yasmah-Addu was fond of wine and how the king of Carchemish, Aplahanda, sent it to him, together with olive oil and honey. Both at Mari and at Karana, wine was the favoured drink; the profession of wine-mixer, XIII 142 *sāmihum*, is known from Mari. Yawi-ila, vassal king of Talhayum, wrote probably to Yasmah-Addu:

"And about the vines of the men of Nagabbini – there are no (suitable) men at Mashum's disposal, so may my lord have a letter sent to Samum, that they may give to him three mixers, so that the vines be not ruined and lest Mashum complain."[12]

The cupbearer was already an important man, who sent his XIII 149 own servant to deal with acquiring wine. He was in charge of K 85 the silver goblets out of which wine, and perhaps also beer, were drunk. He may also have distributed drinking vessels as presents to visiting celebrities. His wine supplies came from many different localities, and it is clear that viticulture was widespread at this period. Not only did Aleppo and Carchemish supply wine; it was also produced in the regions of the Upper Habur, and in the towns Zarbat and Shirwun which lay within the kingdom of Karana during Aqba-hammu's reign. Further to the east it was produced and K 251 exported from Talmush, which lies not far due north of Nineveh.[13] This very extensive area of production meant that wine was not restricted to the royal family's cups: it was also consumed by messengers and foreign envoys, by troops and K 252, 255 by female singers. No doubt remarkable vintages were the subject of royal gifts: Zimri-Lim sent to Hammurabi of Babylon X 131 "10 jars of wine of the sort that I myself drink"; but many tax records from Mari show a regular, copious trade down the XIII 99 Euphrates.

The qualities of the different types of wine are described as "red", "of good quality", "second-rate" and "old". The wine was stored in the palaces at Terqa and Mari, and a man named Sammetar was in command at both places. It was also stored in the temple of the goddess Belet-ekallim. Perhaps this store was for religious offerings, for as we shall see, Iltani and the goddess of Karana both drank wine.

Here is a letter in which the governor of Terqa Kibri-Dagan describes to Zimri-Lim how he helped the cupbearer of Atamrum, the king of Andarik, to select wine:

"My lord gave me an order about taking some jars of wine XIII 126 from the boats of the men of Emar for Atamrum (king of

Andarik), so I and Mannu-balu-Shamash the cupbearer of Atamrum – he was with me – had the jars of wine from those boats, all that there were, brought up (on to the quay), and they selected 90 jars of wine out of all those jars of wine, and sent back the rest. Now, I have embarked those 90 jars of wine on another boat, and I have appointed a boatman as escort for Mannu-balu-Shamash (for the journey back) to Atamrum."[14]

Ice

When the summer is at its height in northern Mesopotamia, the temperature often rises to over 100°F. In such weather a cool drink is a delight. To reach this peak of luxury the rulers of Mari and Rimah built ice-houses, where they stored ice, *šurīpum*, that was collected during the winter. The foundation inscription of such an ice-house at Terqa has been discovered; and if we are to believe it, Zimri-Lim established the practice of keeping ice in that area.

"Zimri-Lim, the son of Yahdun-Lim, the king of Mari, Tuttul and the land of Hana, (was) the builder of an ice-house, which no previous king had ever built, on the bank of the Euphrates. He had ice brought and built an ice-house on the bank of the Euphrates at Terqa, the city beloved of Dagan."

Two fragmentary letters from the governor of Terqa to Zimri-Lim describe the problems of preventing the ice melting, although unfortunately they do not give a continuous text. In a third letter he asked Zimri-Lim to send an official to II 91 be in charge of gathering and storing the ice at Terqa. We know, however, that iced drinks were not unknown at Mari before the time of Zimri-Lim, so perhaps only the type of construction or the placing of the ice-house was new, for Aplahanda, the king of Carchemish, wrote to Yasmah-Addu, during the Assyrian interregnum that preceded Zimri-Lim's reign, saying:

V6 "Now, there is ice in Ziranum. It is plentiful. Set some of your servants to guard it, that they may guard it for you, and while you are staying there, have them bring it to you regularly. And if you have no good wine with you to drink, write to me and I shall send to you good wine for you to drink."

I 21 Shamshi-Adad, the king, wrote to his son about collecting ice:

"About collecting ice: is it good when porters have to bring ice from 20 or 40 miles away? Give orders to the cup bearer's servants or to the *ušmum*–officials, and make them collect the ice! Let them wash it free of twigs and dung and dirt."

These texts show plainly that ice was not formed in the ice-house by flooding and freezing, as it is made in Iran in modern times. Whether or not Yasmah-Addu had built an ice house at Mari, is uncertain. Zimri-Lim was not content, however, to build one only at Terqa: he ordered Yaqqim-Addu
II 102 to build one at Saggaratum too, and sent him a builder to
XIV 25 complete the work. But Yaqqim-Addu did not have any timber beams big enough for the job, and had to send a working party off to a wood to find some. There must also have been an ice-store at Qaṭara, within the kingdom of Karana, for Aqba-hammu wrote to Iltani saying:

"Let them unseal the ice of Qaṭara. The goddess, you and
K 79 Belassunu (Iltani's sister) drink regularly, but make sure that the ice is kept safe."

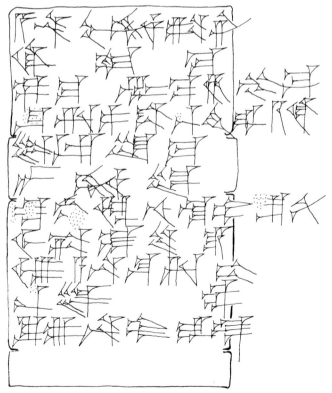

Figure 33 A letter to Iltani telling her to use ice in drinks

This letter does not actually say that the ice was used with wine, but ice comes with wine in a Mari text about food and drink for visiting Elamites. It is probable that fruit juices were also iced for drinking. So this practice of transporting and storing ice, common in the Eastern Mediterranean in mediaeval times, is now known to go back at least to the time of Hammurabi in northern Mesopotamia. It is a practice which shows a high standard of living and respect for the luxuries of life reinforcing the evidence of the excavated palace architecture.[15]

The palaces at Mari and Karana hummed with the activity of IX 25 kitchen staff. Both men and women did the work of grinding flour. As baker, *epītum*, at Mari, only a woman, named IX 27 Ashumiya-libur, is known from a ration list, but the same list CB 42 gives four cooks, *nuhatimmum*, all men. At Chagar Bazar there are two male *epûm*-bakers in the rations lists. At Mari there p. 259 were specialised pastry cooks or cake-makers who were women. A profession not attested in these texts in the masculine form is *abarakkatum*, which is usually translated "steward"; the texts show that fruit, spices and oil were all for their work, but it is clear that they were not just menials, for at CB 41 Chagar Bazar an *abarakkatum* is also a scribe. Brewing seems to have been largely a man's work, although there are "women of the *alappānum*–"mead". Men only are attested as "wine-mixers" *sāmihum*, probably to be understood more generally as "wine steward" according to the letter quoted on p. 90 above.

A banquet for Ashkur-Addu, King of Karana

We shall take leave of the food and drink at Mari and Karana with an imaginary banquet, held on a warm summer evening in the Courtyard of the Date Palms, in the palace at Mari. The king of Karana, Ashkur-Addu, brother of Iltani, is coming to dine with Zimri-Lim. Orders go out to Mukannishum, who makes due preparations: he takes out of storage a silver, XIII 22 high-back throne and an elaborate silver *kaniškarak-kum*–table. On it he sets out gold and silver goblets, some in the shapes of animal heads – bull, gazelle and ibex – placing them on highly ornamented stands, the king's stand being silver decorated with lion heads and stag horns, the stands of lesser men being of ivory, plated with gold or silver. The aromatic fragrance of cedar doors is wafted into the courtyard,

and the little silver stars with which they are studded twinkle
in the background. The throne bearer brings in the king's chair
and a footstool that has a patterned inlay of mother-of-pearl.
The royal party enters and sits. While the visitors admire the
prancing winged bulls and other fabulous monsters that
decorate the walls, servants come in to wash the visitors' feet
and to anoint them with perfumed oils. Attendants bring in
trays of sandalwood and pistachio-wood, piled high with
food: choice cuts of mutton, venison, gazelle and beef from
animals specially fattened for the king's table, spicy
confections of pulses, bread loaves of many kinds and shapes,
cakes made with honey, nuts and dates. A huge wooden bowl
is heaped with juicy, fresh fruit – grapes, pears, pomegranates
and apples; small bowls of burnished bronze and silver hold
pistachios. Circular dishes of food impressed with a wide
variety of patterns decorate the table. Each guest has an
individual spoon made of ivory or sissoo wood to eat with, and
a fragrant flower to delight his senses.

Figure 34 A goddess smelling a flower

The royal cupbearer distributes the precious goblets and fills them with iced wine. An enormously heavy goblet of red gold is filled with the best wine from Carchemish, and the king lifts it to his lips, a sign to the guests that they may begin to feast. Girls sing softly to the accompaniment of the lyre and the lute. Every member of the royal party, including visitors, wears the best garments that the workshops can produce, newly made and now worn for the first time, with the characteristically decorated borders and fringes of Zimri-Lim's kingdom. As the shadows lengthen the banqueters are entertained with VII 91 jugglers, wrestlers, and a performing bear from eastern Iran.

Notes to Chapter Four

1. Epic of Gilgamesh, tablet 2 lines 39'–40'.

2. According to Pliny (*Natural History XVIII xiv*) the Romans made a porridge out of pounded linseed, barley grain and coriander seed.

3. A. H. Layard, *Discoveries in Nineveh and Babylon*, London 1853, p. 325.

4. For the possibility that these shrimps were not for eating but for textile work, see note 8 to Chapter 3.

5. Bees are shown in Egyptian painting before this period; and bees may have been kept in Minoan Crete; see K. F. Kitchell, "The Mallia 'wasp' pendant reconsidered," *Antiquity* vol. 55 no. 213 1981, pp. 9–16.

6. See H. Helbaeck, in Mallowan, *Nimrud and its Remains* (London 1966) p. 618; also *Notes on the evolution and history of linum, Kuml* (Aahus) 1959, p. 103ff. For resistance to this identification see F.R. Kraus Sesam in "Alten Mesopotamien", *Journal of the American Oriental Society* 88 1968, p. 112ff. The identification with linseed is now accepted by the *Chicago Assyrian Dictionary*.

7. It has the disadvantage that wrong processing produces a poison from it. Various uses and processing are discussed by P. L. Simmonds, *Tropical Agriculture*, London 1877.

8. But an olive stone was found at Tell Taya, near Karana; see J. G. Waines, "Plant remains from Tell Taya", in *Iraq* 35 1973, p. 185.

9. At Karana a broken storage jar that measured 74.3cm in height, and with a maximum diametre of 58.5cm, was uncovered with its ancient capacity inscribed on the outside. When the whole was reconstructed and mended it was filled with dry rice and its modern capacity (for dry rice) was measured. The result showed

that the *qû* "litre" measure was in fact between 0.79 and 0.82 of a
litre. See J. N. Postgate, "An inscribed jar from Tell al Rimah",
Iraq 40, 1978, pp. 71–75.

10. S. Dalley, "Old Babylonian dowries", in *Iraq* 42 1980, p. 53ff.

11. Ilu-kanum took charge of stock-taking when the accounts were
    done; huge quantities of cereal and pulses are listed: "7,170 litres
    of barley; 5,390 litres of *burrum*–cereal; 1,765 litres of chick peas,
    stock of Ilu-kanum when the accounts were done, to Ilu-kanum."

12. It is likely that this man Mashum is the same official as he who put
    his stamp on Chagar Bazar tablets, to authorise the movement of
    barley; for Yawi-ila was the vassal king of Talhayum, a city-state
    which, like Chagar Bazar, lay in the Upper Habur region.

13. For the location and identification of this place, which is disputed,
    see Groneberg, *Répertoire Géographique* Band 3, p. 233.

14. For a comprehensive study see H. Finet, "Le vin à Mari", *Archiv
    für Orientforschung* 25, 1974–7.

15. The word for ice, *šurīpum*, was thought to be a mineral ore in the
    early publications of Mari tablets. See S. Page-Dalley, "Ice
    Offerings and deities in Old Babylonian Rimah", *Actes de la XVII
    Rencontre Assyriologique Internationale,* Brussels 1969; also H.
    Freydank, *bīt šurīpim* in Bögazköy, *Welt des Orients* 4 1967–8.

Chapter Five
Women

The tablets are full of good information about women, their status and behaviour, their dress and manners. No other archives throughout two thousand years of early Mesopotamian history has so much to tell.

The Queens

At Mari the personal letters that passed between Zimri-Lim, his queen Shibtu and his many daughters are well preserved, and they can be compared with the Rimah correspondence that passed between Aqba-hammu and his queen Iltani. We know more about them than about even the Assyrian queen Semiramis, for we still have few contemporary details about her life. For lesser females and their occupations within the palace walls the great ration lists are a mine of information.

Queen Shibtu

Shibtu[1] was the daughter of Yarim-Lim and Gashera, the king and queen of Yamhad (Aleppo), where Zimri-Lim had probably spent his years of exile during the Assyrian interregnum. Shibtu and Zimri-Lim produced many daughters who, like their parents, made dynastic marriages to secure alliance or loyalty in other states. For instance, a daughter named Ibbatum married Himdiya, the king of Andarik; another daughter, Inib-sharri, married Ibal-Addu, ruler of Ashlakka. Zimri-Lim had at least eleven daughters, perhaps all by his queen Shibtu, but the letters are almost silent on the subject of sons. There is a letter from Shibtu to Zimri-Lim saying:

X 26   "I have given birth to twins, a boy and a girl: may my lord rejoice!"

It may strike the modern reader as odd that the queen

should give her husband the news in writing; but it serves to emphasise that letters were being written continually, and passed to and fro between different wings of the palace. Letter writing embraced domestic matters and daily trivia no less than weighty matters of state. Whether or not the twins survived, we cannot be sure; one letter referred to the death of a daughter, in which one man writes to another to say:

"Before the king reaches Mari, tell him that that daughter is dead, and may he understand; perhaps if the king were not to hear about the death of that daughter until he entered Mari, he would be too distressed."

Zimri-Lim probably had a son whom he named Yahdun-Lim after his famous father; but this son died. There is AREC a record of one silver *memmum*–crown or fillet, weighing about 4 g, and a silver ring weighing 8 g, "for the grave of Yahdum-Lim the king's son."

Shibtu was a loving wife, often concerned for the health and safety of her husband, never complaining to him about her own condition, never angry nor causing him to be angry.

X 17   "May my lord conquer his enemies and enter Mari in peace and joy of heart! Now, may my lord put on himself the tunic and coat that I have made!"

She wrote to him regularly, even if it was only to say: "Mari, X 22 the temples and the palace are well." At other times she discussed in some detail prophecies or omens that might affect his welfare, or provisions for the palace kitchens and storerooms, or how newly-won captives were to be distributed in the palace workshops. She was no lady of leisure. Personnel problems abounded in the many departments of the palace, and the queen was often requested to settle them. Zimri-Lim took the trouble to keep her informed of his movements:

X 121   "As I send this letter to you, I have received the people of the town of Shenah, and have made them give allegiance to me. I have set a governor in the citadel. After this letter, I shall depart for Urkish and promote goodwill. Then straight away I shall proceed from Urkish to Shuna and promote goodwill there. I am well, and the troops are well. May news of the palace reach me regularly."

This letter in particular shows that Shibtu was no ignorant and secluded wife relegated to a place of unimportance, but a well-informed participant in a large organisation.

To enable her to carry out her responsibilities to her husband

and to her numerous children, she had help. The wet-nurse *mušēniqtum* for infants and the nanny or governess *tārītum* for weaned children were established in society. One lady wrote desperately to Zimri-Lim to say:

"I am being robbed here: wipe away my tears![2] Sin-mushallim robbed me: he took my nanny and now she is living in his house. If my lord had taken her, and if she were living in my lord's house, I wouldn't mind, but it is Sin-mushallim who has robbed me. Now, because you make light throughout all the land, make light for me too, and give me back my nanny; let me say a prayer for you before Teshub and Hepat" (the chief Hurrian god and goddess).

On a lower level of society, children of working mothers accompanied the mother to work; the ration lists for groups of female textile workers – spinners and weavers – show that the mother was given an extra ration for her child, payment according to need and not just a standard wage for the job. The lists do not tell how old the children were, except for the occasional "unweaned child" DUMU.GAB, but probably there were simple tasks that they would be given from an early age.

When Shibtu wrote to her husband she usually addressed him as "my lord", and called herself "Shibtu your servant". However, in the occasional letter to Zimri-Lim and to palace officials she calls herself by the epithet "Lady of the Land", which leaves us in no doubt that she was the queen. Zimri-Lim's daughters, on the other hand, write to him as "my father, my star", calling themselves "your daughter".

Evidence for a Harem

Scholars are at present divided on the question of whether Zimri-Lim had more than one wife, or whether he kept a harem.[3] Not long ago the matter seemed dependent on a crucial word that was thought to mean "veil"; Zimri-Lim wrote to Shibtu asking her to select girls from a new group of captives, girls who had no blemish or brands (which were marks of a previous dedication to a temple, or of slavery). It now seems certain that these girls were to be trained as singers, perhaps for a particular type of cult singing, hence the emphasis on physical perfection, and that Shibtu was not being asked to choose a harem for her own husband. There is no clear evidence for segregation of women within the palace. Shibtu wrote to male officials and conversed directly with x 18 Mukannishum, the workshop manager, when her husband was not there. There is no evidence for eunuchs at this date, nor evidence for bolting off sections of the palace, with a particular official in charge of the locks. However, there is a possible term, damaged and occurring in a single text, for

VII 206 harem women, and "serving women of the king" are given a wine ration together with female musicians. [4]

In my opinion the royal harem as an institution probably came in during the Middle Assyrian period, several centuries later, when for the first time there were royal edicts that governed very strictly the behaviour of palace women and the behaviour of male palace staff towards them; at the same time a new code of public laws dealt savagely with women's rights and sexual behaviour, quite different from the laws of Hammurabi. [5] A culmination of the severe Middle Assyrian laws is as follows:

"Apart from the penalties for a man's wife which are written on this tablet, when she deserves it, a man may pull out his wife's hair, mutilate or twist her ears, with no liability attaching to him."

At this period, therefore, there is no definite evidence for an organised harem. There is clear evidence, however, that the queen could travel without her husband within his kingdom; Zimri-Lim wrote to Shibtu saying:

x 137 "Now, I am coming towards Mari; come to meet me in Saggaratum."

The same is true at Karana: there is no evidence for an organised harem, for eunuchs or for a system of segregating

K 71 palace women; Iltani travelled without her husband within the kingdom of Karana. So the two groups of records give the same impression of women's liberties.

A woman who was closely associated with Zimri-Lim is Adad-duri. Her form of address is: "Speak to my lord, thus your servant", and she is full of pious hopes for Zimri-Lim's

x 54 safety. "The city Mari, the temples and the palace are well", she wrote, echoing the reassurance that Shibtu often gave. "May the heart of my lord not be troubled ... may my lord not neglect to guard himself!" Her letters chiefly contain information about omens and presages, and the minutiae of the cults, and Zimri-Lim's letters to her are also preoccupied with religious observances. There can be no doubt that Adad-duri was second only to Shibtu in importance among Mari women, and for that reason some scholars would see her as a second wife of Zimri-Lim. [6] But in my opinion this is unlikely; she sends no news of children, no handmade garments, and there is nothing in her letters that would not fit a powerful dowager, an energetic, elderly relative who took on the responsibility of ensuring that Zimri-Lim observed the will and needs of the deities in every way. Here is one of her letters; others will be found in the chapter on religion.

X 52 "Speak to my lord, thus your servant Adad-duri. About the golden breast ornaments of the goddess Anunitum, Ahum the priest came and said to me: 'It is not the appropriate time to give them'. So when the throne of the goddess has been made, let an omen be taken and then let that gold be taken and manufactured for the throne of the goddess."

8, 9, 10 Shibtu was more often concerned with food supplies and personnel, although she also reports on portentous visions and prophetic utterances.

Queen Iltani

With Iltani, Shibtu's counterpart at Karana, we clearly have an entirely different personality in a similar environment.
K 119 Possibly she was older, and had spent years in uncertain exile in eastern Mesopotamia, in the city of Eshnunna. She worked hard at running the palace industries, in particular textiles and food, and had to meet her husband's frequent, urgent demands for goods and personnel. In addition she had to deal with many begging letters. She was concerned with her own health, worried, harassed, mean, querulous and indignant, as the following extracts from her letters show. Her husband
K 58 wrote: "Hammi-ṣuri told me that you have celebrated a festival and that nobody took any notice of you. What is this? I myself shall certainly take notice of you . . . I shall come myself, and you will see what I will do to whoever ignores you!"

An unknown correspondent who calls himself "your
K 131 brother"[7] wrote: "Don't worry; I instructed Igmil-Sin before his journey, and he will put your anxieties and my anxieties to my lord's son, and will do all he can to ease your worries. Until he comes be quiet, and let no word that you are worried escape from your mouth to anyone!"

A man named Rish-Adad, who sent a letter begging Iltani for two men-servants or two female servants wrote to her saying:
K 119 "May Adad and Geshtinanna heap honours on your head in the city where you dwell. I have written to ask how you are: send me news of yourself. You used to live in Eshnunna, yet

you have never remembered to mention my name, and you have not given me new life. Now you are living in Karana, and there is not a single one among my brothers whose names you have not brought to attention, yet not once for me, not even in the slightest respect, have you ever remembered my name, nor given me new life. I am not writing this letter to you for any specific favour; I am writing to you because you have never remembered my name."

Another correspondent, Yasitna-abum, complains to Iltani that the servant boy whom Iltani gave him is hopeless, far too young.

K 152　"Speak to Iltani, thus Yasitna-abum your son. May Shamash and Marduk grant that my mother live forever for my sake. My mother called my name, and my heart came alive. Now, do send me a letter saying how you are, and give me new life. Whenever I reread your letter, the dust-storms of Adad (the weather-god) are forgotten; my heart is replenished with life. The servant boy whom my mother sent to me is far too young. For that servant boy does not keep *me* regularly supplied; it is I who have to keep *him* regularly supplied! Whenever I go on a journey, not even so much as 2 litres of bread for my ration is carried behind me. May my mother send me another servant boy who will be able to carry 10 litres of bread for my ration behind me, and who will be able really to help."

Not only was Iltani harassed with letters begging for slaves or food, but also she was the recipient, as Shibtu apparently was not, of appeals against injustice. Here is an example:

K 141　"Speak to my lady; thus Belassunu. Ever since the harvest I have written frequently to you, but you have never sent me a reply of any kind. The king had spoken to me saying, 'Stay in Zarbat. As soon as I come, Uşi-nawir will come with me, and he will let you plead your innocence.' Now, why are you silent? He neither lets me plead my innocence nor lets me go. You are near the ruler where you are: write, that they may take me back to the ruler. What have I done wrong? Why have you frowned upon me, and not pleaded my cause? Who will deal with the matter, and who has turned to help me?"

Clearly Iltani's life was not easy, and her husband's urgent requests must have been an extra strain.

K 67　"Now, I have sent you 25 kg of wool for 50 garments. Make those garments quickly. I need those garments."

K 70　"I shall take many garments with my tribute to Babylon . . . Send me as many as are available, immediately."

K 80   "Send to me quickly the belts(?) that you have made."

K 82   "Send me quickly any cloth that you have available whether of first or second quality."

No doubt life was hard for him too, as the ruler of a petty state trying to juggle with numerous alliances and to fulfil his obligations as vassal of Hammurabi. One letter shows that he had a savage temper that was directed at poor Iltani:

K 158   "Speak to my lord; thus Iltani thy servant. My lord wrote to me about letting go the oxen, sheep and donkeys belonging to Tazabru, saying: 'If you do not let them go, I shall cut you into twelve pieces.' That is what my lord wrote to me. Why has my lord written my death sentence to me? Only yesterday I spoke to my lord saying it was his own shepherd who had in the past kept his oxen and his sheep; he was pasturing them in Yashibatum. That is what I told my lord. Now, let my lord simply write that they are to take his oxen and sheep away from Yashibatum. If I have taken any of his oxen or sheep, may my lord inflict the punishment on me. Would I, without my lord's permission, would I have laid hands on and taken anything? Why then has my lord written my death sentence?"

Iltani's work as overseer of the textile business is known in some details from her archive. In the palace at Rimah was the "department of Iltani", which comprised some 15 women who spun and wove (2 of them brought a child), and 10 male textile workers. In addition she employed 2 millers, and a brewer named Samkanum; and 6 girls who worked under Mutu-hadki in an unknown capacity. 13 more women, 3 of them with a child, worked for Iltani, again with an uncertain task; she had a doorman named Kibsi-etar, and a man called Anda in charge of pack-asses, also 4 other men. In the textile department wool was the material mainly used, and Iltani was supplied by Aqba-hammu and by a man named

K 107   Kiṣṣurum. Kiṣṣurum did the accounts of the textile department, which had to be checked and sealed by Iltani, using her personal cylinder seal. He also helped her to fill

K 105   Aqba-hammu's urgent orders. Iltani also had an agent in the textile trade, perhaps her sister, named Lamassani, who lived in Ashur. Lamassani reported to Iltani on the regular progress of caravans and was in charge of servants who included female textile workers. Perhaps because she was a younger sister (this is only a guess), she regarded Iltani as under some obligation to send her rations of oil and barley when those commodities became expensive in Ashur, and to provide her with a slavegirl who could spin or weave, when some of her own women died.

Lamassani was trying to find a lapis-lazuli necklace for Iltani in Ashur in return.

K 120   "Speak to Iltani, my sister; thus Lamassani. I am well. The caravan comes regularly. You have never written to me to say how you are. I am still looking for a necklace of lapis lazuli, for which you wrote to me, and I shall send you a serving woman (with it), but until now I have not found what you wrote for, and so I have not yet sent a slavegirl. Are you not aware that I am receiving short rations of barley? For in the city of Ashur, barley is expensive and linseed oil is expensive. Your son Sin-rimeni often comes and goes, but you have never mentioned me to him; you have not heaped honour on my head in the household where I am staying. As you must be aware, I am receiving short rations: please provide me with barley and linseed oil."

The role and position of women

The queens' activities were not restricted to the traditionally distaff side of production: to textiles and food. They were in some ways connected with metals too. Iltani, Queen of
K 109   Karana, personally received copper from her subordinate Kiṣṣurum, and Gashera, Queen of Halab, received an allocation of "tin" separate from the allocation of "tin" to her
RA 64   husband Yarim-Lim. We may infer from a letter in which
K 85   Aqba-hammu tells Iltani to deliver drinking vessels to his messenger that Iltani was trusted to handle precious goods, although there is no direct evidence that she had a say in the design of these luxury items.

We do not know for certain whether royal women joined the king for state banquets or main meals. It is established,
K 263   however, that the queen drank wine with ice with her sister
K 79   Belassunu, and that the wet-nurse was allowed a ration of ten
K 271   litres of best beer, doubtless as an aid to lactation.

That women could own land is well known from southern records of this period, in particular records from Sippar, but this aspect of Old Babylonian life is ill-documented at Mari and
VIII 15   Karana: a single tablet so far published from Mari shows that a woman owned land, but the terms of reference are completely obscure. On the subject of land tenure in general there is very little information.

At Sippar there was a class of woman called *nadītum* who lived in a cloister attached to the temple of Shamash and his divine spouse Aya. These women came from royal or very wealthy families, inherited and bought considerable amounts of real estate, and owned many personal possessions. When they entered the cloister they received a dowry from their parents, just as another girl could receive one at marriage. They probably took a particular name when they entered the cloister, two common *nadītum* names being Amat-Shamash "servant-girl of Shamash", and Erishti-Aya "request of Aya".[8] By great good fortune it has been possible to connect these ladies of Sippar with the royal families of Mari and Karana: from Karana a sister of Iltani, Amat-Shamash, was a *nadītum* at Sippar, and from Mari a daughter of Zimri-Lim, Erishti-Aya, likewise.

K 134   Amat-Shamash upbraided her sister for meanness. She emphasised by contrast the generosity of Aqba-hammu and pointedly sent presents to Iltani.

"Speak to Iltani my sister, thus Amat-Shamash your sister. May my divine lord and lady grant that you live forever for my sake. Previously when Aqba-hammu came to Sippar I gave him cause to honour my priesteshood, and he honoured me greatly, for he said to me: 'When I go back to Karana, write to me and I shall send you a boat full of whatever you need. Offer a prayer for me to your divine lord.' Now, I have written, and he has provided me with two servants. But you have not recalled my name; you never even sent me so much as a single jar of perfume; you never said: 'Approach and offer a prayer for me to your divine lady.' Instead you say: 'What do you think I am for?' Apart from you, does a girl who has washed her husband's feet for one day not send her own sister provisions from then onwards? And the slaves whom my father gave me have grown old. Now, I have sent half a mina of silver to the king. Allow me my claim, and let him send to me slaves that have been captured recently, and who are trustworthy. Now, in recollection of you, I have sent to you five(?) minas of first-rate wool and a basket of 'shrimps'."[9]

Erishti-Aya, the *nadītum* from Shibtu's family at Mari, made similar requests for slaves from her parents; perhaps these requests were part of a competition for status among the cloistered princesses. Erishti-Aya has a fulsome literary style, calling her father "my star" or "my sun" and calling upon her divine lord Shamash and her divine lady Aya to "guard you for my sake like heaven and earth". Her requests were endless:

X 39   "I am always, always crying out, always!... When I wrote to you last year, you sent me two servant girls, but one of them died, and now they have brought me two more servant girls, and one of them has died too. I am the emblem of your father's house, so why am I not provided for? They have not given me any silver or oil."

She reproached her mother Shibtu, writing:

X 43 "Speak to the lady my mother, thus Erishti-Aya your daughter. May my divine lord and lady grant you long life for my sake. Why didn't you ever wear my dress, but sent it back to me, and made me dishonoured and accursed? I am your daughter, and you are the wife of a king. . . . Your husband and you put me into the cloister; but the soldiers who were taken captive pay me more respect than you! You should pay me respect, and then my divine lord and lady will honour you with the good opinion of the city and its inhabitants. I am sending you a nanny. Do send me something to make me happy, and then I will be happy. Don't neglect me."

These two letters serve to highlight the point that a daughter wrote just as freely to her father as to her mother. The mother did not act as an intermediary in matters between daughter and father.

The terms that may describe women's garments are still difficult for us to understand in detail; we do know that a woman commonly had twice as many headdresses as dresses and coats, and that variety was introduced by means of detachable trim.[10] But shape, colour and detail of decorative work are unknown, and there is a marked lack of statuary and relief showing women from this period. More promising in the present state of knowledge is the evidence for jewellery. We have already seen that Iltani asked her sister Lamassani to find and buy a necklace of lapis lazuli in Ashur – the famous deep blue stone that was mined in distant Badakhshan and

K 136 imported into Mesopotamia. A man named Yarkiba-Addu (who may have been her brother) sent Iltani a mina of silver, about 0.5 kg, for a pectoral, an enormous weight of precious metal to be used for a single ornament. From cylinder seals and from the statue of the goddess with the overflowing vase we know that very heavy necklaces with several rows of beads were fashionable with a counterweight that hung down the back to avoid pressure on the back of the neck. Women of the royal families ordered their own jewellery, either through members of their own family, as Iltani with her necklaces, or through a palace official, as a letter from Princess Bahlatum to the chief goldsmith(?) Ili-idinnam reveals:

Figure 35 Front and back views of a goddess with a flowing vase. (Height approx. 152 cm)

X 109   "Speak to Ili-idinnam, thus Bahlatum. You behave as if you and I had never spoken and made an arrangement! I gave you barley some time ago to buy a necklace, but you haven't bought it for me. Four years ago I gave you silver, so now the goldsmith has got gold and silver, yet those pectorals still have not been made. Now, if you are really my 'brother', do the god and goddess a favour and send me the work soon; don't delay. If he doesn't finish that work soon, there won't be any work; I won't agree to it. If the 2⅓ shekels of gold and 4 shekels of silver that they gave you were not enough for that work, put 4 shekels of bronze in the middle."

There are a few lists of ornaments, mostly fragmentary, from the Mari archives. They are probably delivery notes, quite brief and laconic, but from them can be gleaned these items:

VII 244   "An iron buckle with an inlaid 'opening'
VII 245   A silver mirror
VII 246   21 small stars of lapis lazuli
VII 246   1 oval bead of lapis lazuli
VII 247   Kidney-shaped beads, and beads in the shape of a coriander seed, made of gold and of alabaster."

These fine ornaments were not always destined for female finery, but were also made to decorate royal or divine statues or thrones. However, they give a small idea of the variety that must have been available to queens and princesses.

At Mari perhaps more than at Karana it seems to have been the habit for palace women to note and report presages and ominous occurrences, and to write and tell the ruler – not that he always took much notice. A daughter of Zimri-Lim named Kiru, who married the king of Ilansura, wrote:

X 31   "Speak to my star, my father and my lord, thus your daughter Kiru. It really was a sign when I spoke to you in the courtyard saying: 'You are going away, and so you will not be able to direct the country; the country will become hostile behind you.' That is what I said to my father and lord, but he didn't listen to me . . . . Now, if I am truly a woman, may my lord and father pay heed to my words – I am always writing the words of the gods to my father!" Kiru had trouble with her husband, and some of her presages may have been designed to draw her father's attention to her.

X 33   "If my lord doesn't fetch me back to Mari, I shall 'hold my nose'[11] and fall off the roof!'', she wrote to Zimri-Lim in a moment of desperation. Probably she wrote to the king her father rather than to her mother because he alone would have the authority to recall her.

Similar is the case of Inib-sharrim, another of Zimri-Lim's daughters, who complained of disgraceful treatment in the kingdom of Ashlakka.

X 74

"About my worries I have written twice to my lord, and my lord has written to me saying: 'Go into Ashlakka and don't cry'. My lord wrote that to me, and now I have entered Ashlakka and my worries have been fully justified! The wife of Ibal-Addu is queen all right; that woman takes it upon herself to receive personally every delivery for Ashlakka city and its towns. She made me sit in a corner holding my head in my hands like any idiot woman. Food and drink were regularly put in front of her, while my eyes envied and my mouth watered. She put a strong guard on me, and took no notice at all of appeals in my lord's name. So my fears have been fulfilled here . . . May my lord send someone to fetch me back to my lord, that I may look upon my lord's face." This text does imply that the king of Ashlakka took several wives, but it also implies that Inib-sharrim found the situation unacceptable, possibly because it was a foreign custom. When a coppersmith from the Hurrian town of Kahat was working at Mari, he had three wives with him, which called for comment from the *65 p. 62 normally terse list of workmen.

So far we have surveyed the concerns of royal and high-ranking ladies, revealed in detail in their letters. But the ration lists in particular allow us to distinguish the occupations followed by ordinary women, although they lack the detail that letters provide. Some of the occupations are predictable, but two may cause us some surprise.

Female spinners and weavers were common, but men also worked with textiles. The details of their work are not yet known or in what ways the different kinds of work were divided . This is partly because the profession *ašlākum/ašlāktum* seems to be a general term that embraces spinning, weaving, dyeing, fulling and stitching. At Karana Iltani had 15 female and 10 male textile workers working in her palace workshop.

In private houses it was a woman's work to grind grain, and every girl at marriage received an assortment of millstones for different types of flour as part of her dowry. Azzu-ena, a woman of Ashala, wrote to Mutu-hadki at Karana saying: K 160 "May my father and lord give me a slave-girl, and may he free my hands from the millstone, or else may my father and lord write to Iltani."

But in Iltani's palace the millers were men, probably for heavier work on a much larger scale.

At Mari many women worked in the kitchens preparing food under the indomitable Ama-dugga. A kitchen maid XI 262 called Eliza was in charge of the drink *himrum* and the XII 203 containers in which it was stored, as well as being the recipient of barley for making *pappāsum*-pudding.

Many singers were female, although they were trained by a X 126 male chief singer named Warad-ilishu. They may also have played musical instruments; again, the term used is a general

one that probably encompasses all kinds of musicians. On
RA 50 what occasions they performed is uncertain, but they were
allotted cereal among the rations of palace workers, and wine
along with the king's serving girls. In one ration list there are
35 senior lady musicians, 14 junior and 7 very junior lady
musicians. The seniors and juniors received the same amount
CB 40 of food, but the very junior girls received less. A ration list
from Chagar Bazar lists 8 young boy musicians.

X 18   One lady doctor occurs in passing in a letter from Mari. That
she was not simply a midwife is likely because there is a more
specific word for that profession.[12] But the greatest revelation
RA 50 in the ration lists has been to find female scribes, *ṭupšarratum*.
The evidence gives no more than their names, 9 of them,
with no details of social standing, training or type of work.
However, this is enough to show that men did not hold a
monopoly of literate skills, and that in the days of Hammurabi
the female secretary flourished in Zimri-Lim's palace at Mari.

Notes to Chapter Five

1. It may be preferable to read her name as Shiptu, see Dalley,
    Bibliotheca Orientalis, 36, 1979, p. 289.

2. See K. Deller – K. Watanabe, "Šukkulu . . . abwischen" in
    Zeitschrift für Assyriologie 70 1980, pp. 202–3.

3. Kibri-Dagan appears to have had two wives named
    Dam-huraṣim and Hushutum, but with the long time-span of the
    Mari letters in mind we cannot be certain that they were
    concurrent, nor do we know whether the earlier wife was barren.
    According to Hammurabi's Code a man with a barren wife might
    take a second wife in order to have children.

4. See also *CAD* sub *esirtu*. B. F. Batto, *Studies on Women at Mari*,
    (Johns Hopkins 1974) assumes the existence of a royal harem
    without discussing the evidence, p. 8 ff.

5. For instance, a woman's dowry could never be taken by her
    husband. It remained her property for life, and then went to her
    sons or back to her father's family. She could buy, own and sell
    real estate. If she married a bad husband she could not be pledged
    to pay off debts that he had incurred before marriage. If he
    illtreated her, she could leave him and take her dowry with her. A
    widow could not be driven out penniless. Orphaned brothers
    were compelled to provide a dowry for a young sister out of the

deceased father's estate. A husband who wanted to divorce a barren wife had not only to let her take her dowry, but also had to pay her separation money. If a husband was long absent without providing his wife with enough livelihood, she could enter another man's house without blame. She could not be punished for suspicion of adultery. There were many circumstances in which a girl could marry "the husband of her heart".
See Pritchard *ANET*, third edition, for a translation of the various laws, and A. K. Grayson, *Assyrian Royal Inscriptions* vol I, p. 130ff. for a translation of the Middle Assyrian harem edicts.

6. A. Finet, *Rencontre Assyriologique Internationale* 18, p. 69. The view of Batto, op. cit., pp. 64–72, may be preferable.

7. This can be either an expression of kinship or one of equal status.

8. R. Harris, "Biographical notes on the *naditu* women of Sippar", *Journal of Cuneiform Studies* 16 1962, pp. 1–12; "The organisation and administration of the cloister in ancient Babylonia", *Journal of Economic and Social History of the Orient* 6 1963, pp. 121–57; "The *nadītu* – women", in *Studies presented to A. L. Oppenheim*, Chicago 1964, pp. 106–35.

9. See note 8 to Chapter 3.

10. S. Dalley, "Old Babylonian dowries", *Iraq* 42 1980, especially p. 72.

11. The expression means "to sneeze" literally, but probably has an idiomatic meaning such as "in a twinkling", or "all of a sudden".

12. *Šabsūtu*; this word is not yet attested in the published texts from Mari.

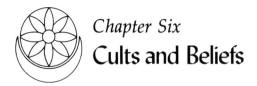

Chapter Six
Cults and Beliefs

In those days each city had one or two deities of particular importance, who were the patrons and guardians of the city and its kingdom, and to whom the king credited his successes. In the city of Mari, probably Itur-mer (a god of little significance outside Mari) and Shamash the sun god were supreme; at Karana, probably the storm god Adad and the goddess Geshtin-anna.[1]

Some cities or towns that were in close communication with Mari and Karana boasted deities who had a more extensive influence, often due to early historical or prehistoric events of which we know nothing; but the influence is clearly present in the palace archives. Adad, the great god of Aleppo, is one of them; because Zimri-Lim married into the royal family of Aleppo, perhaps also because Adad was "the lord of omens", Zimri-Lim accorded him great respect. This may in part account for the emphasis on omens that we have observed among the women of Zimri-Lim's court, but no doubt the queen's childhood influences in Aleppo had their effect too. Shamash and Aya at Sippar also had influence. We are certain of this because royal families in surrounding kingdoms so often sent one of their daughters to be dedicated as a *nadītum*–priestess at Sippar, to spend their adult lives praying for the success of the family dynasty.[2]

But most important of all for the Middle Euphrates region was the god Dagan, a weather god whose two main shrines both lay within the kingdom of Mari during Zimri-Lim's reign. At Terqa, where Kibri-Dagan was governor, and at Tuttul, which lies at the mouth of the Balih river,[3] the cult of Dagan was clearly regarded with the utmost respect. Dagan guarded the road from the south-east into Syria, and Mesopotamian kings with western conquests in mind made sacrifices to Dagan, so that he would look favourably upon their march along the Euphrates passing Terqa and Tuttul.[4] Dagan was the patron deity of the Amorite kingdom of Hana, a state which attained some eminence both before the reign of Zimri-Lim's grandfather, Yaggid-Lim, and in the period following the sack of Mari by Hammurabi's troops. Hana was Mari's closest rival; so when kings of Mari defeated kings of Hana, they took the title "king of Mari and king of Hana", and claimed to have the patronage of Dagan. His name is paired on seal inscriptions of Hanean kings with that of Ilaba, a war god.[5] Less influential at this period was the god Ashur, whose time of overwhelming glory, based on the power of Assyrian kings in the city Ashur, was still to come. At this time he was just another city god, without international standing.

The temples at Karana and Mari

The main temple at Karana was built probably during the reign of Shamshi-Adad. Centrally situated within a circular walled city, it stood high up on the compacted remains of many previous temples that extended back into the prehistoric

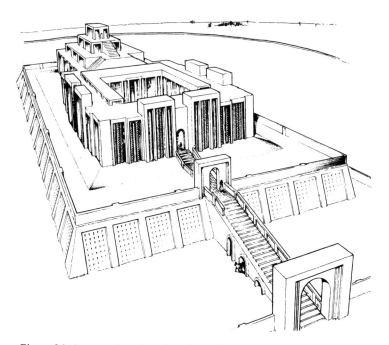

Figure 36 A reconstruction drawing of Karana temple

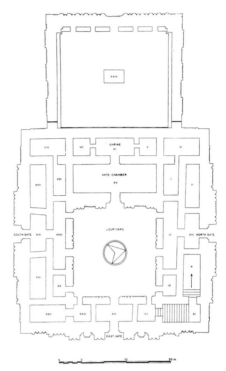

Figure 37 A reconstructed plan of the original temple and ziggurat

period. The approach to the main doorway was up a long and imposing flight of steps, 34 m in length, carried on a succession of three barrel vaults on to the massive terrace from which the worshipper could enter the temple. The façade of the huge, oblong building was built in an elaborate, baroque style: semi-engaged columns in a pattern of great complexity displayed in high relief barley-sugar spirals, diamonds and palm-trunk motifs alternately. These continued around three sides of the temple. The back, western wall adjoined a ziggurat, a solid tower of mud brick that rose impressively in two stages to an unknown height, well above the roof of the temple.[6]

Inside the temple, which could be entered either from the main front door or by one of the symmetrically-positioned side doors, the worshipper would find himself in a large, open, central courtyard, the walls of which were crowded with semi-engaged columns on all four sides, similar in general design and effect to the external façade. The actual shrine in which the statue of the deity would have stood could not be excavated, for the walls were preserved to such an astonishing

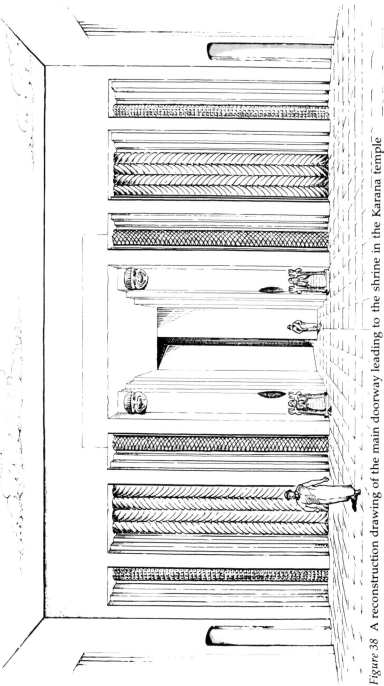

Figure 38 A reconstruction drawing of the main doorway leading to the shrine in the Karana temple

height that the work became too dangerous. Although there were no signs of a second storey, some stairs led upwards, perhaps to a roof walk or even a roof garden. The roof was supported not on a timber construction, but on radial brick vaulting.

The whole extravagant structure was dedicated to the patron deity of Karana; it was his house on earth in which he lived, waited upon by a host of mortal servants who wined and dined him, clothed and entertained him. In most ways the cult in Mari and Karana was similar to that in Lower Mesopotamia, centred on the god (represented by his statue) in his temple which resembled a great, larger-than-life doll's house staffed by priests who provided excursions and holidays as well as daily needs with the utmost care.

At Mari the main temple probably lies beneath a large protuberance known as "le massif rouge" and has not been excavated. However, a secondary temple has been excavated abutting the palace of Zimri-Lim. It was perhaps dedicated to Itur-Mer, since the foundation inscriptions refer obliquely to the god as "king of the land", and Itur-Mer is called "king of Mari".[7] This temple was much less elaborate than the huge one at Karana, and it was completely different in plan, for the building comprised only three rooms (the Karana temple had 25), built right into the core of a solid ziggurat. The approach to this temple was through a large, irregular courtyard. At least 35 great bronze lions stood on guard there; their jaws gaped, their eyes, inlaid with a pupil of black schist in a cornea of white stone, glared at the approaching worshipper, and they were so huge that their heads alone measured some 70 cm in length.[8]

Figure 39 One of the lions which guarded the approach to the temple of the "King of the Land" at Mari

Cult practices

The tablets add different details of cult practices to the architectural evidence. The statue of the deity, however, is seldom mentioned, so that we do not know for certain whether it was life-size, whether there was more than one for each deity (perhaps one in a standing pose and another sitting?) and what materials were used to make them, except that they might be gold-plated. The statue had a throne, a footstool and a standard or emblem, *šurinnum*. It wore a crown

XIII 6
X 52

Figure 40 A metal statuette of a seated god from Qatna. His fringed garment may have been trimmed with fur. (Height 170 mm)

Figure 41   A basalt statuette of a god from northern Syria (Height 87.6 cm)

XVIII 69 and probably also real clothes. If a new statue of a deity was made, the event was very important, and great ceremony attended the entry of the statue into its house. One year at Mari was named: "Year of Yasmah-Addu, when the god Nergal entered his house." Nergal owned a chariot which would have been housed in his temple, and there was a particular festival at Mari for this chariot, at which a special kind of bread called *hūgum* was eaten in enormous quantities.[9]

XII 272 "2,588 litres of *hūgum*-bread, meal of the king and men for the festival of Nergal's chariot."

XII 274 "1,040 litres of *alappānum*-beer, meal of the king and (his) men for the festival of Nergal's chariot."

VII 119 The statue of a deity owned a goblet for drinking, and might also have weapons, probably maces, in one case a bronze weapon overlaid with silver. The images of goddesses were decorated with fine jewellery, rings, necklaces and pectorals.

IS 91, 111 From other texts of the period we know that tiny models of bulls, rings, fish, locusts, and dragonflies made from precious metals and stones were dedicated to deities and stored in the temple treasuries. Some of them may be recognised as having particular significance. At Ur, the main seaport on the Gulf in southern Mesopotamia, a merchant would dedicate a silver model of a boat or some pearls (called "fishes' eyes") in thanks for a successful venture. Others may mark a prayer for the future: a locust model to remind the deity to keep locusts away from his crops, a fish as a request for productive fish ponds.[10]

The meals of the gods seem to have resembled those of the king: meat from young animals, probably specially fattened.

K 200 "One spring lamb, offering of Iltani to Ishtar of Qaṭara... one lamb, offering of Iltani to Sin (the moon god)."

Whether all meat was offered to a deity before being eaten by mortals is not certain, but it seems possible, for that was the K 79 custom in neighbouring Iran.[11] At Karana "the goddess", presumably Geshtin-anna, was given iced drinks, and on one K 269 occasion she was allotted 10 litres of best beer.

It was, of course, apparent that the deity in the form of the statue did not actually eat the meat as a man would. So it was reckoned that the gods to some extent fed on the smell of food. Since their sense of smell was thus an important attribute, they were also probably supplied with fragrant flowers, and bathed in sweet-smelling perfumed oils and resinous extracts. Frankincense, myrrh and other kinds of incense had not yet come into common use, but cedar, juniper and myrtle essences were all used.

Prayer and medicine

The texts do not provide a clear account of who was allowed into the temples, nor of how people behaved in the presence of a deity. Our evidence is usually indirect. When a person entered or left the presence of the deity he (or she) touched his nose. This we know from a rather sentimental letter sent by a man to his two sisters, in which he says:

X 141   "In your entering and leaving, touch your nose to Belet-ekallim. . . . Remember me, don't forget me, and don't be sad from now onwards."

What the significance of this gesture was, we do not yet know. Also the worshipper bowed down when he entered the temple:

RA 42   "I entered the temple of Dagan (at Terqa), and I prostrated myself to Dagan" (i.e. to his statue).

There is not very much evidence for prayers by ordinary people, in contrast to the *naditum*–priestesses at Sippar, who clearly offered regular prayers on behalf of their distant families. Aqba-hammu asked his sister-in-law Amat-Shamash to "offer a prayer for me to your (divine) lord", and Amat-Shamash reproached her sister for failing to say: "Approach and offer a prayer for me to your divine lady."

X 37   Erishti-Aya wrote to her father Zimri-Lim to say: "Am I not the praying emblem who says regular prayers for your life?" The letters of other members of the family, though concerned and reassuring, conspicuously lack this kind of reference, which suggests that prayer was the duty of a *naditum*–priestess, whereas offerings were the duty of the ordinary man, occasionally accompanied by a prayer for the king. One of the rare occasions when a man mentions prayer is a letter sent to Zimri-Lim by Yaqqim-Addu:

XIV 10   "Now, I arrived in Saggaratum, and two servant girls in the house were dead. I looked into the matter, and found out that it was because of the offerings of the god Amu-Tihran. If it pleases my lord, let me satisfy that god. It will only take five days to go there and back, (and I will not be delayed), so that I can pray on my lord's behalf in that offering."

This letter implies that the god was angry either because something was amiss with the original offering, or a person of sufficient importance was not present. The result was the death of two girls and potential danger to the king; the matter could be put right if one of the chief officials of the king went personally to see the god and prayed on the king's behalf.

The power of prayer, according to these letters, was to prevent sudden death and to prolong life. A long and healthy life was the most that favourable gods could grant a man. In another letter Erishti-Aya says:

X 38 "Am I not your praying emblem who makes your *igerrum*–oracles favourable in the temple of Shamash?"

Although we do not know exactly what kind of oracle the *igerrum* was, it seems often to have been an unprovoked word that could be interpreted as significant. In any case, the *nadītum* Erishti-Aya considered that her prayers had the power to make these "oracles" favourable. The course of a man's life depended on the favour of the gods, and the gods revealed their pleasure and displeasure through these "oracles".

To emphasise a statement, or to protest one's veracity, one might swear by a god. A Yaminite chieftain named X 156 Dadi-hadun wrote a vehement letter to Shibtu in which this oath was inscribed: "In the name of Adad the lord of Halab and the god of your father!"[12]

Ancient Mesopotamian beliefs were often different from our own. But there existed also a pragmatic approach to evil and illness, a recognition of cause and effect that may surprise us. The following letter demonstrates that the nature of infectious disease and its control by isolation was understood:

X 129 "Speak to Shibtu, this your lord (Zimri-Lim). I have heard that the woman Nanname is ill with a fever. She has stayed a lot at the palace, and has come into contact with many other women. Now, take strong measures: nobody must drink from the cup that she drank from; nobody must sit on the seat on which she sat, and nobody must lie on the bed on which she lay. She must not have contact with many other women. That fever is contagious." A similar letter speaks of putting a sick X 130 woman in a separate house.

With this attitude in mind, it is easier for us to understand the frequent "post-card" letters, in which people of high rank say only: "I am well. The palace is well. I hope you are well". Early notification of certain diseases would clearly lead to immediate precautions and control. Kibri-Dagan, governor of Terqa, wrote immediately to report an epidemic in Terqa:

III 61 "The city of Terqa and district are well; but in Kulhitum the god has decided to devour men and cattle alike. Today two or three men died."

Similarly in another letter disease is seen as devouring by a god:

v 87   "The family of Bahlu-gayum, your servant, has perished completely in the 'devouring of a god'. All his sons died, and there is nobody left to take charge of that house."

On an international scale, caravans would benefit from early warning of an epidemic; perhaps for that reason Yasmah-Addu sent reassurances to Hammurabi of Babylon saying:

v 14   "Your 'brother' Ishme-Dagan is well and the city of Ekallatum is well; I am well and the city of Mari is well."

The doctor at this time was not a person who specialised in IV 65 exorcism or in rituals of appeasement for angry deities, but a X 18 true medical practitioner of either sex who used bandages VII 23 impregnated with oil, and medicines derived from therapeutic K 113 plants.

"Speak to my lord (Zimri-Lim), thus Yaqqim-Addu your XIV 3 servant. One of my boys is ill. An abscess below his ear is discharging. Two doctors who are with me are bandaging him, but his fever has not changed. Now, may my lord send me the doctor from Mardaman, or some other wise doctor, to examine the boy's fever and bandage him."

Some doctors had a reputation far and wide as healers:

"Speak to Daddy, thus Yasmah-Addu your son. I spoke I 115 before to Daddy about Doctor Meranum coming here. Now Rishiya is in danger of death, terribly ill. If it please Daddy, let Meranum arrive quickly and save Rishiya's life, lest he die."

The code of Hammurabi's laws adds to this evidence, and shows that surgery with a bronze scalpel was carried out even on eyes.

"If a doctor performed an operation on a man with a scalpel, and saved the man's life, or if he opened up the eye-socket of a man with a scalpel and saved the man's eye, he shall receive 10 shekels of silver. If a doctor has set a man's broken bone or has healed a sprained tendon, the patient shall give 5 shekels of silver to the doctor."

Funerary customs

Because Terqa was the major shrine of Dagan in his capacity as lord of funerary offerings, it was also the centre of the rites held for dead ancestors, in particular for deceased kings. A ritual meal called *kispum* was offered regularly to the dead kings, perhaps in the temple of Dagan itself.[13] An inscription of Shamshi-Adad I, King of Assyria, was found at Terqa and records the building of a house or shrine for the *kispum* ceremonies called "the temple of food and drink offerings to

the dead, his house of silence."[14] This was no parochial ritual;
I 65 a Mari letter tells how Shamshi-Adad travelled to Terqa to be
present in person for the *kispum* ceremonies.

By chance, some of the spoken ritual connected with this
ceremony is known from a tablet that probably comes from
Sippar, and is later than the reign of Zimri-Lim when, four
generations later, Ammi-saduqa ruled Babylon (1702–1682
BC).[15] It tells of the invocation of past kings and contemporary
dynasties that was recited on the occasion of these royal
funerary offerings. All the kings of the Amorite dynasty to
which Hammurabi and Ammi-saduqa belonged were called
upon by name, going far back into the remote past. The text
continues:

"The dynasty of the Amorites, the dynasty of the Haneans,
the dynasty of Gutium, any other dynasty that is not recorded
on this tablet, and any soldier who fell while on his lord's
service, princes, princesses, all humanity from east to west
who have nobody to supply them and look after them (with
funerary offerings): Come, eat this, drink this, and bless
Ammi-saduqa, son of Ammi-ditana, King of Babylon!"

Each king, of course, would have had his own version of this
invocation which would name his own ancestors individually
and would call upon the spirits of the dead to bless his own
reign.

The *kispum* ritual was a frequent event, usually held at the
beginning and in the middle of every month, but not always
on a fixed day. Dagan might summon the king to the ritual
through an ecstatic prophet or oracle priest. Kibri-Dagan,
governor of Terqa, reported such an occasion:

III 40 "An ecstatic of Dagan has come and he spoke to me as
follows: 'The god sent me. Hurry and write to the king, that he
may offer *kispum* to the ghost of Yahdun-Lim'[16] That is what
that ecstatic said to me, and I have sent (the news) to my lord.
May my lord act as he thinks suitable."

Thanks to many Mari tablets, we know exactly what food
and drink were offered to the deceased kings and to the gods
of the Underworld *malikū*:

XI 226 "20 litres of KUM-bread, 5 litres of 'sour' bread, 14 litres of
cake, 10 litres of *šipkum,* 2 litres of oil, for the *kispum* of kings, 3
litres of KUM-bread, 2 litres of cake, 15 shekels of oil for the
gods of the Underworld."

Sometimes *alappānum*–beer and honey were included too.

The food was produced from the palace kitchens at Mari;
that is why the records were found there. It is possible that the

food was not always taken all the way to Terqa, but that *kispum* offerings were also made in Mari, perhaps in the palace, or over the graves of the dead kings, although we do not yet know where these were situated. Moreover, a *kispum* offering could be made at any time if any restless, malignant ghost was thought to be causing illness or any other trouble.

All people, not just kings, made this type of offering to dead parents, because restless or malignant ghosts were those who had not received such offerings. In order to ensure peace in the grave, people would sometimes adopt children even if they already had some of their own so that, in exchange for security and perhaps inheritance the adopted children would support them in their old age, and would be obliged by legal contract to perform funerary offerings for them.

This *kispum* ritual, both for kings and for commoners, gives us our clearest evidence for funerary customs and their purpose at this period: the dead must be supplied regularly with food and drink for they had power to harm the living, in particular the king and his dynasty, if they were given cause for grievance by neglect.

No graves of this period have been excavated at Mari or at Karana, but there is good evidence from Ur in southern Mesopotamia to show that the dead were placed in family vaults beneath the floors of private houses. The corpse was laid in a sleeping position, often with a pillow for its head, always with a cup or bowl by the head, but a minimum of other grave goods. Just outside the vault where it was bricked up, a collection of vessels was normally found, and these were presumably the containers in which *kispum* offerings were placed. A deceased man slept, therefore, with his ancestors (whose bones were piled unceremoniously in a heap to make space for a new arrival) and it was easy for the family living above the vault to make the offerings regularly. There is no good reason to connect the *kispum* offerings of ordinary people with the cult or temple of Dagan.

It is characteristic of Mesopotamian archaeology, at almost every historic period and in every region, that public cemeteries and large graveyards are not found. National and domestic income were not invested in monumental tombs nor in professional mortuary arrangements. Death remained largely a private and family matter in which the decomposition of the body and its garments was accepted. Gilgamesh remained with the body of his friend Enkidu until "a worm fell out of his nose"; when he found comfort with the ale-wife, she advised him to make the most of mortal life, for immortality was the fate of the gods alone. Nevertheless, the dead had the power to disrupt the lives of men if they were not properly laid to rest, for belief in ghosts and evil spirits was distinct from belief in godlike immortality.

Two Mari tablets give a small amount of information about grave goods:

VII 58   "One litre of 'pot oil', one litre of cedar oil, for the grave of the woman Ahatani, the bride(?) of Mut-Bisir."

Mut-Bisir is known to have been an army commander who served under Shamshi-Adad and managed to retain his post AREC under Zimri-Lim. The other text lists a silver headdress or crown weighing half a shekel and an armband or bracelet of silver weighing one shekel "for the grave of Yahdun-Lim, the king's son."

The records of food for the *kispum* ritual never mention X 63 Dagan or Terqa by name, but they often allow food and drink II 90 not only "for the *kispum* of kings" but also "for *malikū*", chthonic underworld deities about whom we know very little. Dagan is called the "lord of corpse-offerings"[17] in one letter; in another a man has arranged "to give a (human) corpse to RA 42 Dagan". It is possible, therefore, that human sacrifice played a part in the cult of Dagan at Terqa, and that the *malikū* at Mari are in some way connected with Moloch or Milcom, the abhorrent god of the Ammonites. However, the evidence is still very slight, and open to misinterpretation.

There were several other cultic occasions on which food was offered. One was the taking of the "oath of the god" in which the king might also be involved. A curious text lists more than forty men who are making a legal claim:

VIII 85   "They are claiming a field belonging to the palace saying: 'It is our own field!' The city Saggaratum assembled, and Zimri-Lim gave a judgement in Bit-Hanat, and [he assembled?] the city of Saggaratum for the 'oath of the god' ceremony . . . in our presence they ate the *asakkum*–food of (the god) Itur-Mer, (the goddess) Hanat and (the king) Zimri-Lim."

The oath ceremony, as this text shows, was intended to bind litigants to a decision; they ate food which presumably would "turn against them" if they reneged on their promise to accept the judgement.

The word *asakkum*, which is usually translated as "taboo", covers an important concept in Mesopotamian belief. A relic of it is probably to be found in an Islamic, Arab custom, in which food that is accepted by a guest from a host contains a conditional curse.[18] This curse will become effective only if the guest violates the relationship of hospitality after eating the II 55 food. At Mari, when an oath was taken, *asakkum*–food was the means by which it was enforced. One text implies that this VIII 11 food consisted of "plants", which suggests that the bread and cakes of the "oath of the gods" in the text just quoted were not themselves *asakkum*–food, but accompanied it. A Mari list tells what food might be provided for the ceremony, with the crucial *asakkum*–food of "plants" omitted:

XII 46   "8 litres of KUM-bread, 3 litres of 'sour' bread, 4 litres of cake, 7 litres of *šipkūm*, 5 litres of *sasqûm*–flour for the 'oath of the gods'." Here is an example of a practice with associated beliefs which were certainly widespread, but the texts rarely allude to them, and when they do, they mention them only in the briefest manner.

The "oath of the god"

The "oath of the god" ceremony was used for treaties of friendship and alliance between two states or countries[19], and for many other kinds of agreements and disagreements, great and small.

K 24   "Speak to Iltani, thus Napsuna-Addu. May Shamash and Marduk grant you long life. Concerning the garment belonging to the ruler's servant which was given (accidentally?) to his textile-worker: the men have sworn the oath of the gods here. Give the order that they are to return the servant's garment."

If disputants were unwilling to take the oath or could not be relied upon to follow the correct procedure, certain officials XIII 143 known for the occasion as *mušazkirum*, "commissioners of oaths", would be sent to administer the oath. From southern texts we know that a piece of the god's property was hired out from a temple to be present at the ceremony, as if to represent the god.[20]

XIV 92   To some extent the ceremony was used as a lie detector or proof of innocence:

"They made them swear the 'oath of the gods', and they came out unharmed", says a letter, showing that it was an ordeal in which the gods, who were responsible for justice on earth, would surely punish wrong-doing.

The same divine concern with justice can be found in the river ordeal, which like the "oath of the gods" occurs in

Hammurabi's code of laws, as a means of settling a claim fairly. Rivers were to some extent considered divine: if a man was thrown into the river, the river god would make sure that a guilty man would drown, and an innocent man would come out unharmed.

Lods "Now, I am going to take those two men down to the river-god; and their accusers are being guarded here in prison. Let one of your trustworthy servants take them down to the river-god. If those men come out safe, I shall burn their accusers in a fire. If the men die, I shall give their houses here and their dependents to their accusers."

The river god did not always give a clear-cut result. There is ORD a difficult text which records a dispute over the ownership of a border town, in which it was decided that one man and three women should take the ordeal. The first three survived, but the third woman drowned.[21] In a similar text four villagers took the ordeal by jumping into the river clutching a handful of earth from that village, proclaiming as they jumped: "That village is my village! It was allotted in a share a long time ago, and was not given to So-and-so!"

There was presumably more to the ordeal than simply swimming, but we do not know exactly what happened, except that a particular distance is set for each person, according to that letter. In neighbouring Iran, perhaps at this period, the details of a river ordeal are described in a Sanskrit text: the accused man submerged himself by holding the thighs of a man standing upright in the water. As he went under, he said: "Through truth protect me, Varuna." At that instant an archer shot an arrow, and a runner ran to fetch it. If when he returned with the arrow, the accused was alive, he was innocent; if drowned, guilty.[22]

Prediction and prophecy

Not only could the gods pick out a wrong-doer or bind men to their promises; they also gave indications of coming events. It was believed that they knew the future, and would reveal a possible danger to men in particular ways. One of the most widespread means of prediction was the liver omen, in which an animal was killed and its liver and lungs examined by a specialist priest, the *bārûm*. He would ask a particular question, such as: "Is it the right time for the king to march with his army to a certain place?" The "answer" would be

Figure 42 Drawings of clay model livers. (The inscriptions belong within the dotted areas.)

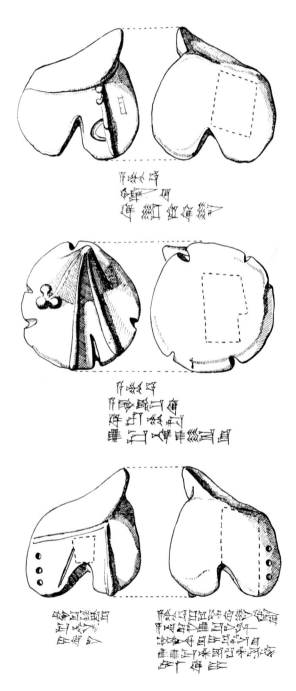

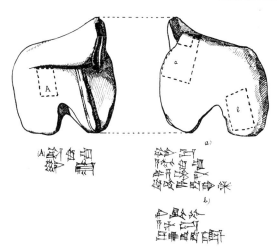

supplied by the interpretation of individual markings or overall configuration of the liver and lungs. A man could then take steps to avoid danger.

Some clay models of livers were found in the excavations at Mari. They have the interpretation written on them to record how the liver appeared and what the significance was thought to be on that occasion. "Omen of the throne(?) of Kish. Undermining will happen in the face of the army, and the army of Ishme-Dagan will be taken." There are many direct references to this kind of omen-taking in the Mari letters:

v 65   "Speak to Yasmah-Addu, thus Asqudum your servant. When I arrived in Terqa, Tarim-shakim arrived too, and I asked him: 'Has Zunan[23] taken the omens for the safety of the land and of the fortress yet?' He answered me saying: 'He has not'. So on the occasion of the census this month I returned to Saggaratum with him and I took the omens for the safety of the city of Saggaratum for the next six months, and the omens were that it would be safe. Then straight away I took them also for . . . Terqa, Ṣuprum and Mari, and now I am writing a complete report immediately to my lord. When I took the omens in Saggaratum for the monthly offering and for the offering of my lord, I looked at the liver and saw that the left part of the 'finger' was detached, and that the middle 'finger' of the lungs was to the right side, a favourable formation. May my lord rejoice!"

xiii 115   There is further evidence that the results of omens had a particular time limit, in a letter written by Kibri-Dagan to Zimri-Lim:

"Dagan and Ikrub-El are well. The town of Terqa and the province are well. Now, I have had omens taken for the safety of the province up until the end of the month, and my omens were favourable."

Many of the king's daily activities must have been restricted or directed by such omen-taking. Adad-duri wrote to Zimri-Lim saying:

x 55   "On the occasion of offerings of the throne of the temple of the goddess Anunitum I made an offering and the (resulting) omens were very favourable.... Now, may my lord guard himself and come to me."

It is easy to understand how vital such omens would be in war, when a defeat could be avoided by careful omen-taking, and how important was the omen-priest who marched with the king. Indeed, Aqba-hammu, the ruler of Karana, was himself an omen priest by profession who had become king; no doubt his special skills helped him to seize power at the right and favourable moment. His letters to his wife Iltani, however, curiously show no particular reliance on omens.

Another way in which a god might warn or advise for the future was through prophetic utterances. From the scattered evidence it seems that each main temple had one or more people, men and women, attached to it whose duty was to "answer" for the god, the person through whom the deity spoke. They occur only, it seems, around Mari and to the west of Mari, and they are not found in southern Mesopotamia or at Karana, as far as our evidence goes. Exactly how they operated can best be seen in an incomplete letter from Mari:

Lods   "During the omen-taking Adad, the lord god of Kallassu town, spoke saying: 'Am I not Adad, the lord god of Kallassu, who brought him up on my lap and put him back on the throne of his father's house? When I had put him back on the throne of his father's house I went further and gave him a place to live. Now, since I returned him to the throne of his father's house, I should receive some property from him. If he will not give it, then as I am the lord of throne, territory and town, I shall take away what I have given. If it is not so, and if he gives what I want, I shall give him throne upon throne, house upon house, territory upon territory, town upon town, and I shall give him the land from one end to the other.' This is what the 'answerers' said, and they kept standing there during the omen-taking. Now, you see, the 'answerer' of Adad, the lord god of Kallassu, is guarding the threshing floor of Alahtum as his property, and may my lord know it! Previously, when I was staying in Mari, I used to tell my lord everything that the male and female 'answerers' said to me. Now that I am staying in another country, shall I not write to my lord whatever I hear and whatever they say to me? If ever in future there occurs some cause for blame, will my lord not say: 'Why did you not write to me the word that the 'answerer' spoke to you, and to say that he was guarding your threshing floor'."

XIII 23   Other deities who are known to have had an "answerer" at
X 9 their shrine are Adad of Halab, Dagan of Tuttul and the goddess Deritum, patron of the town of Der that lay perhaps 15 km downstream from Mari. When Shibtu reported to Zimri-Lim the utterance of the "answerer" of Deritum, she remarked that it happened at the palace gate, which shows that the "answerers" did not only operate inside temples at omen-taking ceremonies.

There were other people who claimed occasionally to be channels for divine utterance through their trances or dreams. Usually the temple of the god in question was the location of their experience, but because they were not usually temple staff a test to verify their authenticity was sometimes held.

First there was the ecstatic trance. This was an experience which could happen either to a habitual recipient of the god's word; or to a common citizen as a unique occurrence. The ecstatic might be male or female, *muhhum* or *muhhutum*. According to his or her standing, or to the potential importance of the message, a piece of the ecstatic's hair and a part of the fringe or hem from the border of his garment might
X 81 be sealed and sent to the king for a verification test.[24] The king might perform an omen-taking ritual in person, to discover whether the experience was "true".

Second, there were dreams, which usually occurred in the deity's temple.[25] Certain people may have made a practice of going to sleep in a shrine expressly to obtain a dream from the god. Like ecstatic utterances, the dreams were usually verified by the hair and hem test. This depended on the character of the dreamer. One letter described the dream that a man obtained in the temple of Dagan in Terqa. Dagan spoke in the dream, to say that he would deliver the kings of the Yaminites into Zimri-Lim's power.

RA 42   "The man who told me this dream will give a corpse to Dagan, and so I did not send him (to you); and because that man is trustworthy, I did not take some of his hair and hem either."

The hem or fringe was a token which represented the whole

person on other occasions. Legal documents were "signed" either with a person's own cylinder seal, or if he had none, VIII 32 with a piece of his hem, impressed on the moist clay. At the end of the text would be noted: "Hem (impression) of So-and-so, cylinder seal (impression) of So-and-so." In one letter military alliance and friendship between rulers is II 71 expressed in the phrase: "to tie one's hem with (that of) an ally".

Another way in which a dream might find confirmation was by the flight of birds (or bats). Two women had an argument about their claim to a priesthood, and one of them claimed to have had a dream in which:

RA 69   "The woman of Shihrum said to the woman of Mari: 'Give me back my priesthood! Either you stay or I stay!'" An official at Mari was called upon to adjudicate, and he wrote: "By means of birds I investigated her claim, and (the result was that) she really did have the dream. Now, I am sending her hair and hem, that my lord may settle her claim." This text shows that the augury was used to establish whether the dream ever occurred; the hair and hem were used to find out whether the content of the dream was a "true" message from the gods.

Some of the reported dreams and ecstatic utterances are quite cryptic and difficult for us to understand. Nor are we alone in this: in one letter the dream reporter asks for the X 94 opinion of a *bârûm*–priest to interpret the message. Others are clear warnings:

X 80   "The friendship of the ruler of Eshnunna is nothing but treachery! Water flows (invisibly) beneath straw. But I shall gather him up in a net . . . I shall destroy his city!" were the words of the god Dagan to Zimri-Lim. A letter from Adad-duri to Zimri-Lim describes a series of portentous experiences, beginning with a dream of her own:

X 50   "In my dream I entered the temple of the goddess Belet-ekallim, but Belet-ekallim was not there, nor were the statues that stand before her. And when I saw it, I kept weeping. That dream happened during the first part of the night. Then I had another dream, in which Dada, the priest of the goddess Ishtar-pishra, stood at the gate of the temple of Belet-ekallim, and his voice was strange, and he kept calling out: 'Come back, Dagan, come back, Dagan'. In addition to this, a female ecstatic got up in the temple of Anunitum and said: 'Zimri-Lim, don't go on the expedition! Stay in Mari.'"

Although it must have seemed that the ecstatic's trance

confirmed Adad-duri's two dreams, nevertheless she had to submit to the hair and hem test, and it was Adad-duri herself who sent the hair and hem to Zimri-Lim, perhaps hoping to give indirect authority to her own dreams.

When Adad-duri mentioned that in her dream the statues in front of the goddess had disappeared, she was probably referring to the statuettes, usually less than lifesize, that were put as portraits or representations of individuals on benches within sight of the divine statue.[26] The purpose of this was to remind the deity of a worshipper's piety at times when the worshipper could not be there in person. Zimri-Lim had a statue made of himself, and sent it to Aleppo to stand in front AREC of Adad of Halab. He used about 14 kg of copper, which came from the temple of Dagan at Terqa, and it was plated with about 350 g of silver. The occasion on which this royal statue was installed in Halab was so memorable that a year was named after it:

"Year when Zimri-Lim dedicated the statue of himself to Adad of Halab."

In addition to named deities in city shrines, Mesopotamians believed that each person had a personal god and goddess, who were not named, and who were like guardian angels. This worked for good if the person behaved properly, but for harm if the person offended or neglected his god and goddess, for they would then turn aside from him so that evil could have access. When a woman named Zibbatum wrote to her brother Abaya, exhorting him to victory in battle, the concept of the personal god was brought to the fore:

x 107   "May Dagan and your god who stands at your side help you; seize the city and win a victory and be famous!"

Offerings and festivals

Offerings were made to deities in several ways. There were the daily meals of a god, the morning meal and the evening meal XII 685–6 given as a matter of routine. Then there were offerings made with a specific request in mind.

x 142   "Now offer sacrifices for the guarding of the palace, and stand before the gods," wrote Zimri-Lim to Adad-duri, implying that it was important to be seen in person by the god, not just to arrange for offerings. For this reason the king himself had to participate personally in many of the festival

offerings, of which there were various kinds. There was the
monthly *essēsum*–festival:

K 58   "I shall arrive there in time for the *essēsum*–festival" wrote
Aqba-hammu to Iltani. Likewise he wrote to her to say: "On
the 15th day of the month Nabrum I shall perform the *elunnum*
festival. Get ready." Some of the month names are the same as
the names of annual festivals; such was the festival of the
brazier, *kinūnum*.

The statues of the gods sometimes left their shrines and
were transported by boat to visit a deity in another town.
Kibri-Dagan reported:

XIII 111   "The gods Lagamal and Ikshudum have arrived in Terqa
from Mari."

A high official named La'um, perhaps based in Tuttul, wrote
to Yasmah-Addu to say that the processional boats of Dagan
V 79 had arrived, but he was postponing their further journey
because "the heavens opened, and it rains unceasingly".

There was some kind of a purification ceremony for the
king, for which Mukannishum supplied from his workshops
XVIII 65 various garments, two pairs of sandals and two musical
instruments, either drums or harps, on which lamentations
were played.

Another occasion, the offerings of Ishtar, was perhaps the
most important event of the year at Mari. It took the form of a
garden party, for which the palace kitchens provided:

XII 268   "420 litres of sweet *alappānum*–beer, the meal of the king and
men on the occasion of offerings to Ishtar, in the garden of the
king."

It has been suggested that this ceremony is the one shown
on a wall painting that was found on the wall of Court 106, by
the main door that led to the throne room, 64. The setting is a
garden with trees and birds, and the king is shown in a framed
centre-piece receiving the insignia of kingship from a goddess
whose right foot treads on a lion, which is well known as the
animal of Ishtar. The scene is attended by lesser, interceding
deities, while below, encapsulated in a lower register, two
goddesses hold overflowing vases of water. These two
branching streams contain fishes and give rise to a new shoot
that grows from each vase.

If these two separate items, the mural painting of the
investiture, and the textual evidence for "offerings to Ishtar"
in the royal garden, are truly connected, we may perhaps have
a version of the New Year festival on the Middle Euphrates. It
included the annual renewal of kingship as the gift of the gods,

Figure 43 An investiture wallpainting from Mari, central panel

and it was known to take place in a garden. An *akitum*-festival, perhaps not yet specifically the New Year festival, was celebrated by the Assyrians under Shamshi-Adad, (probably at Ashur not at Mari); this is known from the Assyrian king's letter to his son Yasmah-Addu saying:

150 "This is the month of Addar, and when the 16th day comes, the *akitum* festival will take place. Some messengers from Eshnunna will be staying. Have teams of your mules and your horses driven to me for the *akītum*-festival. Have the chariots and equipment renewed."

In later times the New Year festival contained some particular elements: the re-investiture of the king, the oath of loyalty by vassals and high officials, a ritual in a special temple built with a garden outside the city walls. There is some AREP evidence that Zimri-Lim summoned his many vassal kings for the "Offerings to Ishtar". This may possibly be a forerunner of the annual oath of loyalty which is well known in the first millennium. If so, the "Offerings of Ishtar" would be the equivalent at Mari of the New Year festival at Ashur a thousand years later.

RA 35   The only ritual text yet published from Mari comes also from the cult of Ishtar. The "title" of the tablet is missing, so we do not know whether it comes from a ceremony that was performed at the "Offerings of Ishtar", or took place on a different occasion. A meal is set before the goddess, and various workers – the brewer, the carpenter, the leather-worker, the textile workers, apprentice craftsmen and apprentice barbers – all dedicate their skills and their tools to her. Ritual songs are sung, jugglers and wrestlers perform, and when they have finished, the king takes his seat. Water is sprinkled three times in various specified parts of the shrine, and then water in metal cups is held out "ready for the needs of the ecstatics". Enigmatic though this fragment is, it combines with the "Offerings of Ishtar" to show how important the cult of that goddess was at Mari, although she was not the patron deity of the city.[27]

In this age of polytheism every deity had its shrine, its attributes and its contribution to the lives of men. The cultic calendar was a flexible one, so that new duties and observances resulting from conquest were readily assimilated into the royal schedule. Foreign gods had their place too – Hurrian or Syrian gods were accorded no less respect than Akkadian deities, nor had that era yet dawned when the god of a conquering nation made the gods of the defeated subservient to him. As far as we can tell from these texts the competitive and exclusive ideologies, first of religious domination and later of monotheism, had not yet come into existence. The many deities of Zimri-Lim's time lived together in harmony, their influence and status hardly affected by the frequent victories and defeats of the cities in which they lived.

Notes to Chapter Six

1. This is known only from indirect evidence, and remains uncertain. See S. Dalley, "Old Babylonian greetings formulae", in *Journal of Cuneiform Studies* 25 1973, pp. 79ff.

2. See note 8 on Chapter 5.

3. To be distinguished from the other place called Tuttul which is near modern Hit, and was of much less importance at this period. See G. Dossin, *Revue d'Assyriologie* 68 1974, pp. 33–34.

4. See for example the inscription of Sargon. I translated in *IRSA*, p. 99

5. The reading Ilaba is preferred by J. J. M. Roberts, *The earliest Semitic Pantheon*, Johns Hopkins 1972, p. 34. The reading Aba is preferred in *IRSA* passim. For the Hanean seal inscriptions see *IRSA*, p. 250.

6. D. Oates, preliminary reports in *Iraq* 27 1965, 28 1966, 29 1967, 32 1970.

7. See Dalley in *Bibliotheca Orientalis* 36 1979, pp. 289–290. Ichiro Nakata, "A Mari note: Ikrub-El and related matters", article in *Orient* XI (Tokyo) 1975, pp. 15–24, has suggested that Itur-Mer was a mortal hero deified after his death as part of the cult of dead ancestors.

8. A. Parrot, preliminary reports in *Syria* 20 1939, *Syria* 21 1940.

9. This festival took place once a year on the seventh day of the ninth month called Lilliatum.

10. See also Chapter 9 pp. 182–189.

11. M. Boyce, *Zoroastrians; their religious beliefs and practices* London 1979, pp. 5–6.

12. For this translation see K. R. Veenhof, "aššum Šamaš", "By Šamas!" and similar formulae, *Journal of Cuneiform Studies* 30 1978.

13. Extensive evidence for the *kispum* ritual at all periods is given now in "Death in Mesopotamia" 26th *Recontre Assyriologique Internationale* 1980, Copenhagen, *Mesopotamia* vol. 8.

14. Complete text given by Grayson, *Assyrian Royal Inscriptions* vol. I, p. 25.

15. Finkelstein, "The Genealogy of the Hammurabi dynasty", *Journal of Cuneiform Studies* 20 1966 and W. G. Lambert, "Another look at Hammurabi's ancestors", *Journal of Cuneiform Studies* 22 1969.

16. This Yahdun-Lim may refer either to Zimri-Lim's father or to his prematurely deceased son who bore the same name.

17. This title may mean either "lord of corpses" (i.e. a god of the Underworld) or "lord of human sacrifices" or "lord of funerary offerings".

18. See C. Roden, *A book of Middle Eastern food*, Penguin 1970, pp. 33–34.

19. See Chapter 7, p. 140f.

20. See R. Harris, "Journey of the divine weapon, in Studies . . . Landsberger", *Assyriological Studies* 16. Compare how in an Old Assyrian text MVAG 33 no. 252: 31 men taking an oath grasp the dagger of Ashur. More examples of this practice are given in *CAD* vol. B, pp. 127–8.

21. The whole of this text is now published by J. Bottéro, "L'ordalie en Mésopotamie Ancienne", *Annali della Scuola Normale superiore di Pisa*, vol. XI/4, Pisa 1981, p. 1041ff, together with an edition and discussion of several similar texts.

22. Described in M. Boyce, *Zoroastrians: their religious beliefs and practices*, London 1979, pp. 8–9.

23. Presumably Zunan was a *barûm*-divination priest.

24. See A. Finet, "Les Symboles de cheveu, du bord du vêtement et de l'ongle en Mésopotamie", *Annales du centre d'étude des religions* Brussels 1969.

25. Geshtin-anna is found as an interpreter of dreams in the myth "The dream and death of Dumuzi". It may be as a dream goddess that she is patron deity of Karana, for there is a curious text in which Karana is named in a list of cities that a man may visit in his dreams. Despite this, the texts from Karana are silent on the subject of dreams.

26. See W. Andrae, *Das wiedererstandene Assur*, Leipzig, 1938, reprint Munich 1977, plate 85; expressed by Esarhaddon: "a representation of myself depicted as king in supplication before the god asking for my good health". (Borger, Inschriften Asarhaddons 87 r.3f.)

27. We have almost no information about the cults of Geshtin-anna or Adad at Karana, and very little about the cults of Itur-Mer or Shamash at Mari.

Chapter Seven
Warfare and Diplomacy

The gods at war

Until Hammurabi united most of northern and southern Mesopotamia, bringing Zimri-Lim's rule to an end, the land consisted of many small city-states, each competing in war or co-operating by means of trade and alliances. Each city-state was protected in peacetime and led in wartime by the main deity of the capital city, and so wars were given religious justification: invasion was either a sin against an innocent country, or divine retribution against a sinner, depending on the viewpoint. The god was victor in a successful war; a victorious power would carry off spoils to enrich the god and his people.

This rationale is expressed very clearly in the letters from Mari and Karana. The deity, speaking through a female ecstatic in the temple of Anunitum in Mari, said to Zimri-Lim:

X 8   "Oh Zimri-Lim, swear that you will not neglect me, and I shall hover over you and deliver your enemies into your power."

At Karana, the woman Azzu-ena of Ashala wrote to beg for a slave-girl from the booty of a recent campaign which was successful thanks to a divine command. She said:

K 160   "You wrote to me saying: 'The booty that is before me will be plentiful. When I enjoy the booty, and you hear about it, write to me that I may present you with a slave-girl'. This is what you said to me. Now, the god has spoken, there was nobody to hinder you; now the booty that is before you is indeed plentiful."

If a ruler believed that a deity was angry with him and had turned against him without good cause, or showed signs of displeasure, he could write a letter to the god in an attempt to exonerate himself and lay the blame elsewhere. One fragmentary letter of this nature was found at Mari. It was

13 written by Yasmah-Addu, and it is clear that he is attempting to point out the "sins" of the dynasty of Yahdun-Lim, in order to prove that his own rule and that of Shamshi-Adad were an improvement on the previous regime and worthy of divine approval even though they had usurped the throne.[1]

Treaties

A treaty of alliance between two rulers was cemented with a religious ceremony in which a donkey foal was usually sacrificed, and both parties swore the "oath of the gods", by which they showed respect for each other's city gods.[2] Ibal-El describes how he went to arrange a treaty between the Hanean semi-nomads and the northern city-state of Idamaraz:

II 37   "The letter of Ibal-Addu arrived from Ashlakka, and so I went to Ashlakka, in order to kill a donkey foal between the Haneans and Idamaraz. They brought me a puppy and a goat, but out of respect for my lord I would not allow a puppy and a goat, so I insisted on sacrificing a donkey foal, the offspring of a female donkey. Thus I made peace between the Haneans and Idamaraz."

The treaty agreement was recorded on a tablet which contained various clauses that had to be agreed in advance. Both parties would seal the tablet since it was a legal contract. Each would possess a copy with identical clauses but a rather different prologue, and we know from slightly later evidence that a copy was deposited in a temple in each country. A Mari letter tells of the difficulties of agreeing about all the clauses; Shamshi-Adad wrote to his son at Mari:

I 37   "There was some clause or other that I took out of the tablet of the 'oath of the gods', and I then sent (it) to Eshnunna. The ruler of Eshnunna is being obstructive, and so far no message has arrived for me. That is why I am held up in this town."

XIV 106   "Remember the 'oath of the gods' and let me come into your district", said the king of Razama to the king of Eshnunna. Such a treaty as this meant that one ally might march through the territory of another, and the clauses regulated their mutual rights there. Usually there were extradition clauses also, for the return of fleeing criminals and escaped slaves.[3] With a treaty the two allies might combine forces for a joint military expedition:

K 1   "Speak to Hatnu-rapi, thus Zimri-Lim. I have read your letter which you sent to me. In the past you have often written that we should meet in Qattuna, saying: 'You there, bring (troops) upstream as far as Qattuna; and I here shall lead out the kings my allies who enjoy good relations with me; let us kill donkey foals; let us put the "oath of the gods" between us.' You often wrote these words to me."

There were rules, perhaps unwritten, about sharing booty when an army of alliance succeeded in capturing a prosperous town. If someone took more than his share, he had to give it back, whether he was a king or not. A king might be persuaded peacefully:

K 5 "Speak to Hatnu-rapi, thus Bunu-Ishtar your brother. Since you are bringing out Zimri-Lim's share from the goods that you are bringing out of Shubat-Enlil (as booty from the sack of Shamshi-Adad's northern capital), why are you still keeping his share? Will he be content simply to look on?"

Obviously bad behaviour might break up an alliance, and would be a good reason to abrogate a treaty. If unfair division II 13 was only suspected, an officer would resort to making the men "eat the *asakkum* – food of Dagan, Itur-Mer, Shamshi-Adad and Yasmah-Addu", and swear an oath by the king. In one case even these stern measures produced no results, and the king was asked to decide the case personally.

Military service

Letters often give the size of an army or a contingent, although the numbers given are not always reliable. They are usually round numbers, probably approximations or estimates, sometimes exaggerated if one king was trying to goad another into action. The largest army known at present for this time is an Assyrian army under Shamshi-Adad, who planned to h. AS 16 besiege the fortress of Nurrugum[4] with 60,000 men. This is I 42 perhaps exceptional; 20,000 men was reckoned to be a strong army by Shamshi-Adad, although we do not know the circumstances that gave rise to that particular levy.

Hatnu-rapi of Karana, Sharriya of Razama and some other petty rulers hoped to raise 4,000 men and to join up with 2,000 others, with the purpose of helping Zimri-Lim, probably against an invasion from Eshnunna.

K 4 "As soon as you have read this letter, you and Sharriya and the kings who are on your side, get together and muster 4,000 men between you, and from here I shall muster 2,000 men. The former plus the latter, 6,000 good men, let us muster between us and let us send them quickly to the help of Zimri-Lim; indeed, let us act in order to save Zimri-Lim. This is no matter for neglect!"

On a later occasion, when Aqba-hammu was king of
K 68 Karana, Hammurabi of Babylon sent a relatively small
K 305 contingent up towards Karana, 1,000 troops. A troublemaker
I 42 led a mutiny in the region of Karana with 2,000 men;
Shamshi-Adad of Assyria sent to Yasmah-Addu at Mari
10,000 troops, to be added to 6,000 from elsewhere. Clearly
troops were reckoned by the thousand. A single letter from
K 302 Karana is written by one Aham-arshi, "commander of a
thousand", and we may suppose that 1,000 was the biggest
unit of men. Smaller contingents were reckoned in hundreds,
II 13 and there was an overseer of 10 men at the bottom of the scale.

The process of enrolment was based on a census. Zimri-Lim
carried out a major census during one year of his reign, and it
was an event of sufficient magnitude for the year to be named
after it. A curious word is used for the census, *tēbibtum*, which
also means "purification"; probably a religious ceremony
helped to confirm the soldiers in their commitment to the
cause of the gods who would fight at their side. The census
was carried out by districts, and the semi-nomadic Haneans
were included. If the locals resisted, they might be made to
swear the "oath of the gods". Yaqqim-Addu had some trouble
XIV 64 with his census in the Saggaratum district which he governed:

"Now, I have sent to my lord a tablet containing the names
of the men whom I have registered in the census. I had to be
severe with the village heads and sergeants and the elders of
the district, and had to make them swear a powerful 'oath of
the gods' . . . I have not yet made a census of the trading colony
of my district – the trading colony of Idiatum, which my lord
ordered me to register; and as for registering the men of
Amnanum and of Sahru, I have written five times to their
village heads, but they won't come."

All the men who were to be registered assembled in one
place and were given a ration of food and drink. There is a
A 926 record from Chagar Bazar listing large quantities of barley for
beer and for bread, "food for 2,770 men of the district of
Qirdahat on the day of the census".

The records from Mari have shown that a considerable
portion of the population around the Middle Euphrates was
tribal and semi-nomadic, people who lacked entirely the kind
of material remains which can be excavated, so they are a
blank in the archaeological record. We encounter them in the
tablets in various capacities: as raiders, as traders, as
pastoralists and as soldiers in the army of Mari, in particular

17 the group known as Haneans. They were induced to gather for
142 the census partly by means of an annual allotment of land for cultivation. Any field whose cultivator had died or deserted was redistributed during the census to semi-nomads, who probably set up temporary encampments near to their fields just for the growing season. If the semi-nomads did not need an allotment of land, it was very difficult to persuade them to come for the census.

16 "You wrote to me about making a census of the Yaminites, saying that they will not agree to the census. You absolutely must make one; otherwise their brothers the Rabbeans who are on the other side of the river in Yamhad will hear . . . be more severe!"

During the Assyrian interregnum at Mari Yasmah-Addu controlled Chagar Bazar, and an official named Ishar-Lim carried out the census on his behalf. Ishar-Lim is found on tablets both at Mari and at Chagar Bazar. He reported to Yasmah-Addu at Mari, saying:

V 51 "About the Haneans who live in the district of Upper Idamaraz, you wrote to the king. Now, I have written the tablet of those men and their names, of the Haneans who live in the districts of Nahur, Talhayum, Qirdahat and Ashnakkum[5] – the area of which I have made a census – and sent it to my lord."

This same man Ishar-Lim made a brief bid for power, usurping the throne of Yasmah-Addu, probably only for a few months or less.[6] To gather such huge masses of men for the census was to control a potential private army for mutiny without, initially, alarming the king. A record from Chagar Bazar shows what Ishar-Lim ate while he was completing his arduous task:

A 950 "55 litres of *sammidatum*-flour, 55 litres of pounded meal, for the meals of Ishar-Lim on the occasion of the census."

The lists of names were kept in boxes in a locked room, which was only to be unsealed in the presence of witnesses.

X 82 "I opened the tablet room which was sealed with your seal, and both Mukannishum and Ṭabat-sharrussu were standing there. Igmillum showed them which were the boxes that they needed, and then they brought out, with their own hands, the boxes containing all the census tablets."

When Bahdi-Lim at Terqa had trouble trying to register the Haneans – they simply refused to assemble – he asked Zimri-Lim for permission to make an example, to encourage the others:

II 48   "If my lord agrees, let a criminal from prison be killed, and his head cut off and paraded around all the town between Hutnum and Appan, to make the men afraid, so that they will assemble quickly."

Several of these extracts have shown that the Hanean people formed a noticeable part of the army at Mari. They were perhaps organised along tribal lines, and their chief man of each group or area, the *sugāgum* "sheikh", dealt with officials from Mari. Two other semi-nomadic peoples of this period were the Yaminites (formerly known as Benjaminites) and the Suteans. For the most part they lived outside the kingdom of Mari, and so are less often found in the army. The Yaminites lived mainly to the north and the Suteans to the west of the Mari homeland. Like the Haneans, they had a *sugāgum*–sheikh for each group or locality, unless they settled in towns where they joined the existing organisation. Because the Yaminites and Suteans lived on the borders of a prosperous kingdom, they are often found as raiders (the Suteans in particular) or as troublesome foreigners. The Yaminites were relatively well organised on the Habur river, and posed a real threat to Zimri-Lim's expansion: he claimed to have defeated them early in his reign.[7]

One passage from a letter shows that a military commander who was victorious in battle might cut off the head of the enemy leader and send it to the king.

II 33   "Shadun-laba[8] wrote to me saying: 'Because I cut off the head of Ishme-Adad, the enemy of my lord, and had it sent to my lord, the men of Hurra and the man of Shinah have come and cut down my orchards!' "

There was a special police force with fortified posts, *bazahātum*, that dealt with criminals and deserters; deserters were harshly punished. When Kibri-Dagan had trouble with a fugitive called Yarim-Dagan, Zimri-Lim wrote to him to say:

XIII 108   "Whether he is in a secret cave, or in the field or inside a town, destroy that man! Whether he goes up to heaven or down to hell, let nobody see him!"

Kibri-Dagan wrote back to say that he was trying hard but still could not find him. "But I have put the police posts under emergency orders, that as soon as they have caught that man, they are to impale him on a stake". Such harsh physical punishments are very seldom referred to, however, and nowhere does one find evidence that cruelty was gratuitous. Generally it seems that able-bodied people were taken prisoner and put to work in the palace workshops;

unnecessary reprisals could be avoided in that way. Besides, this year's enemy might be next year's friend, and important persons could be accorded some respect. Zimri-Lim wrote to Shibtu asking her personally to take special care of the young daughter of Ibal-Addu, King of Ashlakka, who was taken as booty after the capture of Ashlakka after a long siege.

X 124

Captives were listed by name when they came to the palace of the victorious king, and Shibtu generally took charge of women of high standing. Zimri-Lim wrote to Shibtu as soon as he was victorious, saying:

X 123
"Perhaps you will hear some news and be worried; but the enemy proved not strong in fighting against me. There is peace; don't worry at all. Indeed, the god Adad of Kulmish must have organised this disruption for the sake of his priestesses! On the tablet of captives that I have sent to you, the priestesses of Kulmish and the priestesses of other gods are listed separately on a different tablet. . . . Give them clothes to wear."

Another letter tells us that some of these priestesses were set to work in the palace textile workshops under Shibtu; others were sent to train as singers under the chief singer, Warad-ilishu.

X 126

Military tactics

The art of siege warfare had already developed to a fine art at this period, and inevitably towns and cities were heavily defended. Each city had two walls, the outer often separated by a water-filled ditch from the inner, and large gates at the entrances. In addition the palace, centrally situated within the city walls, would have a stout retaining wall of its own. So a siege was often a long business. The besiegers had many weapons at their disposal, including siege towers, scaling ladders and battering rams (one logographic writing of the word for "battering ram" shows that it was thought of as a goring bull). Since defensive walls were usually made of mud brick, which is a relatively soft material, the battering ram was a particularly effective weapon.

VI 29

XIV 45
"My lord wrote to me about sending downstream to Mari some ropes to go around siege towers and battering rams" wrote Yaqqim-Addu. In the palace at Mari, Mukannishum was in charge of making battering rams, and he was also sent beams of pine wood for making siege ladders. The main army would spread its camp right around the city so that nobody

II 17, 24

I 90

could come out unchallenged. Fire-brands would be tossed
VI 69 over the walls to dismay the defenders and to set buildings
alight. The timber and reed matting used for roofs was
particularly inflammable.

Ishme-Dagan was fond of boasting to his younger brother
Yasmah-Addu about his successful sieges:

I 131   "When I had captured the towns of Tarrum, Hatka and
Shunhum, I approached Hurara and surrounded that town. I
set up a tower and a battering ram against it, and in 7 days I
captured that town."

I 135   "As soon as I had approached the town of Qirdahat, I set up
a tower and made its wall fall down by tunnelling, and in 8
days I captured the town of Qirdahat."

The siege was perhaps the main means of victory for one
ruler over another. We have no detailed accounts of pitched
battles, but numerous references to sieges or to negotiated
X 84   surrender. Because the fortified city was the chief defence of
an enemy and a sign of independence, the victor would
destroy the ramparts. Yahdun-Lim, father of Zimri-Lim,
describing his own achievements on a brick inscription, told
how he defeated a coalition of three kings:

"He (Yahdun-Lim) took the three kings captive, defeated
their troops... made a heap of their corpses, destroyed their
ramparts and made them into ruined mounds."

Omens were often taken before a probable confrontation,
and very likely they served as a safety valve, to give an army an
excuse for avoiding a head-on clash when the outcome was
II 22   likely to be unfavourable. So it comes as no surprise to find the
omen-priest Ilshu-nasir marching at the head of Zimri-Lim's
army, and another omen-priest marching with the army of
Babylon. Nor is it surprising, from such a position of power, to
find Aqba-hammu the omen-priest seizing the throne at
Karana.

There is as yet only slight and uncertain evidence to suggest
that a clash of massed armies might be avoided by a personal
X 4   combat between two rulers, or between two prizefighters
chosen from the two opposing sides. The evidence comes from
some kind of prophetic utterances reported by Shibtu to
Zimri-Lim, and several of the words used are still not clear.
When the texts from Mari were first studied, a word read as
dawidum was thought to mean "leader", and to be cognate
with the Hebrew name David. The phrase that indicated
defeat was translated "to kill the David/leader", and it was
thought that a "David and Goliath" combat was a common

way of settling a dispute. Better understanding showed, however, that the word should be read *dawdûm*, meaning "defeat", so that it can no longer be interpreted to show a personal combat between leaders.[9]

Logistics and equipment

When large armies were on the move, feeding and watering were a problem. Zimri-Lim pointed out to Hatnu-rapi the difficulty of joining forces in Qattuna, presumably at a dry time of year.

K 1   "Where would such a numerous force of men find enough water to drink?"

VI 32   Problems of feeding and indeed of arming the men were often resolved with the co-operation of village heads when the army was within its own kingdom. Shamshi-Adad wrote to Yasmah-Addu to discuss the matter of providing for 400 men:

II 1   "Among the Haneans of whom you will make a census, take 400 good men to serve at my palace gate. Of those men, let 200 men be one group, the sons of good men, and let the other 200 men be the other group, of older men.... I shall provide generously for the older men from the palace, and the sons of good men shall be maintained from the households of their fathers. Make the census of Haneans soon, and find out from Yarim-Addu whether there is enough water in Gashim or in Subim for them to assemble there. Let the troops from the banks of the Euphrates assemble in Saggaratum."

On another occasion he gave instructions to Yasmah-Addu, saying:

I 39   "Destroy and burn that town, and then, just as I wrote to you in my last letter, leave for Shuda and secure provisions for the troops for one month, to give them confidence. Let the troops rest for a day or two in Shuda, and then leave for Shapanashum. Stay in Shapanashum, where the troops themselves must supply you with your meals, for the troops will have to take provisions for the coming month from Shuda."

VII 215   The commanders of the army were the *rab Amurrim*–officers, who received payment in silver rings from the palace as well as IV 74 clothing. Other military and local officials – heads of "sections", sergeants, village heads – received similar payments in smaller amounts. But probably the main recompense for service came in the form of booty, an incentive as well as a payment.

Some at least of the soldiers received their weapons from the XIII 54 palace, and were not expected to provide them for themselves. We have already looked at Mukannishum's duties in the supply of some weapons, but in some cases we are hampered by uncertainty over the exact meanings of words. The weapon XVIII 21 *tilpānum*, of which Zimri-Lim ordered six, is almost certainly a bow (rather than some kind of a throwing stick as used to be thought).[10] Certainly arrows were very common: Shamshi- I 38 Adad wrote to Yasmah-Addu asking for 10,000 bronze arrowheads, *samrūtum*, each weighing 6 shekels, (48 g), but there was not enough bronze at Mari, so the Assyrian king had to supply his son with bronze, in exchange for silver at the current rate. Zimri-Lim used lighter arrows, and had a XVIII 5 different word for them, *šiltāhum*; the heads were still made of bronze, but weighed between 1 and 5 shekels (8–40 g).

The sling, *waspum*, was a common weapon too; 500 were ordered in a letter from Shemshara, and 8 are found in a IX 102 supply list from Mari, together with 30 bows. The spear or lance or javelin was perhaps commonly used, but again the terms are not always clear, and there may still be some confusion with a word for a shield. The main representations of arms from this period come from the accoutrements of gods and goddesses, and of course these may not reflect the armaments of the man in the field. As far as body armour is concerned, some of the textile terms may stand for armour. We cannot yet distinguish the items sufficiently, but the linen II 139 *hīrum* seems to occur very often with definite items of weaponry. One of the common headgear terms from the supply lists must mean a helmet: a warrior head sculptured in stone from this period shows a helmet with ear flaps, and that is the extent of our certain evidence. A single text tells of two XVIII 28 hauberks, *gurpīsum*, one in the style of Yamhad, the other Akkadian, but the materials of which they were made are not stated.[11]

Various types and sizes of axe are known from the Mari II 139 tablets, and in one case the weight of the axe is given as 650 g, although we cannot be sure whether it was the blade alone or the whole object that was weighed. The soldier of the rank I 31 *bā'irum* carried an axe, and it is likely that nets were often used, for the god is often described as holding the enemy in a net, and earlier sculptures of the Sargonid period (c. 2,300 BC) show the king's enemies tangled in a huge net.[12] Daggers and swords were undoubtedly used, although there is not yet much textual evidence for them.

Figure 44 Drawings of tools and weapons known from this period: (a) two-edged knife; (b) spade blades; (c) hammer; (d) sickle blade; (e) arrowheads from Kanish; (f) bronze axehead of Rim-Sin, King of Larsa ($\frac{3}{4}$ size); (g) bronze fish hook; (h) lugged axe or adze blade; (i) dagger blade with rivets, Ugarit; (j) pickaxe from Mari; (k) items from Kanish

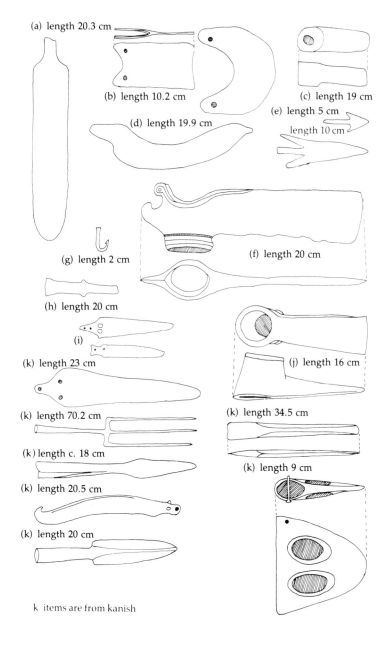

(a) length 20.3 cm

(b) length 10.2 cm

(c) length 19 cm

(d) length 19.9 cm

(e) length 5 cm

length 10 cm

(g) length 2 cm

(f) length 20 cm

(h) length 20 cm

(i)

(j) length 16 cm

(k) length 23 cm

(k) length 70.2 cm

(k) length 34.5 cm

(k) length c. 18 cm

(k) length 9 cm

(k) length 20.5 cm

(k) length 20 cm

k items are from kanish

Various kinds of carts and wagons were in use for transporting heavy equipment, but they were drawn by oxen or donkeys, and did not carry soldiers into battle. The noble art of chariotry in warfare had not yet begun in western Asia. [13]

There are many indications in the letters that communication between the army on campaign and the palace in the capital city was frequent and regular. Messengers were always travelling to and fro carrying the latest information, and so the enemy tried to intercept messages in the hope of gaining useful intelligence. Meptum wrote to his lord Ashkur-Addu of Karana, saying:

II 121   "They have brought in four tablets of the governor of Susa in Elam. . . . I opened those tablets . . . but there was no news in them."

Spies and informers were known; literally "men of tongue", they may often have served only as guides and interpreters. I 29 Shamshi-Adad warned his son against accepting their services, but told him to pay those whom he had hired already, and then to send them away. Where an ambush was planned in unfamiliar territory, such men accompanied the troops:

II 22   "When a large detachment went to ambush an enemy expedition, they could not find a suitable place to lie in wait, so that detachment returned without success, and the enemy expedition continued unchecked – it was not ambushed. Now, let a small detachment go and ambush the enemy expedition, and let them take informers."

The swift raid or ambush by a small party of picked men was probably common, being well suited to the terrain. Trading caravans yielded booty of various kinds, and captured livestock was fresh food on the hoof. To prevent such banditry, escort troops were often provided to see travellers safely into the next state. Raids to steal sheep and cattle, in which the semi-nomadic Haneans and Suteans often took part, may have taken place outside the sphere of military action, but there are many texts showing that the raid was a common practice in the army too. On one particular occasion the men who were caught by raiders were stripped of their II 31 clothing and sent back naked, a source of hilarity to the victors, and of humiliation to the defeated.

Diplomacy

A defeated king might be allowed to retain his throne under certain conditions. First, on the cylinder with which he sealed official documents he had to alter the inscription so as to acknowledge his vassaldom by an additional phrase such as: "Servant of King So-and-so". This is what Aqba-hammu did when he became subject to Babylon; his early seal said: "Aqba-hammu, *bārûm*–priest, son of Himdi-Samas", his later seal said: "Aqba-hammu, *bārûm*–priest, son of Himdi-Samas, servant of Hammurabi". Secondly he had to pay a tribute; Aqba-hammu took large quantities of home-produced textiles to Babylon in person, to pay homage. Thirdly, he may have been forced to accept a governor or provincial overseer, *šapīṭum*. It is possible that Hasidanum held this post while Samu-Addu sat on the throne of Karana as a vassal of

V 45 Shamshi-Adad. Such an overseer may have had responsibility for carrying out a proper census of the population, which a vassal king of suspect loyalty might deliberately falsify. The vassal king Yawi-ila ruled the city state of Talhayum, both during the reign of Shamshi-Adad and when Zimri-Lim was

XIII 143 on the throne of Mari. Under Zimri-Lim he had to accept the presence of a governor, *haziānum*, sent from Mari. Inbatum, a daughter of Zimri-Lim, described in a letter to her father how

X 84 the city Andarik, under its king Himdiya, had to accept two men as provincial overseers. From the same letter we learn that a city might be saved from looting at the hands of the enemy if the defeated king negotiated a surrender in time.

Loyalty could be strengthened by dynastic alliances, as well as by treaties, tributes and provincial overseers. Marriage between two royal families probably indicated that the two kings regarded each other as being of similar status. For this reason we know that the kingdom of Qatna in Syria was important, for Shamshi-Adad arranged that his younger son

II 40 Yasmah-Addu should marry a princess of Qatna. His eldest son, Ishme-Dagan, arranged for his grandson, Mut-Ashkur, to marry a daughter of Zaziya, the powerful ruler of the Turukku tribe, a largely Hurrian people who lived east of the Tigris. Zimri-Lim's wife was taken from the royal family of Yamhad and several of their eleven or so daughters are known

II 113 to have made royal marriages. Shimatum became a secondary wife of Haya-Sumu, the king of northern Ilansura; her sister Kirum visited her but hated what she found there, and asked Zimri-Lim to send someone to fetch her home as quickly as possible after Haya-Sumu said to her:

X 33 "Go away, look towards your father's house, away from my wife!"

We suspect that Zimri-Lim's arrangements went awry here,

that he intended his daughter to take the highest role as queen, but that Haya-Sumu relegated her to a lower rank once the official arrangements were completed. On another occasion Haya-Sumu said to Kirum:

X 32 "Do you suppose you are staying here with the power of a governor? Since I intend to kill you, your 'star' had better come and fetch you back!"

This analysis of the relationship between Kirum, Shimatum and Haya-Sumu is, of course tentative; often we cannot be sure of the difference between a plain statement of fact, a question, and a sarcastic comment, and the interpretation can make enormous differences in reconstructing an event, even when the individual words are clear. The same passage has been taken to show that Zimri-Lim appointed his daughter Kirum as lady-governor to Haya-Sumu.[14]

Another daughter of Zimri-Lim, whose name is not known, wrote to her father, in a letter that is poorly preserved, to say that she had been taken captive by the Assyrians to their X 47 capital Ekallatum on the Middle Tigris. This implies that she was living away from home, and was probably married to a king whose dynastic alliance with Zimri-Lim had not saved him from destruction.

A third daughter, Tispatum, married Ili-Ishtar, the king of Shuna, and wrote to her father Zimri-Lim when her husband was threatened by enemy action, saying:

X 98 "If it is true that my lord loves the city Shuna and his servant Ili-Ishtar, send 100 troops and a loyal servant of yours (to command them) quickly, and save your city and your servant! Because of me, the people who care about him are saying: 'Because he is married to a daughter of Zimri-Lim, he ought to remain loyal to Zimri-Lim!' My father and lord should take heed of this."

So Zimri-Lim, with his plethora of daughters married, it seems, to almost every king of any importance in Upper Mesopotamia, was kept personally informed about pressures and friendships around him. This was surely one of the mainstays of his long reign.[15]

Rich gifts were exchanged when two royal families arranged a marriage. Shamshi-Adad wrote to Yasmah-Addu:

I 77 "La'um, Sin-iddinam and Mashiya are to read this letter with you. I am taking the young daughter of Ishi-Addu for you. The House of Mari is famous, and the House of Qatna is famous: too small a wedding gift would be base, so 5 talents of silver (150 kg) will be given to Qatna as the wedding gift." He adds that he will also provide a pectoral and 100 garments. Later on, however, he had second thoughts and reduced the amount:

I 46

"4 talents (120 kg) of silver will be given as the wedding gift for Ishi-Addu's daughter. I have deposited with La'um a tablet for 1 talent out of the 4 talents of silver, and I personally shall give 3 talents."

Compare this with the wedding gift that Zimri-Lim provided for his sister when she married a nonentity called Rishiya – she was perhaps past her best by then, and had probably been married before – a mere 12 sheep.

AREC

Although one might expect friendship and alliance between kings to be cemented by personal visits with banquets and private discussion, there is very little evidence that kings in person visited other kings. They would send special envoys and delegate their business unless they were in dire trouble and needing asylum. When Ashkur-Addu of Karana visited Mari on the occasion when Mukannishum was ordered to prepare a sumptuous repast, he was perhaps newly usurped, and hoped to enlist Zimri-Lim's aid to regain his throne; for in another letter Zimri-Lim wrote to Mukannishum saying:

XIII 22

XIII 21

"10 women, 2 boys and 2 girls from the households of Ashkur-Addu and Ili-samuh, put them into the textile workshop."

Certainly rulers sent each other presents of which the value was precisely calculated, as the following letter, written by Ishi-Addu King of Qatna to Ishme-Dagan when the latter had become king of Assyria, shows:

V 20

"This matter is unspeakable, yet I must speak and give vent to my feelings. You are a great king; you asked me for two horses, and I sent them to you. And you sent to me two minas of tin. Don't you want to deal fairly with me? This is a paltry amount of tin that you sent me! . . . If you had sent no tin at all, by the god of my father! I would not have been so angry! You are no great king. Why have you done this! Is not this house your house?"

Whenever a party of royal envoys approached Mari, Zimri-Lim was always specifically warned in advance:

VI 23

"A travelling party of messengers from Babylon, Eshnunna, Ekallatum, Karana, Qabra and Arrapha, who are on their way to Yamhad, Qatna, Hazor and X are arriving here. Should I send them on or detain them?" wrote Bahdi-Lim to his master.

Several texts of this sort imply that royal envoys travelled together as much as possible, and that the king had a network

VI 14, 15

of swift messengers.

The king was often absent from his palace, busily fulfilling his religious obligations in cult centres situated in other parts of his kingdom, or leading his troops in war, or taking a caravan to the court of an overlord. Therefore the queen reported to him on the safety of the palace, providing a source of information independent of officials. Aqba-hammu was often away from Karana, and so he corresponded regularly with his wife Iltani. In charge of the palace officially during Zimri-Lim's absence from Mari was Bahdi-Lim, who had discretion to detain envoys pending an order from the king, and who read captured tablets, even correspondence between foreign kings.[16] Hammurabi of Babylon addressed letters to Bahdi-Lim personally; presumably he was well enough informed to know that Zimri-Lim would be absent when his letter arrived.

VI 19

VI 33

The king's main contact with his chief officials as well as with other kings was by letter, and this is one reason for the wealth of information from the tablets. Questions of alliance and troop movements were not always entrusted to envoys, but were written in great detail in royal letters. This is why we have letters sent by Zimri-Lim from Mari and unearthed at Karana, and letters from the king of Carchemish discovered at Mari, yet the king's own letters often ended up in his home town. Everyone wrote in a fairly standard Akkadian, which was the universal language of diplomacy regardless of a ruler's mother tongue. Therefore we have an abundance of homogeneous material with which to reconstruct the political and diplomatic life of that early period.

Notes to Chapter Seven

1. A more up-to-date translation of this text is given by Grayson, *Assyrian Royal Inscriptions* vol I, pp. 27–8. In the present writer's opinion the letter was probably addressed not to Dagan, but to Shamash as chief god of Mari, and divine patron of justice. Cf *CAD* vol. K., p. 480a.

2. See J. M. Munn-Rankin, "Diplomacy in Western Asia in the early second millennium BC", in *Iraq* 18 1956, pp. 68–110.

3. A treaty of this period from the Diyala region, east of the Tigris is now extant, published by S. Greengus, *Old Babylonian Tablets from Ischali and vicinity*, Leiden 1979, p. 74ff. It may only be a draft for a treaty, since it was never sealed.

4. Nurrugum lay west of the Tigris, perhaps quite close to Karana.

5. These towns are all situated in the Upper Habur region.

6. It cannot be proved absolutely that Ishar-Lim is the same man, but it seems very likely.

7. The nomad tribes are analysed by Kupper, *Les nomades en Mésopotamie au temps des rois de Mari*, Paris 1957. A general account of nomads throughout all Mesopotamian history is given by H. Klengel, *Zwischen Zelt und Palast*, Leipzig 1971.

8. Shadun-laba was a vassal king of Ashnakkum under Zimri-Lim.

9. This example serves to highlight the complexities in the cuneiform system of writing, and the dangers of looking for Biblical parallels at too early a stage of study. See also J. Sasson, "Reflections on an unusual practice reported in ARM X 4", in *Orientalia* 43 1974.

10. See O. Rouault in *ARM* XVIII, p. 157 note 217.

11. Leather or felt would have been the basic fabric for the latter. See D. Steinkeller, "Mattresses and felt in early Mesopotamia", in *Oriens Antiquus* 19 1980.

12. E.g. A. Moortgat *The Art of Ancient Mesopotamia*, London 1969 plate 118 victory stela of Eannatum of Lagash; plate 126–7 stela of Sargon (?).

13. Some Syrian seals of approximately this period seem to show a charioteer riding over a fallen enemy, but since the texts never mention military charioteers, either the seals show a victory display rather than a battle, or they may date from a slightly later period. See also Chapter 8 p. 159.

14. B. F. Batto, *Studies on women at Mari*, Johns Hopkins 1974, pp. 42–44.

15. A daughter called Inib-sharri was married to Ibal-Addu, King of Ashlakka in the Upper Habur, perhaps after giving consideration to the governor of the neighbouring state of Nahur. (X 74). Another daughter called Inbatum was almost certainly married to Himdiya the king of Andarik (X 84). The seal of impression of a daughter of Yahdun-Lim, father of Zimri-Lim has been found in excavations at Acemhüyük in Anatolia, a relic perhaps of another marriage arranged with a distant, foreign king. N. Özgüç, in Porada, *Ancient Art in Seals*, pp. 62 and 65.

16. Fully discussed by Kupper, Bahdi-Lim, *Préfet du palais de Mari*, Brussels 1954.

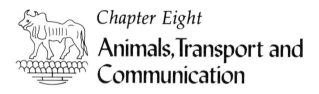

Chapter Eight
Animals, Transport and Communication

Domesticated animals

The earliest remains of settled people in Syria and northern Iraq have shown that stock-raising flourished from neolithic times.[1] The texts of the Middle Bronze Age confirm that the tradition continued, and give some of the details that can never be supplied by material remains.

The ox was an invaluable member of society for it was harnessed to the plough, it was a source of food, and it pulled heavy carts. The ox driver is a profession known from a ration CB 42 list at Chagar Bazar, and plough oxen in other texts from that site are fed on barley:

CB 26 "30 homers of barley, feed for 50 plough oxen, 3 litres each."

This record comes from the palace archives because the palace owned oxen, fed them and hired the ox driver and the ploughman.

Other oxen or bullocks were fattened for the consumption of gods and men.

K 74 "If there is no ox available from the fattening stalls in Zarbat, send one ox from your fattening stalls to Napsuna-Addu", wrote Aqba-hammu to Iltani.

Cows were kept by the palace in large herds:

I 118 "I have got only 3 herd-boys to help me with 1,200 cows", complained a chief herdsman to Yasmah-Addu, explaining that a lion in a wood had carried off five cows, and raiders from the hinterland had stolen another five.

IV 79 Mari was famous for making carts, as Ishme-Dagan admitted in a letter to Yasmah-Addu, saying:

"Mari-made carts are better than any other carts in the country! Send me a carpenter who specialises in making Mari carts."

IX p. 301 For all but the heaviest work, donkeys and asses were used, CB 62 both with carts and as pack-animals. Pack-asses were sometimes clearly distinguished from riding donkeys, and at

Chagar Bazar and Mari there was a further distinction made in
writing between the mule (ANŠE.NUN.NA) which was used
CB 33 at Mari with horses for the Assyrian *akītum*–festival, and the
IX 149 still unidentified *lagum*-mule or donkey.[2] The donkey carried
goods on trading caravans, and there was a donkey park
K 121 known as *kigamlum* attached to every trading station. Donkeys
K 145 were looked after by their drivers, a specific profession; at
K 207 Karana the palace allowed a ration of five litres of barley to
a donkey driver called Anda. A long list of barley feed for
K 314 donkeys, also from Karana, divides the donkeys into two
categories: those of the king (perhaps he owned those that
went on royal or palace-sponsored caravans) and those of a
man named Buniya.

Because the camel had probably not yet been domesticated
as a beast of burden at least in this area of Upper Mesopotamia,
only the donkey and the mule were used for trading caravans
over both long and short distances.[3] The donkey was almost
certainly the commonest mount; Iltani and her sister both rode
K 66 on donkeys provided by the king Aqba-hammu. They were
also used locally for threshing grain and for transporting
cereals.

K 137   "Concerning the sending of the carts and the pack-asses, of
which my lady wrote – the pack-asses are at my lady's
disposal, and so are the carts, whereas the oxen that are at my
disposal have begun ploughing."
K 145   "The donkeys from the country and those belonging to the
donkey-drivers will transport grain from Azuhinnum."

Sheep, shepherds and sheep dogs played their part in the
IX 26, 27 economy of northern Mesopotamia. Employee lists from Mari
show that five shepherds as well as three cowherds were on
the palace payroll; a ration list from Chagar Bazar allows three
CB 13 litres of barley to each of seven shepherd boys, who perhaps
all worked under one shepherd. There can be little doubt that
IX 24 shepherd dogs were in use, since a Mari ration list names five
shepherds who each get six litres of bread followed by one dog
who is allotted twice as much; moreover the dog is added to a
total that is summarised as "shepherds".

With such a flourishing textile industry at Mari, and with
palace workshops needing supplies of wool, it comes as no
XIII 24 surprise to find that Mukannishum at Mari was involved with
the "shearing house", or that Yasim-Sumu assembled and
XIII 30 registered a motley collection of 260 men for the shearing. The
wool was stored and sealed in leather bags or sacks until the
XIII 10 textile workers were ready to begin their work.

We cannot be certain whether dogs were kept as pets or trained for hunting, but the following letter, written by Yaqqim-Addu to Zimri-Lim, shows that the king personally had an interest in acquiring dogs.

XIV 39   ''My lord wrote to me about fetching the/a 'dog of the palace' and a dog of Yazibum to Mari. Of the three dogs that my lord saw in the town of Barhan, one dog has died. Now, in accordance with my lord's message, I have fetched for my lord two 'dogs of the palace', one dog of Yazibum, one dog of a peasant, one bitch of Umu-shakim, ... one bitch of another peasant and two dogs of Ṣilli-X.[4] And about the bitch that was mother of the dog of the town of Barhan – that bitch died.''

Falconry was almost certainly a sport practised at Mari and elsewhere in Mesopotamia. Although there is not yet certain evidence from these texts, an earlier cylinder seal seems to show a falconer with his falcon,[5] and the sport is shown on neo-Assyrian stone sculptures. So there is little doubt that this traditional Middle Eastern pastime was already known and practised, even if we have not yet isolated the Akkadian words connected with it, nor do we know whether it was primarily a means of obtaining food practised by ordinary men, or a royal sport.

Figure 45 A falconer of Sargon II, late 8th century BC

Pigs were kept, perhaps more commonly in the north at Chagar Bazar than at Mari and Karana, for there are few II 106 references to them from the latter two sites. At Mari a pig and a K 95 dog are used to feed a lion in a cage; at Karana pigs come with the possessions confiscated from criminals. Pigs and swineherds are more frequently found in the texts from Chagar Bazar: in a fodder record, 18 homers of barley go to 20 pigs, 3 litres each "which they shall eat in the workshop/pri- CB 32 son", that difficult word *nepārum* again, which is now shown to harbour pigs as well as criminals and the upper class prisoners of war who make textiles and learn singing. At Mari no swineherds have yet been found, even though several personnel and ration lists have been studied; at Chagar Bazar CB 42 however, a swineherd called Nanizu is listed on a closely comparable list.

Of geese, ducks, and chickens we know almost nothing from Mari or Karana, perhaps only because of the types of v 46 record that have been found and published. A single letter mentions that the professional animal-fattener fed birds as well as animals. The more rural records of Chagar Bazar come CB 15 to our help again, with another fodder list, this time with barley at half a litre each for seven gazelle and one-third litre each for seventeen "large birds". It is not entirely clear whether these birds and gazelles were kept and fed in a royal park as pets, or whether they were being fattened up for the next banquet; but one man named Ellanum was in charge of them all.

Horses

When the word for horses was first discovered in the Mari texts, there was great astonishment among scholars. For the general view was that the horse was not domesticated until the middle of the second millennium BC. At that period, it was reckoned on the small amount of evidence then available, that the Indo-European invaders called Mitanni introduced the art of training horses, in particular for chariotry, for the first time. Although it is still true to say that horse-drawn chariots played no part in the warfare of the early second millennium, there is no longer any doubt that horses were bred, trained, traded and used for a variety of purposes at this period. The evidence for this comes almost entirely from the tablets found at Mari, Karana and Chagar Bazar.

Figure 46 Impression from a Syrian cylinder seal, showing an early war chariot

Figure 47 Impression from a Syrian cylinder seal, showing one of the earliest war chariots

CB 17 First, from Chagar Bazar tablets comes a list of barley "fodder, three harnessed teams 1½ litres each, x horses x litres each... in the charge of the trainer". The vital words, "harnessed teams" and "horses" are clearly preserved, and it
A 929 is clear from the quantities of food allotted to the "teams" that a team of horses might consist both of a pair and of a group of
CB 30 three animals. Another barley list registers cereal rations for five grooms, *kartappum*, in the charge of the trainer. However, these two texts do not tell the purposes that those horses and their staff served. A Karana letter gives one clue:
K 85 Aqba-hammu wrote to Iltani:

"May the horses promptly deliver the case of silver cups that are placed in the care of the cup-bearers, to the bearer of this letter of mine."

So horses, whether harnessed or ridden, were used for the swift delivery of small items at Karana. At Mari a variety of evidence has now accumulated to give some perspective on
I 50 the use of horses in that city. We have already seen that Shamshi-Adad asked Yasmah-Addu to send from Mari some of his mules and horses as well as chariots or carts for the celebration of the *akītum* – festival in Assyria. This text implies that the regent in Mari kept a good stable of horses, and that horses were already being used in religious processions. In another letter written to Zimri-Lim by Sumhu-rapi (who probably preceded Yaqqim-Addu as governor of Saggaratum), we learn that Zimri-Lim sent an envoy to the northern land of Elahut, accompanied by a guide from that
II 123 land, with ten donkeys carrying timber, and one horse. This appears to have been a small trading caravan on a relatively short run; the horse was not being used to carry timber, but was probably a gift from Zimri-Lim to the ruler of Elahut.
IX 149 That horses were suitable for royal exchanges is clear from
V 20 the letter of Ishi-Addu, the king of Qatna, to Ishme-Dagan, in which he complained that he received a mean amount of "tin" in exchange for two horses. Another letter, written by
X 147 Zimri-Lim to the lady Adad-duri, also mentions Qatna as a source of horses, from which we may surmise that Qatna was a centre for horse trading and perhaps also horse breeding for many decades, at least from the Assyrian interregnum at Mari well into the reign of Zimri-Lim. Although this letter is broken, it gives instructions about stabling and feeding the horses, which have evidently just arrived.

"About the white horses that are from Qatna, of which you are always hearing: those horses are really fine!" wrote the xiv 98 enthusiastic king. Another white horse is found in a broken context, but this is enough to cause speculation: was the white horse the most valuable and prestigious kind? Is there any connection between these earliest white horses, and the neo-Assyrian Iron Age custom of dedicating white horses to the god Ashur? Or the Babylonian custom of using a white horse to draw Marduk's chariot along the sacred way in Babylon? On another occasion Zimri-Lim tried to obtain white

rha 35 horses from Carchemish, without success. He had to be content with some "red" horses from the Anatolian town of Harsamna, which lay in the vicinity of Kanish. This city Harsamna was associated with a mountain or range of hills that was known in much later times as "the mountain of horses".[6] These letters all give the impression that trading in horses was a royal prerogative; there is not yet evidence that, for instance, Sutu nomads of the Syrian desert owned or traded in horses. We do not know what kinds of horses there were, except that there is now evidence for a very small pony-sized horse from this period.

   As for details of stable staff and gear, grooms are briefly

xviii 55 mentioned in a single Mari text; much more informative is a list of harness items which an official received from Mukan-nishum:

xviii 45   "2 top quality chest-guards, 2 linen *kammakum*-objects, 1 linen *hīrum* for attachment to the seat, 4 pairs of top quality buckles, 4 top quality reins, 1 pair of leather blinkers."

   At this time horses were controlled by a nose-ring with a pair of reins attached; this is known from terracotta plaques and seals, and is true both for draught animals and for horses with a rider.[7] The bit was not invented until the later part of the second millennium, so we do not expect to find a word for it in the lists of harness; indeed, the invention of the bit seems to

Figure 48 Impression from a Syrian cylinder seal, showing an early war chariot. The nose rings are clearly shown

Figure 49 A chariot drawn by two equids with reins attached to nose rings. From a cylinder seal found in the Assyrian trading colony at Kanish

Figure 50 Clay plaque showing an early Mesopotamian horse and rider. The reins are attached to a nose-ring and the rider sits far back on the haunches. Height 83 mm

herald the development of chariotry for warfare. Riders sat far back on the horse's loins in a manner suited to onagers and donkeys, but ill-adapted to the horse's anatomy and very uncomfortable for both man and beast. Some representations seem to show the reins as made of thin cord or string; but a text of this time from Eshnunna shows that an allowance of oil was made for lubricating leather reins.[8]

Another list of chariot equipment gives:

VII 161 "4 *malallu*–wheels, 2 *hallu*– and *malallu*–wheels, 3 wooden *kammāku*–objects, 3 seat attachments, 2 yellow harnesses, 8 reins, 4 pairs of leather blinkers, 10 pairs of buckles."

Near the end of the text, which is broken, two sorts of chariots or carts are distinguished: "chariots", and "swift chariots". Although we cannot be certain that horses, rather

than mules, were being used for these vehicles, the
X 147 accumulation of evidence (particularly with the Chagar Bazar
"harnessed teams" and a word in a Mari letter that may mean a
team) suggests that chariotry was already developing without
any help from Indo-Europeans. However, it must be
emphasised that there is still no evidence for chariotry in
battle, and it may have been restricted to parades and
ceremonies.

A letter from one Ila-salim to Yasmah-Addu suggests that
provincial officials might travel around in a chariot or cart on
official duty, at the king's discretion, since he supplied the
vehicle. The letter omits to mention whether it was
horse-drawn or mule-drawn.

V 66 "The king gave me a chariot, but when I went away between
the country and the mountains, that chariot broke in the
middle, and now as I travel to and fro there is no chariot for me
to ride. If it please my lord, may my lord give me another
chariot, so that I can organise the country until my lord comes.
I am my lord's servant; may my lord not refuse me another
chariot."

Figure 51 Impression from a Syrian cylinder seal, showing a slightly
later war chariot

Another letter suggests that it was more dignified for a king
to travel by mule-drawn cart rather than to use horses,
perhaps because training was not yet perfected and there was
more risk of an upset with horses. Bahdi-Lim advised
Zimri-Lim saying:

VI 76   "My lord should honour his position as king, and seeing that you are King of the Haneans and, secondly, King of the Akkadians, my lord should not ride with horses; my lord should ride in a cart with mules, and thus honour his position as king."

Bahdi-Lim seems here to be trying to restrain an exuberant monarch who was keen to master the arts of horsemanship at the expense of his dignity and of convention.

Wild animals

At this period the Syrian lion, now extinct, prowled the Middle Euphrates, a threat to livestock and people.

II 106   "Speak to my lord (Zimri-Lim), thus Yaqqim-Addu your servant. I wrote to my lord before, saying: 'A lion has been caught on a roof in Bit-Akkaka. My lord should write to say whether that lion should stay on the roof until he comes or whether I should send it to my lord.' My lord's answering letter was delayed, and the lion had been on the roof for five days; they threw a dog and a pig to it, but it refused to eat. I was afraid that that lion might turn nasty, so I put it into a wooden cage and put it on to a boat, and sent it to my lord."

Another letter, from the same man to Zimri-Lim concerns a similar incident in the lion-infested town of Bit-Akkaka.

XIV 1   "A lioness was captured on a roof in Bit-Akkaka during the night, and in the morning I was told, so I went and spent the whole day in Bit-Akkaka so that they would not kill that lion, for I said to myself: 'I may be able to get it to my lord alive.' I gave it [a dog?] and a pig to eat, but it left them alone, and would not eat them. I sent off to the town of Bidaha to fetch a cage, but on the next day, before the cage reached me, the lion died. I had a look at that lioness: she was old and ill. My lord may think: 'They actually killed that lion!' But I swear by the taboo of my lord that nobody touched that lion! Now, since that lion is dead, I have had it skinned and given to be tanned.[9] The lion really was old, and died of exhaustion."

Such great pains were taken to send these lions alive to the king that we suspect the lion hunt was already a royal pastime, and that it was the king's privilege to kill lions that were released from cages specially for his sport. It is a royal sport well known from later times, and it persisted until the Syrian lion was extinct. As an indirect result of this ancient royal privilege, which remained traditional in the Near East into

2

1

4

3

6

5

7

Figure 52 A cartoon strip drawn from lion-hunt sculptures of the 7th century BC of the Assyrian king Ashurbanipal in the royal park at Nineveh. The sculptures are now in the British Museum, and are reproduced here running from right to left.

1. Captured lions at leisure in the royal park 2 are put in cages for the day of the royal hunt. They are released 3 and driven in the direction of the king. 4. The king shoots arrows at the lion, assisted by a shield-bearer. 5. The king delivers the coup-de-grace with a dagger, 6 and the lion falls dying to the ground. 7. The king and his attendants give thanks and sacrifice to the gods over the bodies of the fallen lions.

Sassanian times, the lion became a widespread symbol of royalty, making its way into western Europe by means that are still not certain. Ultimately it found its place on the royal coat-of-arms of England where the animal was never indigenous.

XIV 38   Another letter, again from Yaqqim-Addu to Zimri-Lim, shows that gazelles were hunted and captured with nets, although some of the tablet is broken away.

It is clear that unusual animals were exchanged as gifts between rulers, for a Mari text lists:

VII 91   "12 oxen, 4 roe deer and 1 bear, delivery from Shubram the king of Susa."

These exotic animals – the oxen presumably an Iranian breed not found on the Middle Euphrates – having travelled so far, were surely not destined for the butcher's knife. [10]

Figure 53 The lion as a heraldic symbol: (a) a neo-Assyrian royal stamp seal. The central motif was always used on the King's seals from 8th–7th centuries BC; (b) the Achaemenid Persian King Darius I fighting a lion, c. 500 BC (from a doorway in Persepolis); (c) motif adapted from a Sassanian silver bowl of the 4th century AD; (d) King fighting a lion with a winged, crowned, human-headed horse. Motif on a proto-Bulgarian jug of the 9th century AD; (e) Richard I probably bore these arms on the 3rd Crusade, c 1195 AD

(a)

(b)

(c)

(d)

(e)

The communications network

Mari lies beside the river Euphrates, and almost all the routes that lead to it are river routes. In addition to the rivers, the kingdom was covered by a network of canals which connected the main towns, in particular Terqa and Saggaratum, with the capital city Mari. Therefore the king sometimes travelled by boat, a means of transport which was impossible for the ruler of land-locked Karana. The food lists show that Zimri-Lim sometimes took his meals on a boat:

XII 562   "170 litres of KUM-bread, 60 litres of 'sour' bread, x litres of *isququ*–flour, travel provisions for the boat of the king."

Because water transport played such a vital part in communications at Mari, it was the duty of governors at Saggaratum and at Terqa to report on the condition of the rivers, to maintain barrages to direct the flow of excess water, and to keep the canals that led off the Habur and the Euphrates in good order. This was a local matter, but it was important enough for the king's personal attention. Yaqqim-Addu wrote:

XIV 18   "Previously when the Habur was in spate, because of the swollen waters of the Habur I put the old barrage in good order. Had my lord heard about it when he said: 'The barrage is damaged!'? There really is no damage; I have put it in good order. But before my lord appointed me to the district of Saggaratum, I ordered Kibri-Dagan to build a large barrage . . . and after my lord appointed me, I repaired four breaches. All the other barrages are in bad condition, and I have had to make the embankment 2 cubits bigger. My lord should write sternly to Kibri-Dagan, to gather his workmen, and I shall gather my district, and let us secure that barrage, otherwise there will be damage, and it won't be my fault. That barrage is not my responsibility!"

As the towns within the kingdom of Mari were all ranged XIV 28 along the banks of rivers, all kinds of goods were conveyed by boat. Very heavy items went on rafts that were probably towed by donkeys from a tow-path.

There are three commodities in particular that came down to Mari by boat and were taxed as they passed a point near Terqa. The first is wine.[11] The customs official Numushda-Nahrari took the tax and recorded it in a letter that was sent to his XIII 99 superior officer in Mari, a man named Iddiniatum. The usual rate of tax was 10%, taken either in silver or as a proportion of the goods. The wine generally came in boats that carried 300 ten-litre jars each, and had a capacity of 6 tonnes.

The second is barley. For reasons that are not yet clear, Mari XIII 36 imported quantities of grain: 360,000 litres from Nahur in the III 33, 35 Upper Habur; another 360,000 litres from Emar higher up on the Euphrates. We do not yet know whether the imports were the result of a single crisis during Zimri-Lim's reign, or whether centralisation at Mari had created a demand for food that far outstripped production. But a letter from Yasim-Sumu gives considerable detail:

XIII 35   ''About the boats that were ready to carry the grain from Emar, the boats are no longer available. The harvest time has arrived, and they have not arrived to collect the grain of the palace. From now onwards for five months (or, until the fifth month) the boats will not be made ready. Even if they were ready, and arrived, even if those boats were full of grain, they would not be willing to return empty. Now, if it seems right to my lord, may my lord send me 5 minas of silver and let me and the creditors that live in Emar hire 10 boats of 36,000 litres capacity; that I may get to Mari 360,000 litres of grain.''

It appears from this letter that the normal boat merchants could not hire labour at the time of year when the harvest was safely in, when debts were repaid and stomachs full; moreover, they would not take on a cargo unless they were assured of a cargo for the return journey. The king of Mari therefore stood to lose money in his haste to secure supplies for the capital. But since his own harvest had been poor, he voix was buying grain abroad at the cheapest time, despite the difficulties.

Although the grain was not transported beyond Mari, tax XIII 61 was exacted, in kind, not in silver. 540 litres were taken from one boat, but sometimes the grain was carried in ''small boats'', from which 240 litres were taken as tax.

The third commodity is millstones. ''On the boat of XIII 82 millstones of Beli-liwwer, 200 millstones are loaded. $6^{2}/_{3}$ shekels of silver have been taken as tax.''

XIII 90   ''On the boat of millstones of Kuzzari, 56 millstones are loaded. He is not carrying any silver, so 6 millstones have been taken as tax.''

If Numushda-Nahrari did not manage to inspect and tax a cargo, he sent a swift letter to Iddiniatum at Mari.

XIII 95   ''Now, the one boat of Zumman was not inspected, and was not taxed. Tax it.''

The same happened to a cargo of bitumen: ''Now, the two boats of bitumen of Sin-bel-aplim and Bunene-abi were not inspected and were not taxed. Tax them.''

Each record is precisely dated with the day and the month.

There is a single letter, from Yasitum to the tax controller Iddiniatum, which may describe an unsuccessful attempt to smuggle wine by boat:

XIII 99   ''Of the two boats of wine belonging to Ebatan, one of his boats has its sides filled with wine. It arrived a month ago. Apart from that he has paid his share (of tax). Take 30 jars of wine in tax from the 600 jars of wine that he is carrying."

There is not yet a corresponding group of records dealing with land caravans and their taxes; indeed, we are remarkably ill-informed about the size and composition of these caravans, where they stopped and what they paid. Nor is there any information about the smugglers' routes that are known to have existed among the Assyrian traders of Cappadocia a century or so earlier.[12] But some details can be gleaned from various letters. When Zimri-Lim's provincial governors reported to him on the foreign envoys who were approaching Mari, they gave some incidental detail.

Escorts

The envoys preferred, as we have seen, to travel in groups. Each one had his own personal escort, *ālik īdišu*, which was provided by the king through whose territory they were travelling. Bahdi-Lim reported the arrival of a group of foreign envoys in Terqa saying:

VI 14   "A group of envoys from Yamhad and Qatna has arrived. Ibbi-Ishtaran, Yabanni-El and Utli-Ishtar, three envoys from Babylon, have also arrived from Yamhad with their escort Samsu-ishar, himself an envoy from Yamhad. They are travelling through to Babylon. Sin-ili, an envoy from Ekallatum, with Zawadan, his escort from Yamhad, is travelling through to Ekallatum. Yarpa-Addu, an envoy from Qatna, is being sent to my lord: he came without an escort. Now, I have prepared one man to escort him and I have sent him on to my lord."

Yaqqim-Addu wrote to Zimri-Lim:

II 107   "One envoy from Carchemish, with Napsi-Addu and Mannu-balti-El as his escorts from my lord, has arrived in Dur-Yahdun-Lim."

Envoys travelled with a caravan. Iddin-Numushda spoke of envoys whom he detained until he received orders from his master:

II 133   "The caravan left the day before yesterday. The envoys will have to go with the next caravan." When Hammurabi of Babylon was angry and wished to declare his displeasure to the king of Elam, he is reported to have exclaimed:

II 73   "I shall send the Elamite envoys back to their master without any escorts!"

At Karana, when Napsuna-Addu wanted to send two of his servants to the king Aqba-hammu, he wrote to Iltani to say:

K 45   "Appoint men to escort them (*mušallimī*) and let them ensure their safe arrival."

A king who was paying tribute to an overlord would travel in person with the caravan that brought the goods from which the tribute was paid.

K 70   "I shall take many garments with my tribute to Babylon" wrote Aqba-hammu when he had accepted the supremacy of Hammurabi. But when it was his turn to be overlord, having

K 72   conquered the pathetic, penniless ruler of Shirwun, he received tribute in turn, albeit goods that the poor vassal was forced to borrow from his own overlord.

The men who brought the goods and led the caravans were fed at the palace. One text lists joints of mutton for the man of

XII 747   Babylon, the man of Hazor, the man of Yamhad, the man of Carchemish, the man of Emar and the man of Eshnunna. We do not yet know to what extent the palaces acted as a caravanserai where the travelling merchants could rest as well as be fed.

Trade and diplomacy were very closely linked, since the kings of petty states or their plenipotentiaries travelled with their caravans of merchandise, and it was thus important to treat certain caravan personnel with respect. To detain a caravan or messengers too long was to show displeasure and

II 141   to insult the king of the country from which it came. Equally it was rude for a royal caravan to arrive without a generous stock

K 82   of presents.

The textiles that Iltani manufactured in her palace at Karana often went straight into a caravan load. There was not always a great difference between presents and tribute, and the words used are not always distinct. Aqba-hammu himself paid tribute[13] to Babylon in the form of textiles.

K 70   "Speak to Iltani, thus Aqba-hammu. I shall take many textiles with my tribute to Babylon. . . . Send me immediately as many as are available."

A man named La'um wrote a detailed letter to Zimri-Lim to

II 76   describe how he and his caravan were received at the court of Hammurabi, King of Yamhad.

"Speak to my lord, thus La'um your servant. We went in for a meal with Hammurabi and went into the courtyard of the palace, and they gave us – myself, Zimri-Addu and Yarim-Addu – clothes to wear, and the men of Yamhad who went in with us were all given clothes to wear so that everyone was wearing Yamhad costume. But my lord's servants, the *ša sikkim*-messengers, were not given clothes, so I spoke up on their behalf to Sin-bel-aplim saying: 'Why do you separate us as if we were robbers? Whose servants are we, and whose servants are the *ša sikkim*–messengers?[14] We are all my lord's servants.' "

Compare that treatment of Mari men abroad with this letter xiii 32 about a party of Elamites in Mari.

"Speak to my lord, thus Yasim-Sumu. Just as my lord wrote to me, they have brought a jar of wine and two good rams and some ice from my lord, and had it taken to the Elamites. And my lord wrote to me saying: 'The Elamites are anxious for a meal; they are annoyed about the meal and about their presents.[15] Either you yourself or one of your entourage should look into the matter.' So I sent Yatar-Addu to look at the boat and their provisions, and he found out that they are not annoyed at all about their presents or the meals, they are annoyed about the business of the palace, and they told Yatar-Addu all about it. So now I have sent Yatar-Addu to you that my lord may ask him for a complete report."

If trouble was expected, an escort would be sent with the caravan, or an escort might be sent out later if a caravan got into difficulties in foreign lands. Yasmah-Addu wrote to Hammurabi of Babylon to say:

v 14 "A little while ago your 'brother' (Ishme-Dagan) sent a caravan to Tilmun (Bahrain). Then that caravan set out homewards, but was detained by Ili-epuh in a dispute over a well. Now, I have sent X and Imgurrum: they are to escort that caravan to Babylon to you. Let that caravan be detained with you until your 'brother' writes to you to say that it may depart. Your 'brother' is well, and the city Ekallatum is well; I am well and the city of Mari is well."

Such escorts, sent abroad under special circumstances, were obviously different from the regular escorts who looked after parties of travellers within a kingdom. In addition to them, the ii 134 king might decide to send a military escort, *ṣābum taqribātum*, with a caravan as far as the boundary of his kingdom if there were bad omens. Yaqqim-Addu once reported the arrival of Ṣura-hammu in the town of Huhru saying:

ii 105 "Belshunu and Yawṣi-El, subjects of my lord, his escorts, are still with him, and 100 troops are coming with him too."

It would probably be false to try to distinguish between diplomatic and trading travellers, since so much trade was carried out as the exchange of presents between rulers. But there must have been some independent merchants who did not bring personal news from their ruler. We would not expect to find their records among those of the palace – it is essential to remember that every single record on the subject from Mari, Karana and Chagar Bazar comes from a palace; however great their number may be, they will not give a balanced view.

There was a regular flow of trade along the main routes. K 120 Lamassani, living in Ashur, reassured Iltani in Karana by saying: "The caravan comes regularly." A fragmentary letter from Shamshi-Adad to Yasmah-Addu described how a I 66 caravan set out on a journey: the omens were taken, the men were provided with waterskins (perhaps also with sandals) and with ten days' worth of provisions, to last them until they arrived at their destination of Qatna.[16]

It is not easy to estimate average sizes of caravans. One piece of evidence comes from a letter describing a disaster which overtook the travellers:

II 123 "Ili-iddinam, my lord's envoy, whom my lord sent to Elahut, and Tulish his escort from Elahut, the 10 donkeys who were carrying white cedar wood[17] and the one horse that they were bringing – between the towns of A and B those men were raided. They killed Ili-iddinam, his 4 men servants, and the 2 Haneans who were with him, and Tulish the man from Elahut together with his 5 men servants and his servant girl. They carried off the 10 donkeys and the one horse that they were bringing. Out of those men only 2 men of my lord and 8 men of Elahut escaped."

A party of this size was not big enough to deter bandits. Presumably also the early warning system of omen-taking had failed on this occasion.

RA 66 p. 117 There is evidence for much larger numbers: 50 Numheans and 150 Babylonians accompanied the king of Kurda, Simahlane, to Mari. This may have been an unusual situation, for Simahlane had probably been defeated and driven from his capital city Kahat.[18] One letter gives much higher numbers for RA 60 p. 24 a caravan of semi-nomadic Haneans carrying grain and wool in Upper Mesopotamia: the Haneans have 3,000 donkeys. In a letter to Zimri-Lim we hear about a caravan which was not allowed to proceed intact from Karana to Kanish during Ashkur-Addu's reign:

"50 donkeys and their men (from the caravan) went on to RHA 5 p. 73 Kanish, but the rest are being detained by him."

It can be inferred from the letters that messengers who simply carried tablets from district officials to the king travelled faster than caravans and therefore did not always travel with them. Unfortunately the actual words do not differentiate clearly between such a messenger and an envoy or royal emissary. The former is often referred to only as a servant, *ṣuhārum*. Possibly he travelled alone on mule or horse within his native kingdom; there is no definite evidence for a relay of runners or riders with posting stations. One letter mentions that two runners accompanied an envoy from Carchemish; they may have been post messengers. Another letter says that swift messengers, *ṣuhārū qallūtim*, were sent out to forestall troop movements that were unnecessary:

"Speak to Yasmah-Addu, thus Ishme-Dagan. About the two torch signals that you raised by night, didn't you realise that the whole country might come to help? Have letters sent to the whole country, to the land of Andarik including the district of Hasidanum, including the district of Nurrugum, send your swift messengers, to say: 'A large number of the enemy went to make a raid into the countryside; that is why the two torch signals were raised, but you need not come to help'."

There was a system of defended posts from which policing operations were mounted, called *bazahātum*. These may be frontier posts or relay stations along main roads, or simply police posts; there is still no definite connection between these posts and the messenger mail. They are mainly found helping to track down and arrest criminals and fugitives, but there is a small clue that may point to their use as posting stations. Yaqqim-Addu reports to Zimri-Lim:

"On the day when I sent this letter to my lord, Zu-hatni arrived from Yamhad. I have not asked him for his news yet, but the men of the *bazahātum*–posts have announced (his arrival) to me."

"On the day when I sent this letter to my lord, Dariya and the cedar wood arrived in Tillazibim. The men of the *bazahātum*–posts announced (his arrival) to me, and as soon as he arrives I shall send him to my lord."

In neither letter is there any suggestion of wrong-doing which would explain police involvement and so the better explanation may be that the posts, in addition to their police functions, received envoys just before they reached a city, and so gave advance warning to the governor.

Torch signals

Roads in those days were probably only beaten trackways. There is not yet evidence from these texts for any artificial surfacing or for bridges over wadis, canals and rivers, although bridges are mentioned in contemporary tablets from Lower Mesopotamia.[19] Ferry-boats and fords were presumably the rule. The "royal road" of later times, which may have enjoyed the benefit of surfacing on difficult stretches, is nowhere attested in these letters. Therefore weather conditions affected travel arrangements to a great extent.

II 78 Sharriya, the king of Razama, planned a journey to Mari, but had to delay his departure because of heavy rain. Local weather reports from provincial governors were occasionally sent to the capital, probably because of the effect of wet conditions on travel arrangements, and the punctuality of the post. News of heavy rain was often reported. Rain would also have affected the use of torch signals, another example of which is described in the following letter:

RA 35 p. 178 "Yesterday I went out from Mari and spent the night in Zurubban; and the Yaminites all raised torches: from Samanum to Ilum-muluk, from Ilum-muluk as far as Mishlan. All the towns of the Yaminites in the district of Terqa raised their torches in reply. Now, so far I have not managed to find out the reason for those torches, but I shall try to find out the reason and I shall write to my lord the result. But let the guards of Mari be strengthened, and may my lord not go out of the gate!"

RA 35 p. 182 In a letter quoted earlier it was clear that torch signals covered much of Shamshi-Adad's empire, and could be used to summon immediate reinforcements. Two torch signals meant "Come quickly to help", whereas one torch signal could have more than one meaning, over which there was confusion:

RA 35 p. 183 "Speak to my lord, thus Zidriya your servant. My lord wrote to me about the torch signal saying: 'Why did you raise a torch signal? Was not the order given to raise a torch signal from Hana and from here only?' That is what my lord wrote to me. Well, previously the order was given to raise it if I saw one torch signal. But now, since my lord has written to say otherwise, whenever I see one torch signal I shall not raise a torch signal, but whenever I see two torch signals I shall assemble the country and raise [two torch signals] myself."

The area around the Middle Euphrates and along the Lower Habur river is flat, and the mounds of ancient cities project above the level of the plain, the old citadels even now prominent. Under these natural conditions, fire signals must have seemed an obvious, if inflexible, means of swift communication. But they were dependent not only on climatic conditions, a rainstorm or a dust storm rendering them useless or invisible, but also on human fallibility.

V 68 "Speak to Yasmah-Addu, thus Habil-kenum. My lord wrote to say that two torch signals were raised; but we never saw two torch signals. In the upper country they neglected the torch signal, and they didn't raise a torch signal. My lord should look into the matter of torch signals, and if there is any cause for worry, an official should be put in charge."

Despite many difficulties remaining over individual words, the texts from Mari in particular have shown that communications and travel were highly organised in the early second millennium, and were flexible enough to allow traders and troops, police and messengers, to travel in relative speed and safety, informed about recent weather, epidemics and changes in the political and military scene. The stability and prosperity of the palaces largely depended on them.

Notes to Chapter Eight

1. J. Mellaart, *The neolithic of the Near East*, London 1975, especially p. 135ff.

2. In general, however, a generic term is used, and one cannot be certain whether a mule is meant rather than a donkey, although the word is translated as donkey.

3. For the stages, periods and regions in which the camel became domesticated, see R. W. Bulliet, *The Camel and the Wheel*, Harvard 1975.

4. X indicates that the second part of the man's name cannot be read due to damage on the clay tablet.

5. D. Collon, *Catalogue of the Western-Asiatic Seals in the British Museum*: cylinder seals II London 1982 no. 214, and commentary on pp. 101–102. A literary simile that definitely comes from falconry is used in the 14th-century *Legend of Aqhat,* from Ugarit. See J. C. L. Gibson, *Canaanite myths and legends,* 2nd ed. Edinburgh 1978, p. 112. A probable reference to falconry in the Old Babylonian period is found in the literary text CT. 15 5. ii. 6.

6. E. Reiner, "The lipšur litanies", in *Journal of Near Eastern Studies* 15 1956, p. 129ff.

7. P. R. S. Moorey, "Pictorial evidence for the history of horse-riding in Iraq before the Kassite period", in *Iraq* 32 1970.

8. Unpublished, quoted in *CAD* sub *appatu* A a).

9. Translation of this verb follows M. Stol in *Bibliotheca Orientalis*, 35 1978, p. 218b.

10. A courtyard in the Mari palace is called "the courtyard of the female kids" (IX 31). This could refer either to an enclosure with live animals or to mural decoration. In court 106 a fragment of painted wallplaster depicted two goats rampant on a hill.

11. A. Finet, "Le vin à Mari", in *Archiv für Orientforschung* 25 1974–7.

12. K. R. Veenhof, *Aspects of Old Assyrian Trade* Leiden 1972, p. 316ff; and *CAD* sub *mupazziru*.

13. In this case the term used is unequivocal.

14. The meaning of this term is not understood.

15. VII 221 records the payment of such "presents". It is a list of silver and garments given to named foreigners.

16. From Mari through Tadmer (Palmyra) to Qatna in ten days: compare Baedeker 1912, nine days from Damascus to Palmyra. The text confirms the use of a desert road, but does not mention what animals were used for transport.

17. *Juniperus oxycedrus.*

18. There are administrative lists of men in groups which may refer to parties of travellers, but some scholars prefer to interpret them as purely military groups. The precise meanings in that context of the key terms *piqittum* and *ummatum* are not yet certain. See S. Dalley, review article of ARM X in *Bibliotheca Orientalis* 36 1979, p. 292a, and A. Malamat *"ummatum* in Old Babylonian texts", in *Ugarit Forschungen* 11 1979.

19. See W. von Soden *Akkadisches Handwörterbuch* sub *titurru*.

Chapter Nine
The Late Bronze Age and the Iron Age

The Late Bronze Age

The Old Babylonian palaces at Mari and Karana were sacked and destroyed. Hammurabi, the king of Babylon, had risen from small beginnings to win an empire, and Zimri-Lim was a powerful enemy who could not be content to take the role of vassal king. Hammurabi gave him a chance: a year elapsed between the defeat of Zimri-Lim's army and the final razing of the palace, from which it never recovered.[1] Aqba-hammu presumably was willing to compromise at first; we are ignorant of the circumstances of his downfall, but he may not have outlasted Zimri-Lim by more than five or so years. His palace too was destroyed and never again inhabited,[2] although the main temple continued in use.

The results of Hammurabi's demolitions were far-reaching: not only did Mari sink into obscurity after a thousand years of eminence, but also the old, flexible pattern of trade routes was broken up, and the Assyrian trading colony at Kanish in Anatolia soon ceased its activities after many generations of profitable enterprise. The first Hittite kingdom had its origins in this period.

Assyrian power on the Middle Tigris had already declined during Hammurabi's reign to the advantage of the non-semitic Hurrians, who expanded their influence from Persia to the Mediterranean, and who emerge as the traders par excellence of the Nuzi period, some 250 years later. This period is named after the site of Nuzi, which lies in the kingdom of Arrapha, east of the Tigris near modern Kirkuk. Many thousands of tablets illustrating the transactions of a small group of merchants over several generations give us our very restricted information about these times. Although they all come from the one city, they are not entirely parochial in content, for they mention Karana quite frequently.[3] Two small tablets of the Nuzi type were found at Karana itself.[4]

Mari failed to take advantage of the prosperous times of the Late Bronze Age (from about 1600 BC), if an argument from silence is justified, although the famous "Mari cart" was remembered by school boys at Ugarit.[5] Its history now diverges from that of Karana, which in contrast thrived and remained a major trading post for Nuzi merchants.

Extensive strata for this period were uncovered by excavation at Karana, and they revealed much that was of interest. A large public building stood on top of the Old Babylonian palace; it may have been a palace, for a king of JEN 347 Karana is probably mentioned in a Nuzi tablet.[6] The city as a whole was no longer fortified; indeed, it appears from other excavations that much wealth was stored in huge, heavily fortified buildings standing outside the cities. Through or past the city of Karana ran "the great road of Karana",[7] for transit trade was still the main source of its wealth, combined with the local production of woollen textiles. The texts from Nuzi tell of this continuing tradition of wool manufacture from Old Babylonian times, which indicates that Karana's produce was famed abroad and was not simply destined for local consumption.

Palace envoys headed trading caravans as before, and much trade was still done in the guise of exchanging so-called presents. But travelling merchants doing palace business also traded on behalf of private individuals, for private profit.[8] There was enough wealth to enable the crumbling temple to be repaired; soon after it was built in Old Babylonian times, perhaps because the foundations were not sufficient to take the weight of a roof supported on radial vaults, or perhaps because of an earth tremor, the magnificent temple had partly collapsed, and had had to be propped up with reinforcing walls. By the Nuzi period some further repairs were made, and the old temple with its ziggurat was still the main focus of the city's architecture.

In one room of the temple was found a great store of beads and other objects made of glass and frit.[9] Indeed, the hallmark of these levels for the archaeologist is the presence of glazed frit, which was produced in huge quantities. Another, similar, deposit came from a little shrine in the vicinity of the palace.

Many of these glass and frit objects bear witness to great technical skill. A glass beaker had on a deep blue ground inlaid decoration consisting of a narrow band of oblique stripes around the rim, and two bands of ogival curves around the body. The colours were yellow, grey, blue and white in repeated sequence, and the base was a band of yellow. A fine bottle was made of red, green and white coloured glass cones assembled as a mosaic to make a zigzag pattern. Another glass bottle, 17.5 cm high, was covered with an inlaid pattern of yellow, white and orange festoons on a light blue ground.

Figure 54 Glass beaker. Height 134 mm.

Qatna inventories

The image of a goddess and the jewellery that might belong to her at this period can best be illustrated from a unique text which was excavated in the city of Qatna in 1927.[10] It is "the tablet of the treasures of the goddess Belet-ekallim, the lady of Qatna",[11] and it begins with the statuette of the goddess herself, made entirely of red gold, holding a sword of yellow gold in her hand. Beads strung on necklaces, and ornaments

Figure 55 Bronze statuette of a war-like goddess from Minet el Beida, Syria. (Height 179 mm)

that could be sewn on to clothing, objects inlaid with yellow and blue stone (or with imitations of them in frit) she owned in abundance. They had probably all been dedicated by grateful worshippers; some were inscribed with the names of the donors. Each necklace is listed separately with the types of beads that were strung on it. Some were ovoid or cylindrical, but many were in the shape of animals, and the descriptions in the text sometimes coincide with those actually found in the temple at Karana. Gold, frit, alabaster, carnelian and iron are the materials; the shapes include jackal, vulture, bull calf, fly, frog, a golden eagle of Tukrish workmanship, lion, fish, crocodile, falcon, fig, pomegranate, date, bramble, and an *alum*-sheep overlaid with gold leaf. She also possessed other forms of jewellery: gold plaques, pectorals, earrings, neckrings, bracelets, and a gold mirror;

"Tamarisk of real lapis lazuli;

An imitation lapis luzuli (blue frit) statue of a man named Uşur-pishu;

4 gold beads weighing $13\frac{1}{2}$ shekels, from Sin-adu the king, the son of Naplimma the king;

1 şişşatum-flower of gold inlaid with blue, yellow and red, in the style of the land of Tukrish;[12]

1 statue of the lady Shemunni;

1 Humbaba-face of gold inlaid with blue;

1 plaque with gold leaf, on which is one face of Humbaba, from Durusha the king of Qizza (Qadesh)."

The vulture, crocodile and falcon show an Egyptian influence which is strong in Syria at this period, and Egyptian motifs are also found at Karana. For this is the time when the New Kingdom pharaohs came out of the Nile valley and controlled much of Syria and Palestine. They not only brought with them soldiers and governing officials but also distributed art forms from their own, distinctive material culture. The effect of their expansion is recognisable over a much wider area than that which they governed directly.

In the temple at Karana, among the beads and ornaments, was found a terracotta mould for the production of plaques showing a naked female holding her breasts. This suggests that the temple itself manufactured and sold many of the objects that were offered by worshippers. This naked lady plaque, and a fragment of a terracotta bed model, suggest that worshippers who had problems with fertility, lactation, insomnia or conjugal love would offer one of these objects as a plea for help, having bought it at the temple shop.

Figure 56 Humbaba pendant from Karana. (Height 2.2 mm.)

Among the recognisable shapes of beads at Karana were a sphinx, a lion, a fly, a frog, and a hedgehog; also a miniature mask pendant representing Humbaba, only 2.2 cm high. The theme of Humbaba is common to the Qatna and Karana jewellery, but it is also found in the Karana temple in a quite different way.

Discovered near doorways at two points in the Nuzi-phase temple were two halves of an enormous stone block, sculptured in the form of Humbaba's grotesque face, split down the middle. The two parts were discovered separately in different seasons of excavation, but they fitted together exactly, to the delight of the excavator; indeed, there were signs that the stone had broken in antiquity, and had been mended perhaps when it was reinstalled in the Nuzi period. The original installation probably dated to the foundation of the temple under Shamshi-Adad I. Humbaba was the demon man who guarded the Cedar Forest until he was killed by Gilgamesh and Enkidu, in the epic of Gilgamesh. His face resembled coiled intestines, and he was a ferocious guardian who could ward off evil, hence his position at the doorway of the temple, and his popularity in amulet form. [13]

Figure 57 A terracotta plaque, showing Humbaba heads as they may have been positioned in the temple at Karana (see also Figs 38 and 58)

A second inventory from Qatna lists the treasures of "the king's gods". Together with the beads and jewellery are items of martial import: a gold mace and a dagger of pure gold with a "head" (pommel?) of real lapis lazuli and a gold handle. There were also various drinking vessels with the names of the men

Figure 58   Humbaba block found in the temple at Karana. (Height 580 mm.)

and women who donated them, including a bull-headed example. This last item shows that the tradition of animal-headed drinking vessels had continued, probably unbroken, from the time of Zimri-Lim. Two of the golden vessels came from a familiar town, Shirwun, whose impoverished king was defeated by Aqba-hammu in the 19th century, and which now produced, perhaps 300 years later, a characteristic vessel in a distinctive local style.

The skills of fine glass and frit work continued into the Middle Assyrian period, towards the end of the second millennium. The Hurrian power of Arrapha was replaced by the rising might of Assyria, and Karana was absorbed into the new Assyrian kingdom. Merchants who left the records of their transactions in tin (or lead)[14], in barley and horses, strewn over the temple and palace area, no longer looked towards Arrapha but to Ashur. As far as this little group of records shows, the merchant families flourished for six generations, mainly during the 13th century, during the reigns of the Assyrian kings Shalmaneser I (1274–1245) and Tukulti-Ninurta I (1244–1208).[15]

In this prosperous 13th century the big temple at Karana was patched up again, on top of a level of destruction which perhaps marked the end of Arraphan domination, and the beginning of Assyrian rule. This was virtually a rebuilding upon ancient ruins, and foundation deposits of a small animal and a fine alabaster vase were found in the new walls. The original shrine room was renewed with a new mud-brick dais.

Some excellent glazed frit and glass work was still being produced, including three tiny "masks" of female heads, of which the finest is described by the excavator:

"A female mask of glazed frit with eyes and eyebrows of the same material set in bitumen. Tresses of hair ending in ringlets are represented by spiral rods of frit inlaid in pairs on either side of the neck and terminating in groups of small glass discs. Black, white and yellow discs are also used to indicate a jewelled necklace, collar and diadem, and each ear is pierced with a vertical row of four holes."[16]

At Mari little evidence of occupation was found that could be dated to this period. However, this may well be due either to erosion or to the chances of discovery, for some very fine graves were excavated, dating probably to the Middle

Figure 59 A frit mask from Karana. (Height 118 mm)

Figure 60 Another frit mask from Karana. (Height 62 mm)

Assyrian period. They lay over the remains of Zimri-Lim's palace. The body was placed either in the earth or in two jars placed rim-to-rim, always with an east–west orientation. Beside the body were placed many small vessels made of glazed frit, probably containers for perfumes and cosmetic paint, oils and creams, and jewellery of stone and gold: gold earrings, and beads of several different shapes. Mainly, then, these were female burials; there was also a bronze mirror, so that the dead woman could see to adorn herself with the jewellery, paint and perfumes that were placed around her.

There were also female "masks" of glazed frit in the Mari burials, very similar to those found in such a different context at Karana, and in one case the "mask" was positioned exactly over the sternum of the dead person.[17] The excavator suggested that the holes in each ear of the masks were for threads or cords to attach the frit head to the person's body or clothing, for it was never the fashion in Mesopotamia for women to wear several earrings in more than one perforation in one ear. So the function of the "mask", as with the other grave goods, may have been adornment, the face of the goddess of love attached between the breasts, comparable to the modern rosette or daisy sewn centrally on a brassiere.[18] Since the frit heads were found both in a temple and in a woman's grave, we may speculate that the temple sold or hired these objects to make a woman more attractive. They are very widely distributed, from Palestine to southern Mesopotamia, a fashion craze that swept across the whole of the ancient Near East.[19]

At the end of the 12th century BC Karana still prospered. Incorporated into the Middle Assyrian empire, the city was paying taxes of foodstuffs to the king in Ashur, Tiglath-Pileser I (1114–1076).[20] But Mari became independent, and under its indigenous ruler, Tukulti-Mer, it resisted the Assyrian king, Ashur-bel-kala (1073–1056), who conducted two bloody expeditions against Mari and flayed the luckless ruler for his intransigence.[21]

But around 1050 BC the Assyrians grew weak; the old trade route from Ashur to Karana was abandoned and all the old caravan cities south of the hills were virtually deserted. The purpose of their existence had gone, for the main road now ran well to the north of the old one.

This is the period of transition from the Late Bronze Age to the Iron Age. The change is much more than a gradual shift in ... The great power of the Hittites had come to ... the Hurrians had dispersed. To call ... recognise that there was a marked ... ons of western Asia. Assyria and ... s of the worst upheavals, and many ... were kept alive; but their way of life ... netheless, ending in state control ... nacy over a huge area.

... rana became a ruin. Even the name of ... or the whole region became deserted ... n Tukulti-Ninurta II (890–884 BC) made ... rds from Ashur along the banks of the Wadi Tharthar ... south of Karana, it was as if he were opening up new territory, exploring a wild, deserted area that was scarcely known. This was a time when semi-nomads roamed and raided at will, making travel dangerous because they were not controlled by any organised cities with adequate local government. An era of prosperous trade and fine palaces had come to an end.

The Iron Age

The great and powerful neo-Assyrian empire of the Iron Age was built not upon taxation through trade, but from loot and tribute. So the function of palaces and temples changed. Outside the main cities of the Assyrian homeland they were no longer centres of commerce but of provincial administration which collected taxes to send back to Ashur. In Ashur and the other main cities of Assyria proper they became repositories for wealth that was never redistributed, and the luxuries and surplus produce of the whole empire became centralised in the Assyrian homeland at Ashur, Nimrud and Nineveh. Royal hospitality to foreigners on equal terms and the respectful exchange of presents ceased. Assyria belittled its own distinguished past and looked to Babylon for a cultural heritage, for southern Mesopotamia suffered so much less than northern Mesopotamia in the troubled times. Neither Mari nor Karana had a useful role to play upon so changed a scene.

The area downstream from Mari was known as Suhu, where nomadic Arameans, "enemies of the god Ashur", lived from the twelfth century onwards. They were better adapted to desert life than their predecessors of the early second millennium, for they now increased their range and swiftness by means of the camel. If there was a change in fertility and in water supply in Upper Mesopotamia at this time, nomads with camels were equipped to overcome the difficulties. They could also avoid paying taxes to the great Assyrian state in a way that no settled, urban people could.

Curiously, at this time the whole region seems to have had a population of elephants, for Tiglath-Pileser says:
"I killed ten strong bull elephants in the land of Harran and the region of the river Habur, and I captured four elephants alive."
Yet the copious Old Babylonian letters from Mari and elsewhere never mention elephants, and ivory as a material was not common at that period compared with the wealth of ivory that is found in the early first millennium.[22]

Spasmodic efforts were made to improve the region. In the early tenth century Bel-eresh an independent ruler at Shadikanni on the Lower Habur, restored a canal there and rebuilt a dilapidated temple in an attempt to revive a small area during a period of Assyrian weakness. He worshipped Kubaba, the old goddess of Carchemish, alongside a Hurrian

Figure 61 Basalt relief of the goddess Kubaba (Cybele) from the excavations at Carchemish, 9th century BC. (Height 167.6 cm)

god Samnuha, and the restored temple was their shrine.[23] Around 900 BC the Assyrian king Adad-nirari II rebuilt the town of Apqu, not far north-west of Karana, "which had turned into ruined mounds", although he further depleted the population of elephants north of the Middle Euphrates by killing six and capturing four alive.[24] Tukulti-Ninurta II took tribute from the districts around Mari and visited Sirqu (old Terqa) and went hunting too, but he mentions no elephants.[25] However when Ashur-naṣir-apal II (883–859) took tribute from the governors of Suhi and Lubdu he received five live elephants, "and they came with me on my campaign."[26]

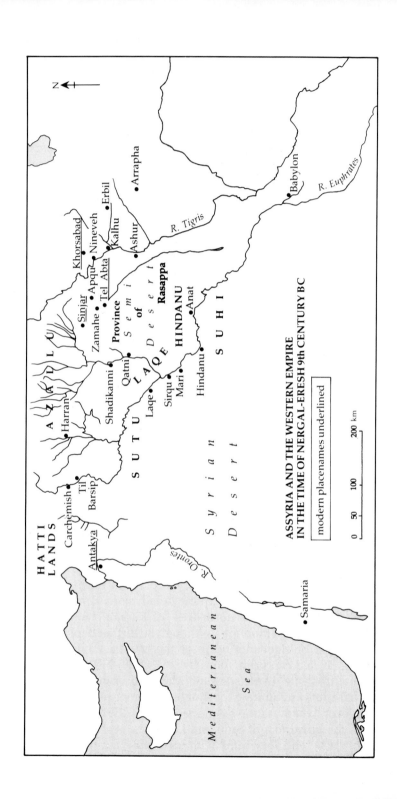

ASSYRIA AND THE WESTERN EMPIRE
IN THE TIME OF NERGAL-ERESH 9th CENTURY BC

modern placenames underlined

0   50   100   200 km

Not until the end of the ninth century did the Assyrians attempt to redevelop and recolonise the land between the Middle Tigris and the Lower Habur on a large scale. By that time either the old cities had fallen into such neglect that their old names were forgotten, or the pronunciation of old names had changed. Terqa was now Sirqu, Qattuna had perhaps become Qatni, Saggaratum was now called Sangarite. A fort that once stood on the borders of the kingdom of Mari had been built by Zimri-Lim's grandfather Yaggid-Lim and named after him "Fort of Yaggid-Lim"; but the once powerful ruler was now consigned to oblivion, the name of his fort corrupted by its ignorant inhabitants to "Fort of Katlimmu."[27]

At that time Karana was part of the enormous province of Raṣappa which owed its size to the fact that huge areas were but sparsely inhabited, needing very little attention, contributing very little wealth, and posing no external threat to the big cities on the Tigris. From Mari to Karana and along the Lower Habur the province of Raṣappa came under the administration of an ambitious man named Nergal-eresh[28] during the reigns of Adad-nirari III (810–783) and Shalmaneser IV (782–773). By then Karana was a nameless ruin that had been abandoned for perhaps 250 years; the old temple and ziggurrat had fallen in and were unrecognisable as anything except a mound of decaying mud brick.

Nergal-eresh

Nergal-eresh was governor of Raṣappa for at least thirty years.[29] The ruins of Karana were given a new name, Zamahe, and were repopulated, probably with deported people from intransigent states on the edges of the Assyrian empire.[30] Probably under the auspices of the governor, the crumbling temple mound was faced on the north side with a massive revetment wall, set into the old temple walls at an angle, into which the corner of a new temple was inserted.[31] This new building was a shrine dedicated to the weather god Adad. At the entrance to the inner sanctum stood a pair of stone orthostats in the shape of lion heads with the elongated tongue projecting downwards and shaped to resemble a dagger blade; another pair was uncovered inside the shrine. They probably formed the bases for a pair of wooden pilasters.

Figure 62 (left) Assyria and the Western Empire in the time of Nergal-eresh

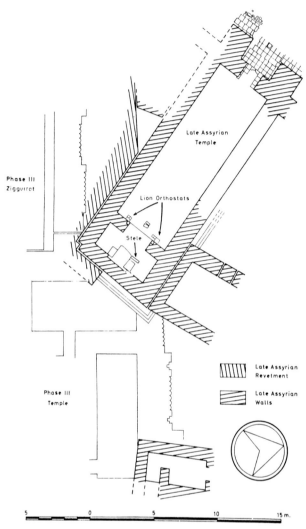

Figure 63 A plan of the neo-Assyrian temple

The motif of lion heads with dagger-tongues pointing into the ground is an old Hurrian motif, found in the famous Hittite rock sanctuary of Yazilikaya, beside the Hittite capital of Bogazköy. It may symbolise the banishing to the Underworld of old gods by the weather god in both shrines.[32] By neo-Assyrian times the deity to whom the main temple and ziggurat at Karana were dedicated would have been

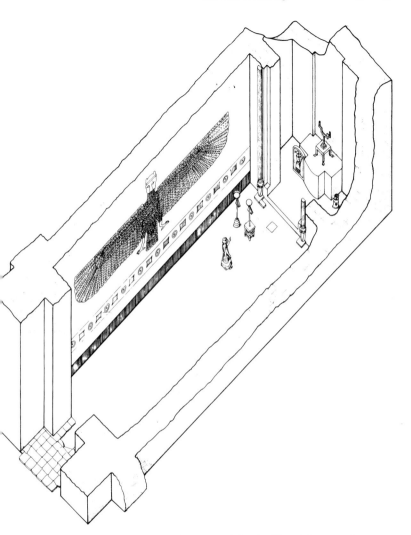

Figure 64 Reconstruction drawing of the inside of the temple

forgotten; perhaps, therefore, the lion-head daggers were intended to avert the wrath of the old deity descending on the new temple that violated its holy territory.

The walls of the temple of Adad were adorned with an enormous bitumen relief representing a composite monster, wings, animal's legs and claw feet. Two objects which are entirely Egyptian in motifs were found in this temple.

Whether they were of Syrian manufacture or imports from Egypt itself, they suggest that the old contacts with the west had been resumed at this time. They were both of frit: a ram's head, and an openwork bead with the "eye of Horus". However, there was no clear evidence to show how long the temple remained in use; if the sack of the building can be associated with the overthrow of the Assyrian cities by the Medes and their allies in 612 BC, these may be truly Egyptian objects, dedicated by men of Zamahe who fought in Egypt under Esarhaddon and Ashurbanipal, over a century after the temple was built.

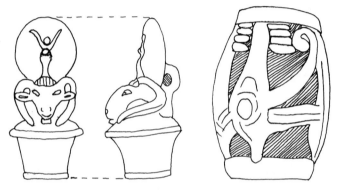

Figure 65 Egyptian beads: (a) ram's head pendant of green glazed frit; (b) openwork bead of blue and yellow glazed frit. (Height both 31 mm)

Inside the cellar of the temple stood a stone altar top, raised on a mud brick platform. Beside it stood a magnificent stone stela, 1.30 m high, in perfect condition, sculptured with a full relief of Adad-nirari III, the king of Assyria whom Nergal-eresh served.

On both sides of his head are the symbols of the great gods. From the king's waist to the hem of his robe was written an inscription, of which the second half had been erased, but could be reconstructed from the small pits left by the cuneiform signs. A shortened form of this inscription was written also on the lion-head daggers, where it had been erased completely.

Because it was possible to read the erased part of the stela inscription, the reason for these unexpected erasures became clear. Here is a translation of the whole inscription:[33]

Figure 66 Limestone stela of Adad-nirari III and his governor Nergal-eresh from Tell al Rimah. (Height 1.30 m)

"To Adad, the greatest lord, hero of the gods, the powerful one, eldest son of Anu, who alone is fiery, the lofty irrigator of heaven and earth, who provides the rain that brings abundance, who dwells in Zamahe, the great lord, his lord:

"I, Adad-nirari the mighty king, king of the world, king of Assyria, heir of Shamshi-Adad (the fifth) the king of the

Figure 67 View into the late Assyrian shrine at Karana-Zamahe. The royal stela stands behind the altar

Figure 68 Stone base from a pillar, a lion-head with the dagger-blade tongue, from the late Assyrian shrine at Karana-Zamahe. (Height approx. 40 cm)

world, king of Assyria, heir of Shalmaneser the king of the four regions, mobilised chariots, troops and camps, and ordered a campaign against the Hatti land. In a single year I made the entire western land, the land of Hatti, kneel at my feet; I imposed tribute and regular tax for the future upon them.

"He[34] received 2,000 talents[35] of silver, 1,000 talents of copper, 2,000 talents of iron, 3,000 multi-coloured garments and plain linen garments as tribute from Mari'[36] of Damascus. He received the tribute of Joash the Samarian, of the ruler of Tyre and of the ruler of Sidon.

"I marched to the great sea where the sun sets[37] and erected in the city of Arvad, which is in the middle of the sea, a stela showing my royal self. I went up the Lebanon mountains and cut down timbers: 100 mature cedars, material needed for my palace and temples.

"He received tributes from all the kings of the Nairi land. (The erased section begins here.)

"At that time I ordered Nergal-eresh, the governor of Raṣappa, Lake, Sirqu, Anat, Suhi and X to . . . 'Fort of Ishtar' with 12 villages,[38] 'Market of Sin' with 10 villages, 'fort of X' with 33 villages, 'Fort of Ashur' with 20 villages, 'Fort of Nergal-eresh' with 33 villages, 'Fort Marduk' with 40 villages, 'Mound of Adad-nirari' with 126 villages behind Mount Sinjar and 28 villages in the district of Azallu, 'Fort of Adad-nirari' with 15 villages in the district of Lake, 'City of Adad' with 14 villages in the district of Qatni; a total of 331 towns of subject peoples which Nergal-eresh founded and built in the name of his lord.

"Whoever shall blot out a single line from among these lines, may the great gods fiercely destroy him."

If this final curse was effective, the man responsible for erasing several lines of this inscription will have met with a violent end!

This inscription shows that Nergal-eresh, at first with the king's authority, attempted to repopulate the region in which the old Karana, the new Zamahe, was situated. His new towns with their numerous villages and farmsteads were almost certainly filled with prisoners of war and deported peoples from the newly-conquered states of the west. This was not the only stela that he put up: another has been found, west of Sinjar, known as the Saba'a stela,[39] which has not been erased; but it does not refer to new settlements, and so may be an earlier monument.

Why was part of the inscription erased? The answer to this question is a matter for speculation on very little evidence. The new settlements must have put a very large number of people at the disposal of the governor as his provincial army, perhaps tempting him to power, certainly offering a potential threat to the king. To name a new town after oneself was normally the prerogative of kings and deities only. But presumably he did not fall from favour until well into the reign of Shalmaneser IV, since he served as governor under that king in 775 BC.

There were perhaps two factions at work late in Adad-nirari's reign. A broken stone tablet from Nineveh dates to Adad-nirari and mentions Nergal-eresh by name.[40] It promises that Raṣappa province shall include the district of Hindanu, and that no successor of Adad-nirari shall move Nergal-eresh from the post of governor there, nor detach Hindanu from Raṣappa. Hindanu was an area on the Middle Euphrates below Mari. Evidently an unsuccessful attempt had been made to reduce the power of Nergal-eresh, even while Adad-nirari still sat on the throne.

Nergal-eresh's example was followed by another high official who was based near Tell Abta, only 25 km south of Zamahe.[41] This man, named Bel-Harran-belu-uṣur, set up a stela that portrayed himself, not the king, full size, and he named the town at Tell Abta after himself: "Fort of Bel-Harran-belu-uṣur". He flourished in the period from the reign of Shalmaneser IV to Tiglath-Pileser III (782–727). It was a time of great weakness for Assyria, when the kingdom of Urartu was expanding and gaining control of vital natural resources. Assyria's military supplies of metal ores and horses were severely curtailed during some forty years; much of the Assyrian empire west of Nineveh virtually seceded for that period.

This was the heyday of the famous Queen Semiramis, wife of Shamshi-Adad V and mother of Adad-nirari III, whom Herodotus mentions as one of the outstanding personalities of ancient Mesopotamian antiquity. A stela recently found in Turkey has shown that Semiramis crossed the Euphrates in 805 BC, and that she was closely associated with the powerful Shamshi-ilu, who was the highest official in Assyria during the first half of the eighth century.[42] Shamshi-ilu set up stelae in his own name and recorded his personal achievements at his provincial capital Til Barsip,[43] not far east of Carchemish, and probably also at Karabur which lies 25 km south-east of modern Antakya.[44] It may indeed have been this man, rather than Nergal-eresh, who set the trend for independence among western governors.

Shamash-resh-uṣur

The region of Mari has produced a fine stela of the first millennium too. It was discovered in Babylon, whither it was carried as booty by a neo-Babylonian king, perhaps the famous Nebuchadnezzar II (604–562).[45] New evidence from recent excavations on the Middle Euphrates has enabled us to date it at last, to approximately 760 BC, when a weak king, Ashur-dan III, ruled Assyria.[46] It commemorates the deeds of a governor called Shamash-resh-uṣur, engraved in cuneiform in the dialect of Babylonia, not Assyria. The stone is not the usual Assyrian, round-topped shape, and the gods are shown standing on plinths that represent stylised mountains, not as symbols but in human form with the king. Each deity grips an emblem of power: Adad the god of thunder brandishes forked lightning in each hand, and there are divine symbols above as well: the pointed "spade" of Marduk, patron of Babylon, beside the stylus of Nabu and the winged disk of Shamash, the sun god, beside the lunar disk of Sin.

The inscription is nothing short of astonishing: chatty, repetitive, and quite wrongly organised according to the format of the period. In one place an afterthought was added

〰〰〰 represents lines of inscription

Figure 69 The stela of Shamash-resh-usur, governor of Mari. (Height 118 mm)

to the inscription, quite disrupting the lay-out of the lines and columns. According to the rules of the time the curse, on whoever may destroy the monument or any of its words, should end the inscription, thus embracing all the words that were inscribed; but here the curse comes in the middle of the text.

The text makes it clear that Mari and its vicinity was, like Zamahe, underpopulated, and that this governor was intent on injecting new life into a depressed area. But here the old place-names have survived: Mari is still Mari, and Terqa is only modified to Sirqu. Shamash-resh-uṣur founded new towns, and chased off 400 marauders of the Tu'manu tribe and killed 350 of them when they interfered with his celebration of a festival in a new town.

"I am Shamash-resh-uṣur the governor of the land of Suhu and the land of Mari. The main canal of the land of Suhu had become old, the workforce too small (to maintain it). From the town of Harze as far as the town of Yabi' it had become too narrow, and I put the middle of it in order, along a length of 1,000 'reeds' (perhaps about 3.50 km). I widened that canal by 22 cubits, and I removed the bridge at the mouth of the canal so that I could send along it a cargo boat 25 cubits (wide). I and my officers went for a ride along it and brought the boat out of the countryside at the weir, at the mouth of the water.

"I planted palm trees in the courtyard of the palace in the town Riba-sharru and installed a throne and footstool in Riba-sharru.[47] I built a new town and named it Gabbari-built-it.[48] I set up Adad, Apladad,[49] Shala and Madanu (as its gods), and arranged for them to live in a fine dwelling.

"Whoever comes in the future and approaches[50] this stela, or who erases the written name and writes his own name instead: may the great gods of heaven and earth make him forfeit his name, his seed, his heir and his offspring from the people. May he never do such work as I have done! May the curse defeat anyone who transgresses this and does not fear the words.

"I planted palm trees in the courtyard of the palace in the town 'Shrine of god'. I planted palm trees in the courtyard of the palace in the town 'Market-of-Nabu'. I improved the date (production) below(?) my city, the suburbs of the city, and I planted palm trees. I built a new dyke 370(?) cubits (195 m) wide over the old one, and in it ran water from the Suhu canal – from the dyke to the weir. I planted all the willow trees that now grow above the canal, in order that corvée baskets for (work on) the canal may be woven from them[51] (i.e. made on the spot) and so that I can cut planks from them, and use them for bank reinforcements,[52] I planted the willow trees, every one of them, above the canal only, so that the Suhu nomads could not get into the palace from above.[53] . . .

"I am Shamash-resh-uṣur, the governor of Suhu and the land of Mari. Bees that collect honey, which none of my ancestors had ever seen or brought into the land of Suhu, I brought down from the mountain of the men of Habha, and made them settle in the orchards of the town 'Gabbari-built-it'. They collect honey and wax, and I know how to melt the honey and wax – and the gardeners know too.

"Whoever comes in future, may he ask the old men of the town, (who will say) thus: 'They are the buildings of Shamash-resh-uṣur, the governor of Suhu, who introduced honey bees into the land of Suhu."

How greatly the land and culture have changed since the days of Zimri-Lim! Gone are the old gods, Itur-Mer, Shamash, Anunitum and Belet-ekallim. Different gods are installed in their place. The land is deforested, the irrigation neglected, the nomads an ever-present threat to the very palaces. If honey bees were known in the days of Shamshi-Adad I, they have long since returned to the wild, the skills of apiculture lost. Shamash-resh-uṣur was ignorant enough of the past to suppose that his good works were innovations: he was much more interested in the present and the future than knowledgeable of the past. The languages of the Middle Euphrates have changed too: no longer is Old Babylonian the main written and spoken tongue, with Amorite and Hurrian also spoken but seldom written. Now the Aramaic language is ubiquitous, Babylonian is reserved only for formal writing, and Shamash-resh-uṣur betrays his difficulties and unfamiliarity with Babylonian in his inscription. This last inscription marks the end of Babylonian culture as it is known from Mari and Karana.

Mari was abandoned, and a new city arose a short distance upstream, Dura Europos, to fill a similar role.[54] A ghostly echo of late neo-Assyrian, Aramaean gods is found, slightly garbled, in the dedication inscriptions and personal names of Hellenised Aramaeans who lived there: Apladad, the patron sun-god of Anat, was worshipped as Aphlad, and Shamash is found too among newly arrived Arab deities.

No new cities have emerged in the vicinity of Karana, which has remained desolate ever since.

Notes to Chapter Nine

1. The year formula for his 33rd year says that he defeated the army of Mari; the formula for his 35th year says that he destroyed the wall of Mari. See *Reallexikon sub Datenlisten*, pp. 180–1.

2. It is generally assumed that the latest tablets found in a building are very close in date to the destruction of the building. But there is a good possibility that this is wrong. If the letters of Hatnurapi alone had been discovered, one might have assumed, wrongly, that he was the last ruler before the destruction.

3. See *Reallexikon sub Karana*.

4. See D. J. Wiseman, "The Tell al Rimah tablets", 1966, in *Iraq* 30 1968, pp. 186–7.

5. See *Syria* 12 1931, p. 147.

6. D. Oates, *Iraq* 30 1968, pp. 135–6.

7. Text AO 10887, line 7; see *Revue d'Assyriologie* 28 1931, pp. 33–4; corrected reading kindly supplied by K. Deller, Heidelberg.

8. C. Zaccagnini *The merchant of Nuzi* in *Iraq* 39 1977.

9. Frit is a crystalline compound of silica, copper and calcium, and was used to imitate precious and semi-precious stone, either as whole objects or as inlays in other materials.

10. J. Bottéro, "Les inventaires de Qatna", *Revue d'Assyriologie* 43 1949 (part I and II) and 44 1950 (part III).

11. Because of a confusion due to the system of writing she is often referred to wrongly as Ningal, wife of the moon-god. Her name is written NIN.É.GAL, and should be "translated" from Sumerian into Akkadian Belet-ekallim, as the Hittite version of her name Pentigalli clearly shows. The name of the moon-goddess was not "translated" into Akkadian, and was probably pronounced Nikkal.

12. See P. R. S. Moorey. "The location of Tukrish and its role in W Iran in the 2nd millennium BC" *Festschrift for B. de Cardi*, ed. E. During, Caspars, London 1982.

13. In the years since excavations at Karana came to an end, a new stone Humbaba block has been washed out of the temple mound. It is now on display in the Mosul Museum, in a very fine state of preservation and is illustrated in *Iraq* 45 1983 pl Va. Humbaba was known at an earlier period as Huwawa.

14. There is still a problem at this period over the Akkadian word *annakum* "tin". Lead must have been traded in quite large amounts for producing (as chemical analysis has proved) yellow-gold colouring in frit, glass, cosmetics and other paints, as well as for riveting stone objects, for making popular little figurines, and for adding to copper or bronze to improve casting.

"Tin" was now often used as currency alongside silver, and it is doubtful whether it was ever abundant enough for uses other than in bronze making. But there is only one possible word in the merchants' texts. Perhaps, then, for the traders both tin and lead had the same name (this confusion is found in later languages see note 2 to Chapter 1) but the bronzesmiths, cosmetic-makers and glass-makers called lead by its more specific name, *abārum*, in manufacturing contexts.

15. H. W. F. Saggs and D. J. Wiseman, "The Tell al Rimah tablets 1965–6" in *Iraq* 30 1968, pp. 154–206.

16. D. Oates, *Iraq* 28 1966, p. 125.

17. A. Parrot, *Syria* 18 1937, p. 83.

18. E. Peltenberg, "Faience Face Masks", in Astrom, Hult and Olofsson, *Hala Sultan Tekke, Studies in Mediterranean Archaeology* 45/3 1977, thinks that these objects may have been souvenirs of pilgrimage to one particular temple. H. Kühne, Baghdader Mitteilungen 7 1974, p. 110, suggests that they may be connected with the worship of the goddess Kubaba.

19. Peltenberg, op. cit., collects the examples then known, to which add now an example from Isin in S. Mesopotamia: *B. Hrouda, Isin-Išan-Bahriyat II* München 1981, p. 67 and Tafel 26.

20. H. Freydank, Mittelassyrische Rechtsurkunden und Verwaltungstexte, no. 56 in Vorderasiatische Schriftdenkmäler der Staatlichen Museen zu Berlin, *Heft* XIX, Berlin, 1976.

21. A. K. Grayson, *Assyrian Royal Inscriptions* Vol. II Wiesbaden 1976, p. 49. Cf. also p. 60 § 278–280. A newly published chronicle fragment mentions a rebellion in Mari which was quelled by a king of Babylon in the 12th century BC. See C.Walker, Babylonian Chronicle 25, in *Zikir Šumim, Assyriological Studies presented to F. R. Kraus*, Leiden, 1982, p. 398 ff. This is a further indication of the importance of Mari at the turn of the millennium.

22. The anomaly is discussed by D. Collon, Ivory, in *Iraq* 39 1977.

23. Grayson, op. cit. pp. 72–3.

24. Grayson op. cit., p. 87 and p. 92.

25. Grayson op. cit., p. 103.

26. Grayson, op. cit., p. 175. He also built a palace at Apqu.

27. W. Rollig, Dūr-Katlimmu, in *Orientalia* new series 47 1978, p. 419ff. and H. Kühne, Zur historische Geographie am Unteren Habur, *Archiv für Orientforschung* 25 1974–7, pp. 252–255.

28. He is also known as Palil-eresh.

29. He held the office of eponym in 803 and 775 BC. See *Reallexikon sub Eponymen*, p. 422.

30. S. Dalley, A. "Stela of Adad-nirari III and Nergal-ereš from Tell al Rimah" in *Iraq* 30 1960, especially p. 140. The town had a herald named Gabari who was involved in land transactions with Nergal-eresh: J. N. Postgate, "A neo-Assyrian tablet from Tell al Rimah", in *Iraq* 32 1970, p. 31ff.

31. D. Oates, *Iraq* 30, 1968, pp. 122–133.

32. See K. Bittel, *Hattusha*, Oxford 1970, pp. 109–110.

33. For corrections and improvements since the first publication see Dalley, *Orientalia* 38 1969, p. 457f; Brinkman, *Revue d'Assyriologie* 63 1969, p. 96, Postgate, *Journal of Economic and Social History of the Orient*, 17 1974, p. 238.

34. The inscription changes from first person narrative to third person at this point, probably because it was composed from several longer accounts, some written in the first person throughout, others in the third person.

35. 121, 200 kg or 60,600 kg, depending whether the heavy or light talent is used here.

36. "Mari" is a title of king Hazael or of his son Ben-Hadad.

37. The Mediterranean Sea is meant.

38. This word could also be translated "farm" or "agricultural estate".

39. E. Unger, "Reliefstele Adadniraris III aus Saba'a und Semiramis", *Publicationen der Kaiserlich Osmanischen Museen* no. 2, Constantinople 1916.

40. Most recent editions by Postgate, "Neo-Assyrian Royal Grants and Decrees", *Studia Pohl*, Series Maior 1 1969, pp. 115–117 without translation for which the older version is found in J. Kohler and A. Ungnad, *Assyrische Rechtsurkunden* no. 3, Leipzig 1913.

41. E. Unger, "Die Stele des Bel-harran-bel-usur", *Publicationen der Kaiserlich Osmanischen Museen* no. 3, 1917.

42. O. A. Taşyürek, "Some new Assyrian rock reliefs in Turkey", *Anatolian Studies* 25 1975, p. 169 and especially p. 180.

43. F. Thureau-Dangin, *Til Barsip*, Paris 1936, pp. 142–151.

44. Taşyürek, op. cit., p. 180.

45. F. H. Weissbach, Babylonische Miscellen, No. IV, *Wissenschaftliche Veröffentlichungen der Deutsch – Orient Gesellshaft* no. 4, Leipzig 1903.

46. Information from a paper on recent excavations on the Euphrates in Iraq, read by M. Roaf at XXIX Rencontre Assyriologique Internationale, London 1982.

47. This means that it became a centre of provincial government.

48. An alternative suggestion for reading this name is "Town of Gabbari-Il".

49. Apladad, literally "son of Adad" is known to have been worshipped on the Middle Euphrates in the 8th to 6th centuries BC, particularly in the city Kannu. See E. Lipinski, Apladad, in *Orientalia* NS 45, 1976.

50. The verb is taken here as an Aramaic loan in Akkadian. See von Soden, *Orientalia* new series 46, p. 192.

51. This meaning is taken by connection with *CAD harû* F. Mari had been famous for its willow trees in the time of Shamshi-Adad I, who wrote to his son in Mari (ARM I 98): "When I stayed there I noticed poplars 3 *akalu* (thick) for 10 cubits (high) . . . Have 20 or 30 such willows cut down for me, and send them by boat to me."

52. Taking *arāti* as a form of *erretum*, a word from Old Babylonian Mari surviving with a change of vowels after 1,200 years.

53. The translation of this phrase is doubtful. It seems to mean that the palace was situated below the canal where there were no trees, so that the palace could not be attacked using the trees as cover.

54. Dura Europos probably existed as a village or small town called Damara in Zimri-Lim's time, but it was of little importance.

Key to editions of texts and abbreviations used

Throughout the text, abbreviated marginal references are employed to refer to the following texts which will be of interest to specialists in the field. The conventions adopted are outlined below.

Roman numerals refer to volume numbers of *Archives Royales de Mari, textes transcrits et traduits*, Paul Geuthner, Paris, by G. Dossin et al. The following Arabic numerals refer to text numbers within the volume. The editions of these texts are as follows:

ARMT I   G. Dossin, *Correspondance de Samsi-Addu*, 1950
ARMT II   C. F. Jean, *Lettres diverses*, 1950
ARMT III   J. R. Kupper, *Correspondance de Kibri-Dagan*, 1950
ARMT IV   G. Dossin, *Correspondance de Samsi-Addu*, 1951
ARMT V   G. Dossin, *Correspondance de Iasmah-Addu*, 1952
ARMT VI   J. R. Kupper, *Correspondance de Bahdi-Lim*, 1954
ARMT VII   J. Bottero, *Textes économiques et administratifs*, 1957
ARMT VIII   G. Boyer, *Textes Juridiques*, 1958
ARMT IX   M. Birot, *Textes administratifs*, 1960
ARMT X   G. Dossin and A. Finet, *Correspondance féminine*, 1978
ARMT XI   M. L. Burke, *Textes administratifs*, 1963
ARMT XII   M. Birot, *Textes administratifs*, 1964
ARMT XIII   J. Bottéro, M. Birot, M. L. Burke, J. R. Kupper, and A. Finet, *Textes divers*, 1964
ARMT XIV   M. Birot, *Lettres de Yaqqim–Addu*, 1974
ARMT XVIII   O. Rouault, *Mukannišum*, 1977
ARMT XIX   H. Limet, *Textes administratifs*, 1976

Reference is also made to the following works:

A   A, followed by a number refers to texts in C. J. Gadd, *Tablets from Chagar Bazar*, in *Iraq*, 4   1947 and 7 1940
AHW   W. von Soden, *Akkadisches Handworterbuch*, Harrassowitz, Wiesbaden, 1965–1982

AREC   G. Dossin, *Archives économiques*, article in *Syria*, 20, 1939

AREP   G. Dossin, *Archives épistolaires*, article in *Syria*, 19 1938

Sh.AS16   J. Laessøe, Shemshara tablet, edited in *Assyriological Studies*, 16, 1965

CB   CB, followed by a number refers to texts in *Text aus Chagar Bazar* by O. Loretz in *Festschrift w. von Soden*, Neukirchen-Vluyn, 1969, ed. W. Rollig

CAD   *Chicago Assyrian Dictionary*, 1956 onwards (still unfinished)

CAH   Cambridge Ancient History (2nd ed.)

EXCE   *Excerta de la correspondance*, C. F. Jean, article in Revue des études sémitiques, 1938–9

IRAQ   *Iraq* (Journal of the British School of Archaeology in Iraq)

IRSA   E. Sollberger and J-R. Kupper, *Inscriptions royales Sumériennes et Akkadiennes*, Paris 1971

IS   *Old Babylonian tablets from Ishchali*, S. Greengus, Istanbul, 1979

JEN   *Joint Expedition to Nuzi*, vol I, E. Chiera and E. Lacheman, American Schools of Oriental Research, Publ. of the Baghdad School, Philadelphia, 1934

K   K, (Karana), followed by a number, refers to texts in OBTR, below.

LODS   *Une tablette inédite de Mari*, article in *Studies in Old Testament Prophecy*, dedicated to T. H. Robinson, G. Dossin and A. Lods, Edinburgh, 1950

OBTR   *The Old Babylonian tablets from Tell-al Rimah*, S. Dalley, C. B. F. Walker and J. D. Hawkins, London 1976.

ORD   *Un cas d'ordalie*, article in *Symbolae P. Koschaker dedicatae* by G. Dossin, Leiden, 1939.

RA   *Revue d'Assyriologie*

RHA   *Revue Hittite et Asianique*

SYRIA   *Syria* (Journal of French archaeology and history of art and architecture in Syria)

TEM   *Textes économiques de Mari*, articles in *Revue d'Assyriologie*, 47–50 by M. Birot

VOIX   *Une opposition familiale à Mari*, article by G. Dossin in *La voix de L'opposition en Mésopotamie*, edited in Revue d'Assyriologie 58, 1964

List of Akkadian words used

Further reading

M. Birot, J. R. Kupper and O. Rouault, *Répertoire Analytique*, ARMT XVI/1

J. Bottero and A. Finet, *Répertoire Analytique*, ARMT XV, 1954

E. Ebeling, B. Meissner et al (eds), *Reallexikon der Assyriologie*, Berlin and Leipzig, 1932 onwards

A. K. Grayson, *Assyrian Royal Inscriptions*, (vols I and II), Wiesbaden, 1972 and 1976

J. R. Kupper (ed), *La Civilisation de Mari, XV Rencontre Assyriologique International*, Liege, 1966

Naval Intelligence, *Geographical Handbook Series*, 1944, on Iraq.

D. Oates, *Studies in the ancient history of northern Iraq*, London, 1968

A. Parrot, *Mission de Mari* (vols I–III), Paris, 1956–67

J. B. Pritchard, *Ancient Near Eastern Texts relating to the Old Testament*, Princeton U.P., (Third edition) 1969

G. Roux, *Ancient Iraq*, Pelican books (revised edition), 1981

J. M. Sasson, *The Military Establishments at Mari*, Rome 1969

E. Sollberger and J-R. Kupper, *Inscriptions Royales Sumériennes et Akkadiennes*, Paris, 1971

A bibliography of articles publishing Mari texts outside the main volumes will be found in J. G. Heintz, A. Marx and L. Millot, *Index documentaire des textes de Mari* pp. 24–38, ARMT XVII/I 1975

Articles in which Shemshara tablets are published are listed in R. Borger, *Handbook der Keilschriftliteratur*, Band I, 1967, and Band II, 1975 sub Laessøe

Index